MY SPLENDOR

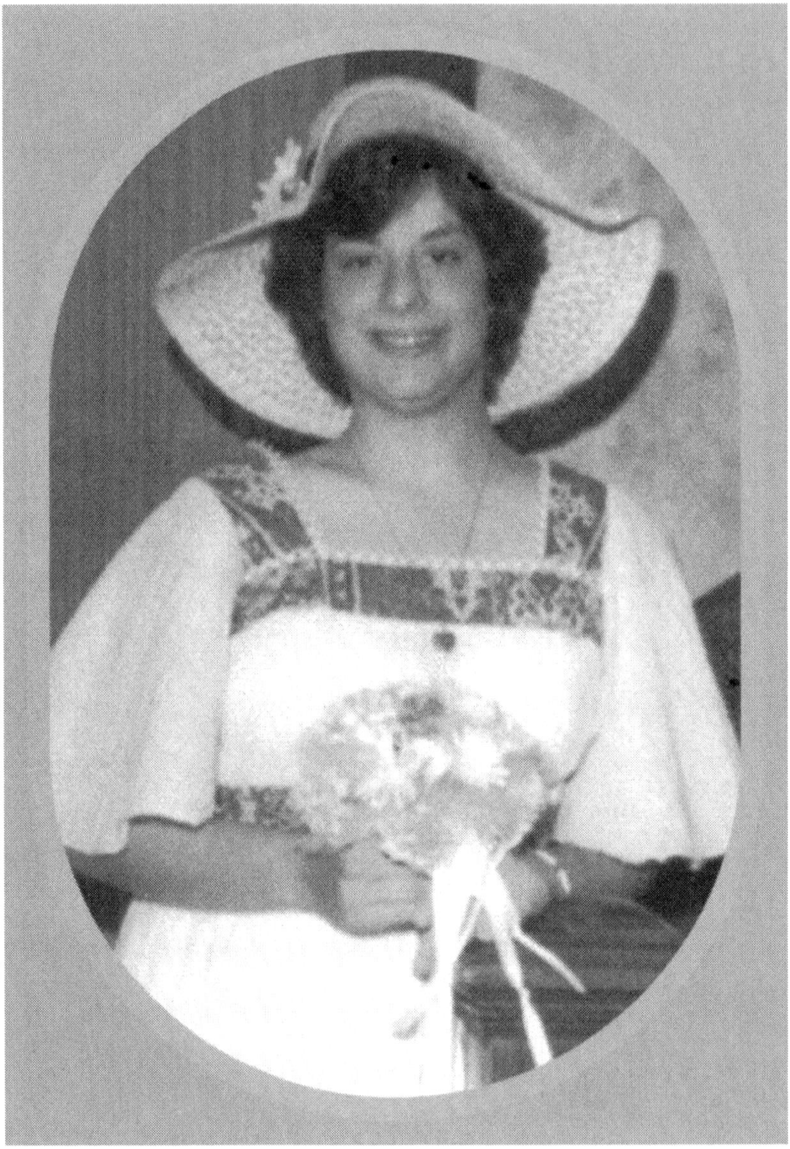

MY SPLENDOR

Forty Years of Love and Loyalty

To a Beautiful Deaf Woman

By

JC Saffell

Copyright © 2019 by Jack C Saffell.

All Right Reserved.

978-1-7010-8617-3

No part of this publication may be reproduced, distributed, or transmitted in any form or by any means, including photocopying, recording, or other electronic or mechanical methods, or by any information storage and retrieval system without the prior written permission of the publisher, except in the case of very brief quotations embodied in critical reviews and certain other noncommercial uses permitted by copyright law.

This book was published thanks to free support and training from:

EbookPublishingSchool.com

This book is dedicated to our children and grandchildren. As the years drift by, the memory of their mother and grandmother, will always be just one turned page away.

We love you.

This is Danielle's Story

Edited by

Christine LePorte

*P*ROLOGUE

"Little girl, hey, little girl, you have to take the baby chicken out of the plastic bag or it will suffocate," the frustrated carpenter hollered for the third time. He was atop the adjacent building's roof repairing its recent water leaks.

Hearing the yelling, Danielle's mom rushed out of the washroom, her hair tousled, and ran through the back door and into the fenced backyard. "What seems to be the problem?" she inquired, loudly and with much distress. She was upset because she was right in the middle of folding the barber shop aprons and frightened that something terrible had just happened to her precious daughter.

"That little girl over there has a baby chicken in a plastic bag and I have been trying to tell her that the chicken will die if she doesn't let it out of the bag, but she keeps ignoring me," shouted the carpenter to the lady, whose name was Alice.

"My daughter can't hear," snapped Alice, awkwardly, and a little louder than she had intended, as she looked up at the carpenter on the roof. Danielle's mom was always on the defensive when it came to criticism of her precious little deaf child.

"Oh, I'm sorry, I didn't know, I was just trying to help," said the now embarrassed carpenter, who quickly returned to the task at hand. Then he sheepishly turned back to the little girl's mother, smiled, and uttered, "That daughter of yours sure is a pretty little miss."

Realizing the carpenter was just trying to help, the guarded mother shyly looked back at the lean man on the roof and threw him a somewhat forced smile.

Danielle watched wide-eyed as the two adults had this exchange. She really had no inkling what, if anything, had just played out. The mother gazed lovingly at her daughter, leaned down, and carefully removed the yellow baby chick from the plastic bag.

CHAPTER 1

It may seem strange now, but visiting each other in one another's homes was common during the early years of television. Danielle's family would usually come by Nonna's house to eat on Sundays after Mass. During the weekdays, friends would stop by just to say hello, and the old Italian ladies (those whose first language was of the old country) would sit around and share stories before deciding whose house would be visited next week.

Danielle and her mom often visited Danielle's beloved Nonna. Nonna, whose name was Emma Malfatti Mela, was a first-generation immigrant from Capannori, Italy, who came to America via Ellis Island in 1918. Emma came from a very, very poor family.

Family lore states that Emma's mother would first feed a meager dinner to her ten children, all the while busying herself in the kitchen, having not eaten anything so her beloved children could get their fill.

When Danielle was nearly two and a half years old, Nonna said to Alice one day, *"Non-me para che la bambina possa sentire."* I don't think the little girl can hear. Emma always spoke in Italian and was probably the first person to verbalize whether Danielle could hear or not.

"Ma, I know something's not right," Alice answered in Italian with great sadness. "Danielle should be talking a little bit by now. The only thing I've ever heard her say is, thump, pha-thump, thump, pha-thump as she lays next to the warm clothes dryer with a load of clothes drying in it." Alice looked dolefully at her beautiful dark-eyed toddler.

One gorgeous sunny day in Rio Dell, a short time after their visit to Nonna Emma's house, the caring mother placed her precious toddler down for her afternoon nap. After an hour, she heard the little girl crying from the bedroom just down the hall. She walked toward the bedroom and called out, quite loudly, "I'm coming, Danielle, I'm coming!" When Danielle's mom pushed open the door which was ajar, Danielle, seeing the door open unexpectedly, jerked back with a start.

The dark-eyed girl never heard her mother calling from down the hall. Quite shaken, Alice slowly picked up her crying baby from the crib and hugged her tenderly. She patted her baby's back as tears started to flow from her eyes. Alice realized that Nonna Emma's hunch was right, and that tragically, this beautiful toddler could not hear.

Alice Mary Mela was born in Scotia in 1923 and lived all her life across the Eel River in the town called Rio Dell. Rio Dell (pop. 2700) is a very small, tight-knit community in Humboldt County, California. Having lived her whole life in such a small town, the proud mother recognized that finding resources to help her beloved deaf daughter could be daunting. This discomfiture soon turned into determination as in time, many obstacles presented themselves.

Danielle's mom opened the thin, 1958 Humboldt County telephone book and searched through the yellow pages under hearing aids. From five possible listings, Alice called the Eureka Hearing Aid Service in Eureka proper, the largest city in Humboldt County (pop. 28,000), to ask questions and to find out what she could do about getting the needed tests so her treasured daughter could hear.

Upon speaking with a receptionist, she was told that Danielle was too young to have any testing done and that she would have to wait at least another year, preferably longer. The resolute mother would not wait.

Next, she phoned Chalmers Hearing Service, pleading with the receptionist in her extreme frustration. She questioned the woman as to what, if anything, she could do to get some tests done for her precious little girl. The sympathetic receptionist responded, "Hold on, please hold."

The compassionate receptionist laid the telephone receiver down. With her elbows on her tired desk, she placed her face into her hands and questioned herself as to how desperate she would be had she ever found herself in this same situation. The receptionist then picked up the telephone and said to Alice, "Ma'am, the first thing Mr.

Crichton would want you to do is to have your daughter's ears checked out by a physician just to make sure everything is physically okay with them."

The desperate mother, not realizing she had been holding her breath, breathed a sigh and said to the caring receptionist, "Thank you so much, you'll never know how much this means to us."

Danielle's primary care physician was Dr. Treadwell, the local general practitioner in Rio Dell. Dr. Treadwell was also the physician who had delivered Danielle at birth. At Dr. Treadwell's office Danielle's ears checked out fine and the kind doctor, having known the family for a long time, said, "Alice, Danielle is very young and there are a lot of things that can be going on here. Please try not to worry too much."

Danielle's mom again called the hearing aid center. "Chalmers Hearing Service, can I help you?" said the cheerful receptionist. Alice told the lady that she had called before and that they asked her to get her daughter's ears examined by a physician. She also relayed everything Dr. Treadwell had told her and said that she was hoping to see the hearing aid specialist as soon as possible.

"From all the information that you have given me, ma'am, your daughter is much younger than most of our other patients. I'll have to talk to our office manager, could you please hold a minute while I find out a few things?" The receptionist turned her swivel chair around and said to the office manager, "Gloria, the lady from Rio Dell with the toddler is on the line and wants to make an appointment."

Taken up with another significant task, the busy office manager was looking downward at her desk. She raised her head and mouthed: "Okay, hold on." Gloria, a well-seasoned office manager, finished jotting down a few things and looked back to the receptionist and said: "Okay, what did you say?" The receptionist repeated her question. The distracted office manager replied, "Um, how old is this little girl again?"

"Two and a half," was the reply.

The office manager shook her head slightly as she thought over the question then said, "Okay, ask the lady to wait a moment and let me go talk to Mr. Crichton first."

Alice waited on the telephone for several minutes and then finally she heard a voice.

"Ma'am, my name is Gloria, Mr. Crichton's office manager. Mr. Crichton said that he would be willing to see your daughter, but because of her age, he needs to figure out a few things first. Give me your phone number and I'll call you back as soon as he has a plan." The desperate mother was truly elated.

While Mr. Crichton ate his lunch that day, a tuna sandwich with cheese, some potato chips, and a Coke, he reread the notation on his desk: "2½ year old with possible hearing loss needs testing." The shrewd Mr. Crichton needed to formulate a plan as to how he might examine this very young patient. He felt he was definitely up to the challenge.

In his thirteen years of service, Mr. Crichton, a good-looking, dark-haired thirty-eight-year-old with a young family at home, had treated many kids of all ages with varying levels of hearing loss, but this one, being so young, would require some exceptional, very imaginative planning.

It was the end of a long and tedious day, and Mr. Crichton was headed out the back door when the office manager said, "Mr. Crichton, I hate to be repetitive, but have you thought about the little toddler from Rio Dell?"

"I'm still working on it, remind me tomorrow," said the harried man as he hurried out the door.

The following morning Mr. Crichton said, as he walked into the office, "Gloria, I think I have an idea how to test the little toddler, would you please set them up with an appointment?"

The day for Danielle's much-anticipated hearing test had come and Alice was elated and very hopeful that this audiologist would be able to help Danielle hear.

Alice was holding Danielle in her arms as they entered the tidy office. Danielle was frightened yet curious and kept looking about the multi-chaired reception room. Alice walked up to the receptionist window and said, "Danielle Silbernagel to see Mr. Crichton."

The two waited for what seemed like a long time. As was his routine for new patients, Mr. Crichton walked into the waiting room, looked at Danielle and Alice, smiled, and greeted them warmly.

Danielle immediately looked away and laid her head on her mother's shoulder. Danielle loved people and always liked having them around, but meeting a new person was always chancy.

Alice gave the man a small smile and followed him into a somewhat large room which contained a smaller, greatly insulated booth. This booth had in it, a thickly padded door which reminded Alice of the freezer door she had often seen at the butcher shop at the market in Rio Dell. Inside this thickly padded room was a chair which faced a double-insulated five-foot-by-five-foot window.

Mr. Crichton told Alice that because the child was so young, he wanted Alice to sit in the chair and hold Danielle on her lap while he sat opposite them on the other side of the window.

Alice took a seat, with Danielle on her lap, then looked out of the large plexiglass window and studied the many knobs and gadgets that were located facing them. Mr. Crichton's chair was visible to Alice and to the right of the chair, Alice noticed a sign on the wall which read, "Do you see what I'm saying?" This unusual sign made Alice think of the many times she had realized her beloved daughter watched her lips intently as she talked. Alice was disheartened that she hadn't even thought a hearing loss could be affecting her child.

Mr. Crichton carefully placed the stout headphones on Danielle's head while she sat curiously on Alice's lap.

Immediately, Danielle pulled the headphones off and began to cry, a piercing, troubled cry that could be felt as well as heard. Mr. Crichton was aghast at the little girl's terrified response. He quickly grabbed the headphones from the crying girl's hands and stood back.

The young audiologist's first thought was that this infant was much too young for testing, but he quickly had another idea that he hoped might work.

Mr. Crichton hung the earphones back on their peg, looked at Alice, and said, "Be right back." He then pushed the enormous door open, walking out of the room and quickly down the hall.

Alice soothed her little toddler with hugs and kisses and patting as she had always done when Danielle became so upset. After some time, Danielle finally calmed down, but she was still whimpering.

When Mr. Crichton came back, as soon as Danielle saw him, she started crying all over again. Even with tears in her eyes, it didn't take long for the toddler to finally discover the young man was holding up something in his hand. It was a large grape sucker that he was waving back and forth in the air. She finally calmed down.

With tears flowing down her sweet cheeks Danielle quickly reached for the purple-paper-wrapped treat. Alice recognized this sucker as a "winner sucker." These large hard-candied suckers, which came in two flavors, cherry and grape, could be purchased at any market for five cents and once you opened it, if there was a little band of waxed paper across the back of the sucker with the word "winner" on it, you'd take the sucker back to the store proprietor and show him that you had a "winner." Having a "winner" allowed you to get another sucker for free.

The young man handed the sucker to Danielle. Alice showed Danielle, with gestures, that they first had to remove the paper wrapper. All the while, Danielle, being two and a half years old and well known for not being very patient, began to make indistinct noises which sounded very odd and guttural. Alice quickly removed the wrapper and let the baby take the sucker from her to avoid further tears. The toddler eagerly started licking the sucker and finally began to settle down.

"Let's try putting the headphones on you first, Alice, then hopefully Danielle won't be so afraid of them. We can then try to put them on Danielle," said Mr. Crichton, thoughtfully and with great hope.

Mr. Crichton waited a few seconds for Danielle to finally look at the other people in the room, then slowly and with a big smile, placed the headphones on Alice. With the headphones on her head, Alice smiled at Danielle as though she was having fun. Danielle was still afraid, but after a few minutes, after looking at the headphones on her mom, stuck the whole grape sucker in her mouth and reached for the bulky headphones.

Danielle roughly pulled the headphones off from her mom's head and, knocking Alice's glasses askance, the curious little girl examined the heavy, black plastic headphones and then, after a short time, placed them crookedly on her own head. Alice straightened the headphones and looked face to face with Danielle and nodded her head up and down with exaggeration, as if to say, "Yes, that's a good girl."

Mr. Crichton quickly left the padded room, closed the bulky door, and settled down in his chair facing this very imposing console filled with dials, digits, and gadgets of many different kinds.

The hearing test began. Hearing tests work by letting out a tone into the ear from the headset and then the audiologist will watch the patient for any out of the ordinary reaction. For instance, the first tone, let's imagine a low audio frequency is emitted extremely quietly. The examiner will then adjust the tone progressively louder until the patient responds. In turn, higher tone frequencies will also be emitted extremely quietly, until the patient again responds. These tones are emitted throughout the entire human hearing range, from low sound frequencies to high.

The hearing test proceeded without too much interruption. Danielle did once drop her sucker on the floor, which gave Mr. Crichton a scare. He exited the room and returned very quickly with a new grape sucker.

After he completed the hearing test Mr. Crichton told Alice that he would call her in a few weeks with the test results. He then told her that after a more thorough examination of the test results they could then decide, if she needed one, what kind of hearing aid would be the best for the little girl.

The subsequent test results were very troubling.

"Danielle has a profound hearing loss," said Mr. Crichton. "She has a ninety percent hearing loss in the right ear and an eighty-five percent hearing loss in the left," he reported to the little girl's parents.

Pete, Danielle's gentle father, had accompanied the duo to the audiologist's office that day so the parents might learn of the test results together.

As the beautiful, dark-eyed girl played joyfully with toys on the ground, both parents gasped upon hearing the news from the young audiologist. These devoted and dedicated parents were shaken to the core.

"Are you sure?" Alice blurted out to Mr. Crichton, not believing the terrible news that she had just heard. Slowly, the audiologist responded, "Yes, I'm quite sure." He looked at both of the grieving parents and then said sympathetically, "I truly am very sorry."

While trying to digest this completely foreign concept, as to simply how little her precious daughter could really hear, Alice tried, with great struggle, to form a suitable question. She asked very slowly and with great difficulty, "What, um, um, how do you think this could have happened?"

The good man paused for what seemed like several minutes before he answered with a question of his own. "Has Danielle ever had German measles or endured a really high fever?"

"Why, yes," answered Alice quite slowly. "When she was born, she suffered a high fever for three days."

The shrewd young man replied, "That could be the cause. I've seen his happen before, but it's usually in older children."

Chapter 2

Transistor radios were all the rage in 1961.

Immediately after Christmas that year teenagers and even some of the younger kids could be seen walking around town in their galoshes, splashing in the many puddles and carrying their new transistor radios.

Some of these radios were placed on the kids' windowsills in their bedrooms or under their pillows at night, with the volume turned up way too loud.

Surprisingly, some of these radios were small enough to be worn in a shirt pocket or, with some homemade holders, worn about the neck.

If a kid was really lucky, they also received an earpiece which could be plugged into the radio as not to bother the people around them with the loud noises emitting from the box.

When Danielle was five, it was one of these transistor-type radios that had become her first hearing aid. Danielle's Beltone hearing aid was made of special components with a built-in microphone. The microphone would then pick up sound from the environment and send this sound through the transistor hearing aid, which would then amplify the sound and run the sound through a wire into the earpiece that was placed into Danielle's ear.

Mr. Crichton was quite proud when he fitted Danielle with this special hearing aid. "Top of the line," the kind man reported as he showed the small box to Danielle and Alice for the first time.

When Danielle came to the hearing aid office to be fitted for the hearing aid Alice told him, "We want only the best." Mr. Crichton then showed Alice all the latest choices he had for giving Danielle the best prospect at hearing.

"Will she hear everything we say?" asked the hopeful mother.

"I'm not sure," said the cautious Mr. Crichton. "She does have a very severe hearing loss, but each child is different when it comes to the outcome of these body aids. Time will tell," he added hopefully. "Come back and see me in four weeks."

The duo left his office and the kind young man was left pondering as to precisely how much this new aid would really help the beautiful deaf girl.

Danielle had what is known as nerve deafness. The parts of the ear that make up the "hearing system" are the outer ear, the middle ear, and the inner ear. The middle ear consists of three of the body's smallest bones, the hammer, the anvil, and the stirrup. The inner ear consists of the cochlea.

A damaged cochlea was why Danielle was extremely hard of hearing. Within the cochlea stands an array of tiny nerve hair cells that send the sound, like a tag team or a line of firefighters in a bucket brigade, through the cochlea and to the brain. It seemed that the high fever that Danielle had three days after birth had caused many of these nerve hair cells to lie down; that is to say, become useless. It can be described as some of the electrical poles in a big city being knocked down after a terrible storm, resulting in none or few of the customers down the line from the storm damage to have limited or no power at all. The hearing aid would, in a way, produce such a loud increase in volume so as to send a small spark from one working electrical pole to the next working electrical pole all the way up to the brain.

It took time, patience and many treats from Alice to convince Danielle to use the new hearing aid. When the device's handmade strapped holder was first put around her neck, Danielle shook her head in protest. Alice would then place the earpiece into Danielle's ear and turn on the apparatus. Danielle would pull the earpiece out of her ear, make a face, and point as if to say, "It hurts my ear."

Alice always encouraged Danielle to wear the hearing aid simply because she needed to learn to use it. If Danielle complained too much Alice would put her finger in front of Danielle's face and pointed her finger down as if to say, "We'll turn down the volume of the machine." Danielle was more content with the volume turned down low.

It was a painful and very slow process, but after some time Alice could see Danielle using the aid more and more. Alice always tried talking to Danielle, but the aid, Alice would eventually learn, helped with speech very little, if at all.

At first, Alice would notice Danielle using the aid when watching Bugs Bunny, or she'd catch Danielle squealing when her favorite cartoon, Pepé Le Pew, came on TV.

It seemed that repetition and doing tasks over and over were the only ways that Danielle was going to get some, if any, benefit from the aid.

Danielle was extremely impatient. This impatience caused Alice to be frustrated many times while trying to get little Danielle to practice "listening."

Danielle had an aunt Flora, who was married and had two kids. Danielle loved Flora. Flora's kids were Dana, a girl one year younger than Danielle, and Kelly, a boy three years younger. Danielle and Dana could often be found playing dolls together, but when little Kelly Boo Boo came around Dana would make sure that Kelly was forced to leave and that Kelly couldn't play with them.

Danielle, being very observant, learned that it made Dana happy to make Kelly leave. Soon after they started their play time together, Danielle too would learn to chase Kelly off so the "girls" could play dolls without being bothered by the curious little brother.

Danielle also had an uncle, Albert. Danielle loved Uncle Albert. Albert worked at the Pacific Lumber Company as a saw-filer. He had four kids—Ronnie, nine years older than Danielle; Janice, about six years older; Jon, two years older; and Paul, about a year older.

On Sundays after Mass, all the Melas would come together at Nonna's home for home-cooked Italian meals, and all the grandchildren would get to play together.

Danielle, being sight oriented, was at her happiest when all the family was together. She would go from one person to the next, to the next, just touching and looking at them and showing them her love with her very unique and kind gesticulations, showing them that she loved them and that she enjoyed just having them around.

Chapter 3

Alice registered Danielle for kindergarten when she reached the age of five. Alice and Pete had no idea if going to school would be beneficial for Danielle because she was not speaking much. The loving parents talked it over and decided that they should try school in order to see what Danielle was capable of when it came to education.

Danielle's kindergarten teacher was named Mrs. Miller. Mrs. Miller was a tall, stately lady who was very kind, bore a small speech impediment, and had a heart of gold. Danielle loved Mrs. Miller.

Mrs. Miller was the kind of teacher who treated each child with great dignity. Each youngster was a gift in Mrs. Miller's eyes. If a child came to school clean or unclean, with a snotty nose or not, Mrs. Miller made them feel good about themselves and that they were significant.

Alice often stayed over during class time to observe how Danielle interacted with the kids and to see if she was learning anything at all. One such day when Alice was in Danielle's class, she noticed a particular little girl who had come into the classroom. This small girl was evidently very poor and it seemed to Alice that the girl's mother was greatly negligent in training and the very basic care of this hapless child.

As the little girl walked by Alice, Alice cringed at the fact that this poor little child reeked of the smell of urine. Alice tried not to show any reaction and smiled when the little girl looked her way. The little girl then walked shyly over to where Mrs. Miller was standing next to her desk. The little girl waited patiently until Mrs. Miller noticed that she was standing there. The teacher looked down and as she stooped to the little girl's level, smiled into her beautiful brown eyes and promptly gave the little girl a great big hug. Alice heard Mrs. Miller state, "My goodness, Ella, don't you look beautiful today."

It had taken Mrs. Miller a long time to teach Danielle that she had to sit down in her seat in class while the other children were seated. While in school it seemed none of the other kids could understand Danielle's speech. Danielle also had a hard time understanding the alphabet, so Mrs. Miller would often give Danielle "special" coloring assignments with crayons in order to keep the child's inquisitive mind occupied. Sometimes the other children objected that Danielle could color all day while they had to do "schoolwork." Mrs. Miller would patiently explain to them that Danielle couldn't hear very well and that she was doing a "special assignment."

Then came play time. Danielle's favorite activity was swinging on the swings. When it wasn't raining and Mrs. Miller let the kids out of class to play, Danielle could always be found swinging, swinging, and swinging, always happy with a smile on her face. It was during one of these fun times on the swings that Danielle learned that children could be brutal.

Alice made sure that Danielle had her hearing aid on each and every day while she attended school. Alice had made a special hearing aid holder out of heavy white burlap cloth. In those days most moms would sew some or all of their children's clothes. This hearing aid holder was a "pouch" with straps tied to it so Danielle could wear it over her shoulders, similar to a backpack worn in front, leaving her arms and hands free. The hearing aid fit neatly in this pouch with the wire from the aid going into the earpiece in Danielle's left ear.

It was recess and Mrs. Miller had let the kids out to play. Danielle immediately ran over to the swings so she could have fun. She watched all the other kids playing and swinging and riding bikes. Danielle was quite surprised when two boys came over to her and started talking to her while she was on the swing. Before she knew it, the boys had taken her hearing aid from her along with the wire that led to the earpiece.

Danielle wasn't used to kids being mean or rude, so she just kept swinging and having fun on the swing. It was time for recess to be over, but Danielle kept swinging and swaying. Mrs. Miller found Danielle on the swings and came over to her. Danielle smiled at her. Mrs. Miller tried talking to Danielle and then noticed that her hearing aid was missing. She took Danielle by the hand and brought her into the classroom. Mrs. Miller gave Danielle some crayons, a piece of paper, and a smile.

"Children," said the joyful Mrs. Miller, while standing at the front of the class, "could any of you please tell me if you have seen Danielle's hearing aid, the 'radio' that she wears around her neck in the white pouch?" Mrs. Miller looked around the class and a boy reluctantly raised his hand.

"Teacher, me and Frankie asked Danielle if we could listen to her radio and she said yes," the boy confessed to Mrs. Miller. The fact was that this couldn't have possibly been the truth because Danielle could not hear speech and Mrs. Miller knew it. "Do you have the radio, Clarence?" Mrs. Miller asked. "No, but Frankie does," said the boy, pointing to Frankie.

Mrs. Miller walked over to Frankie's desk. She stooped down beside Frankie and asked, sweetly and quietly, "Do you have Danielle's radio?"

Frankie nodded. He lifted his desktop and grabbed the "radio" and handed it over to Mrs. Miller. "Teacher?" Frankie said quietly. "That radio don't even work." Mrs. Miller smiled at him and thanked the boy for being honest and went back to her desk.

"Children," said the statuesque figure holding up Danielle's hearing aid. "This is not a radio. This is called a hearing aid. A hearing aid helps Danielle hear better because she cannot hear without it. Please, children, this is a very important thing and no one is permitted to use it except Danielle. Does everyone understand me?" said the kind teacher with a smile.

"Yes, Mrs. Miller," the class replied in unison.

The school year continued and Danielle had fun watching and sometimes playing with the other students. The happy Danielle made friends easily, but communication was always strained, at best, when it came to dialogue.

Over time Danielle learned that some of the kids weren't so nice. One young girl in particular took great pleasure in trying to make Danielle talk. Lorie, an only child whose dirty-blonde hair was always perfectly coiffured, could often be found teasing Danielle's attempt at speech by repeating, "Mum, mum, bah, mum, mum, bah," back to Danielle, which made the other kids laugh.

At first, this just made Danielle smile back and continue playing. But some kids are simply mean-spirited and obtain pleasure by hurting others either by teasing or inflicting bodily pain. Lorie was this type of kid. Once Lorie found out that Danielle could be the object of a laugh by repeating the sounds that she tried to say, Lorie would instigate Danielle and tease her incessantly.

Sometimes the sneaky Lorie would gather two or three of her friends and they would look toward Mrs. Miller and make sure she was busy with other tasks before they would slither over and corner Danielle while she played. Lorie would then seek to make Danielle mimic her speech and have Danielle repeat the sounds they would produce. Danielle, being extremely hard of hearing, would, with great difficulty, monkey their lip movements and add throaty, guttural sounds to the lip movements, which gave these girls great pleasure.

At first, Danielle was just happy that the other girls wanted to play the talking games with her, but after a while, Danielle grew to detest some of these mean girls because, when they tired of all the teasing, they would hit Danielle in the arm or pinch her just to hear her cry. Danielle, being so deaf, would cry with a piercing screech, a sound that is indeed indescribable. This crying too would give those mean girls great pleasure.

Veronica, a small-statured Catholic girl whom Danielle had often seen at Mass, had once found Danielle crying in the corner of the playground and desperately tried to calm the abused girl.

On this occasion, Veronica attempted to take Danielle by the hand. Danielle, having been harshly teased by the other girls, was very reluctant to go with Veronica and pulled her hand back, but Veronica just smiled, slowly reached for Danielle's hand again, and patted Danielle's hand very gently. Danielle decided that this nice girl wouldn't hurt her and finally went with her.

"Mrs. Miller, Danielle was crying in the corner of the playground and I brought her to you," said the kind, gentle girl.

Mrs. Miller said, "Honey, did she fall or hurt herself playing?"

"I don't know, she was just crying and I wanted to help her," said the sweet Veronica.

"That was very kind of you, sweetie," said Mrs. Miller. "I'll take care of her now, honey, you can go play."

The sweet Veronica looked at Mrs. Miller and then at the crying kindergartner and said to Mrs. Miller, "Is it okay if I stay with her? I just want to help her."

"Of course you can," said the joyful teacher. "Veronica, you are very kind to want to help her. Danielle needs special friends like you, Sweetheart, thank you," said Mrs. Miller.

Veronica and Danielle became fast friends, and Danielle discovered that not everyone would be brutal to her. The petite Veronica soon became Danielle's savior.

When Veronica eyed Lorie and the other kids trying to tease Danielle, Veronica would quickly walk over and grab Danielle by the hand and the two would simply stroll, hand in hand, around the playground. Danielle just smiled. It made Danielle feel comforted that Veronica was her friend.

One time, while Danielle and Veronica played, Veronica tried to get Danielle to say her name. "Veronica," she said, slowly mouthing her name and pointing to herself, in hopes to get Danielle to say her name.

Danielle, knowing this game from the many times Alice had done the same thing at home, repeated, "Voah-CA."

"No." Veronica shook her head. "Let's try again," said the patient little girl. "V-E-R-O-N-I-C-A," mouthed the petite girl, much slower this time.

Danielle smiled greatly and repeated deep within her throat, "V-O-A-H-C-A."

Veronica smiled back, patted Danielle on the shoulder, and said, "Good job."

Mrs. Miller would often find Veronica pulling Danielle to different areas of the classroom and showing her different objects with hopes of getting Danielle to repeat the word. "B-i-c-y-c-l-e," mouthed the patient little girl to Danielle as she grabbed hold of one of the tricycles in class.

Danielle repeated a throaty "P-u-c-k-l-e."

Veronica nodded her head yes and said, "Good."

Danielle came to love her kind friend, the sweet Veronica.

Toward the close of the school year, Alice met with Mrs. Miller to evaluate how Danielle had done in school.

"She is going to need special help, Alice," replied the concerned teacher. "She has a very difficult time making the kids understand her and one of the girls especially takes great delight in teasing her."

"I was afraid things like that would happen," said the disappointed Alice.

"But on the bright side," said the cheerful teacher, "Danielle gets along very well with Veronica Johnson. Veronica holds Danielle's hand and brings her everywhere she goes. Now, I've had a lengthy talk with Principal Waldner," Mrs. Miller continued, "and he wants you to call this number. It's the phone number of Marshall Elementary School in Eureka. They have a hard of hearing class which Principal Waldner believes is ideal for Danielle." Mrs. Miller was very hopeful; Alice was not.

CHAPTER 4

Alice was greatly upset when she called Marshall Elementary. Marshall was in Eureka and they indeed had a hard of hearing class for ages six to twelve. If Danielle was to attend the deaf and hard of hearing class this would mean uprooting everything they knew, and Pete and Alice would have to move their family to the Eureka school district in order for Danielle to be eligible to attend.

Danielle's father, Pete, was a barber in Rio Dell. Pete, a South Dakota native, joined the Coast Guard and moved to Ferndale in 1942, and was stationed at Table Bluff's Coast Guard Station. Pete met Alice at a dance in Fortuna and they soon fell in love. Alice and Pete married in 1943 and subsequently the war ended and Pete set about working for the Pacific Lumber Company.

While at the lumber company, Pete loaded boxcars. This heavy, exceedingly trying job took its toll on Pete. Pete was intelligent and a really hard worker. He had a long talk with his father-in-law about an idea he had. Pete's father-in-law, John (Giovanni Mela) kindly lent Pete the money so he could enter and finally graduate from barber school in San Francisco.

Moving from Rio Dell to Eureka was something Alice hated doing, but she and Pete were willing to do practically anything in order to get their beautiful, deaf daughter an education.

Pete, a self-taught do it yourselfer, had just built, three years earlier, a unique, beautiful, completely modern, three-bedroom, two-bathroom house in Rio Dell on South Sequoia Avenue. This home that Pete single-handedly built from the ground up, with little or no outside help, had taken more than two years to complete. This new home even received an award from Pacific Gas and Electric Company. The PG&E inspector presented Pete with a certificate for the high-efficiency electric radiant heat, which Pete had personally researched and installed in their home.

Alice loved this radiant heat. This type of heating had wiring embedded in the masonry of the ceiling which released warmth downward. Each single bit of furniture was warm to the touch as this radiant warmth gently settled. When one sat, this warmth would then embrace one's body. Humboldt County, with its cold and rainy winters, was well suited for this type of innovative home heat.

Pete and Alice now had to decide if and how they would move to Eureka so Danielle could attend Marshall Elementary's class for the hard of hearing.

After much debate and many difficult conversations, Pete and Alice reluctantly decided to sell their beautiful new home in Rio Dell and buy a used home on Summer Street in the Eureka school district. Pete would drive to and from work—a sixty-five-mile round trip—daily.

Danielle was so excited, but her excitement didn't last. Alice took Danielle to school on the first day and her teacher, Miss Parrish, a middle-aged, serious-looking woman, took Danielle by the hand and said to Alice, "Okay, I'll take over from here, you may go now."

Alice, aghast, was reluctant to leave her young deaf child alone in this classroom. She was hoping she might observe Danielle's interplay with the other students, but it seemed Miss Parrish wasn't going to budge until Alice departed.

Alice finally waved good-bye to her beautiful Danielle and left. Danielle tried to pull away from Miss Parrish to run after her mother, but Miss Parrish held on all the harder to Danielle's hand and then quickly steered her onto a cold, hard, wooden student desk and plopped her down.

Miss Parrish then looked straight into Danielle's eyes and said sternly, with exaggerated lip movement, "BE QUIET." Danielle had no idea what Miss Parrish had mouthed. Danielle whimpered most of the day, not knowing at all what was expected of her.

Getting Danielle to get up and get ready for school became a nightmare for Alice. She knew that Danielle didn't like school but it took Alice a few years before she finally caught on to the fact that Miss Parrish was very impatient and possibly an alcoholic.

Miss Parrish was discovered to be hateful and intolerant, not just with Danielle but with all of her hard of hearing pupils. Danielle learned that even if she didn't understand the words, that if she would make a sound and move her lips similar to the teacher's lip movement, then she would not be punished. If she just looked at Miss Parrish and then turned back to her writing work and purposely tried not to copy Miss Parrish's speech, it was common for Danielle and the other students to get a sharp slap to the face. "Pay attention," Miss Parrish would mouth, harshly. Miss Parrish was especially impatient with Danielle.

Miss Parrish had a degree from a college in Connecticut. Her degree was in language development for the orally handicapped. She luckily found a much-needed niche at Marshall Elementary in teaching the hard of hearing children.

Miss Parrish was not married and had no children of her own. All the parents of the deaf kids knew, by the way the children reacted to the teacher, that she was not very patient with them, but the parents had no recourse because teaching deaf and hard of hearing children was such a specialty.

Alice would often ask the brash Miss Parrish if she needed help in her class. "If you ever need help in any way, please, just ask," Alice told the grouchy Miss Parrish. The teacher was always quick to answer, "No thank you!" Alice learned, after many attempts, until she could figure out another alternative to Danielle's oral education, not to make waves and just to let things go on as they were. She thought to herself, *A bad education is better than no education at all.*

Danielle began to learn some words at school, but being so hard of hearing, she very much needed extra one-on-one time from Miss Parrish. Sometimes Miss Parrish was patient; most of the times not.

Danielle, being the sort of girl who enjoyed the companionship of others, soon became fast friends with another hard of hearing girl from her class. This older girl would eventually become Danielle's lifelong friend. Janey Quinn was a black-haired effervescent girl with great patience and of Yurok Indian descent. She had a fast smile and was very kind. Janey was paramount in eventually helping Danielle learn to express herself by teaching her words and proper lip movement.

Danielle would mimic Janey's mannerisms and her way of talking. Danielle learned from her, that in order to have hearing people understand, speech was the key to communication. Danielle would copy Janey in many things and thus she learned what to do and what not to do in order to stay out of trouble with the hateful Miss Parrish.

At home, Danielle would often use some homemade signs to communicate with her mom and dad. She quickly learned that if she used any of these signs at school, Miss Parrish was quick to punish.

Miss Parrish only allowed speech as the form of communication between her young deaf students. If Miss Parrish ever caught any of her hard of hearing students using signs or gesticulations with another student, she—

appearing to be deriving great pleasure from this—would sneak up on the students and administer a fast, hard slap across the hands with a wooden ruler. This came to be what Danielle would learn as the primary source of punishment for her and the other kids when they were caught using signs instead of speech.

The first year in Marshall's hard of hearing class finally came to an end. Danielle was ecstatic when she learned that summer had finally arrived and that she would be able to see her cousins and other family members down Rio Dell way.

Danielle soon discovered that they would shortly be going to Ettersburg for their summer holiday. Ettersburg is an extremely remote area of the King's Range in southern Humboldt County and the family often stayed there during the summer to camp. Danielle greatly enjoyed the swimming and fishing, especially in the Mattole River, and playing tag with her many cousins. These vacations at Ettersburg were some of Danielle's greatest joys in life as she reached the age of seven.

Summer was over too quickly and Danielle was very reluctant to go back to school.

"No, no," and shaking her head was all that Danielle would say and do when she learned that starting school again was just around the corner. Oh, how Danielle hated Miss Parrish.

On the first day of her second year at Marshall, Danielle noticed a new girl in class. She learned from Janey that this young girl's name was Sandra Weeks. Sandra was similar to Danielle in that she liked to be close to other people, but Sandra was of a timid nature and very shy.

Danielle and Janey learned that Sandra was a year older than Janey and two years older than Danielle. Danielle soon learned that although she herself was greatly challenged in learning speech, Sandra, who was completely deaf, was already a capable talker.

Danielle, Janey, and Sandra would hang around with each other all day at school and when they went out for recess, they would hide so they could communicate with gesticulations. This made it easier for the trio to get along. It might not have been American Sign Language but it was what some would call a natural inclination to do, for those who could not hear to make their inner thoughts known.

It seemed to Danielle that Miss Parrish was even less patient this year. Janey told Danielle that it looked like Miss Parrish got married. Janey pointed to her own ring finger and told Danielle to look at Miss Parrish's finger. Janey explained to Danielle that when a woman had a ring on her ring finger it meant that person was married. Danielle was surprised that anybody so old would want to get married. *Who would want to marry that mean lady anyway?* she thought.

As hard as Danielle tried to learn proper lip movement, Miss Parrish would scold her and have her do extra schoolwork in the spelling and writing of these new words. New words were never easy for Danielle.

Alice again offered her time and talents to Miss Parrish in order to get a firsthand look at how Danielle was doing in school and how she was relating to the other students. Miss Parrish always responded with, "Thank you, but you would be a distraction to the class instead of a help." Knowing how unhappy her daughter was in Miss Parrish's class, Alice began to look for alternatives to Danielle's deaf education.

As time went by, Danielle did learn more words, but it seemed that no one outside her family could understand Danielle's speech. Try as she might, with such a profound hearing loss, Danielle was not capable of good, easy to understand speech.

Alice was distressed. Time was passing by and Danielle was nearing eight years old and she was reading at a less than first grade level.

Alice spent many long hours reading and writing, and more reading and more writing, trying to teach Danielle that words meant something. Alice would pick up a stuffed animal and slowly pronounce the name of the beast. They worked and worked on this game over and over until Danielle could somewhat pronounce the word.

Alice would point to a clock and pronounce the word slowly and with extremely exaggerated lip movement until Danielle finally produced the correct lip movement. Now came the hard part. Danielle would have to produce the vocal part of the new word. Most of the time the sound Danielle produced was guttural and harsh. Sometimes the sound was too soft or too loud. She had to learn through repetition how much vocal effort was needed to make a word understood. She was learning, but each lesson was grueling for the little deaf girl.

Frustration was the rule when it came to teaching Danielle new and especially complicated concepts at this age. "The boy read the paper," Alice said during one especially long reading lesson.

Danielle looked at Alice with a quizzical expression and shook her head no, saying, "No, paper not red."

Alice, habitually, and without thinking, repeated, "No, the boy read the paper." Danielle again shook her head no. Alice finally understood what Danielle meant. "You're right," Alice said with a huge smile, "the paper is not red, it is white."

"Why you say paper red?" muttered Danielle.

Concepts such as these were very complicated and unclear when it came to learning these simple yet profoundly different meanings.

Danielle continued her education at Marshall Elementary for the next two years. Danielle, due solely to Alice's dedication in teaching her beloved deaf daughter as much as she could, learned many more words and also how to write. Drill and repetition, and more drill and repetition was how Danielle had to learn at this young age.

Carrying on a conversation had been always quite difficult for the young girl. Alice was one of the few people who could understand Danielle's speech. She was always in on the conversation when Danielle attempted to express herself to others.

When Danielle was nine years old, Alice enrolled her in Blue Birds, a fledgling group of Camp Fire Girls. Danielle loved Blue Birds. Here Danielle could be herself. She truly enjoyed just being close to other girls her age and tried to show the girls her ideas when it came to their many group projects. It was during one of the group projects that Alice discovered that Danielle was very creative.

Making bead necklaces, bead vests, and bead bracelets was so much fun for the young Danielle. She made necklaces for her cousins, her dad, and even her friends at school, Janey and Sandra.

Most of the Blue Bird girls were very inclusive toward Danielle, but verbal communication was still difficult, if not impossible, and Alice had to tell the girls most of the things Danielle was trying to tell them.

Danielle made many scrapbooks of her experiences in Blue Birds and enjoyed showing her achievements to all who would "listen."

Danielle graduated to Girl Scouts and had many friends there. Some of these girls being a bit older, were more patient with her and really tried to understand her speech. One girl, Mary Ann, was Danielle's age, ten years old. Mary Ann was an only child. When Danielle would try to explain something to the other girls in Girl Scouts, Mary Ann was the one who would interpret to the other girls what Danielle was trying to say.

Danielle came to respect and truly trust this kind girl. She often asked Alice if Mary Ann and she could have a slumber party together. Mary Ann and Danielle would make tents out of blankets in Danielle's bedroom and pretend to make campfires out of old Lincoln Logs that Danielle had played with when she was a little girl.

Danielle taught Mary Ann some of the signs she had devised while trying to communicate with her mom throughout the years. Danielle later called these made-up signs "homemade" signs. Danielle knew she could not use these "homemade" signs in school, or Miss Parrish would whack her.

It was when Danielle was eleven that Alice made up her mind to change the course of her daughter's education.

Chapter 5

Rio Dell is a very modest, close-knit community. Alice was aware, by hearsay, that there was a young deaf boy, a little older than Danielle, who lived in Rio Dell. She knew his last name was Chittenden but that was about all she knew.

Alice sat down with Pete one day at dinner time and asked, "Pete, do you cut the hair of the dad of that deaf boy we've heard about in Rio Dell?"

Pete said, "I cut the boy's hair during the summer when he's home from school, nice-looking kid as well. If the dad comes in for a haircut, I'll ask him for his wife's name and their phone number, if they have one."

It might be hard to grasp, but in 1966 some households in Rio Dell still did not own telephones.

Time slipped away and Alice had nearly forgotten that she had asked Pete for this information, but one day after work, while eating dinner, Pete handed Alice a folded-up bit of paper with a name and a telephone number on it. The paper read: Edith Chittenden RO 4-6789.

The very next morning Alice called the number on the paper.

"Hello," said the juvenile voice from the other end of the line.

"Is your mother home?" Alice asked.

"No, she's at work," was the reply from the youth on the other end of the line.

"OK, I'll ring later, thank you," Alice said and hung up.

After dinner, Alice called the phone number again and a woman answered this time. "Hello," said the gentle voice on the other end.

"Hello, is this Edith Chittenden?" Alice asked.

"Yes, it is," was the reply.

"Hello, Edith, this is Alice Silbernagel, I used to be Alice Mela, I am Pete the barber's wife."

"Oh, hi, how are you?" replied Edith.

"Okay, thank you. The reason I'm calling you," Alice went on, "is to ask you about your deaf son's school. That would help us determine whether we should send our daughter Danielle, there as well."

"Yes, I have heard from my husband that you have a deaf daughter. How is she?" Edith asked.

Alice and Edith spoke for a very long time. Edith assured Alice that her son was doing very well at the school, which was in Berkeley, California, that he had lots of friends, and he too had a hard time using only speech in his communication. Edith also told Alice that their son, Danny, rode the bus home several times a year—almost 250 miles—and was home during summer break.

Alice eventually got a phone number for the deaf school from Edith, and decided that she would call them in the future if Danielle didn't have better results this year at Marshall.

Danielle went to Marshall from the ages of six to eleven, and Alice had had enough. She knew Danielle was a bright girl and she was not happy with the slow progress Danielle had achieved so far in Marshall's hard of hearing class. While at Marshall Elementary, Danielle did learn how to read and write, but due to her deafness, she was working at a third-grade level. No one knew better than Alice, that under the right conditions, Danielle's possibilities in learning could be endless.

In the early spring of Danielle's eleventh year, Alice contacted the California School for the Deaf in Berkeley. Pete, Alice, and Danielle visited the school in May of 1967. Alice was still trying to determine what, if any, change would be best for Danielle's education.

Danielle was in awe at what she saw at the deaf school. Hands flying in all different directions was one of the things she remembered most from the visit.

Alice and Pete asked many questions of the staff and counselors as to how their deaf daughter would learn sign language. The hearing staff showed Pete and Alice the dormitories and the cafeteria, and they even took them into a schoolroom.

The trio was brought into a working classroom through the back entrance so they might watch a class in session. As they quietly slipped into the class it was apparent to Pete and Alice just how sight perceptive the deaf pupils were. As soon as the teacher in the classroom turned around from writing on the blackboard, she looked to the back of the class as the visitors walked in. To Alice's amazement, every student turned around to peer at the visitors. When sight is one's main sense, where another one faces is a dead giveaway to activities and perhaps a very significant issue that is currently taking place.

Pete and Alice had a lot to talk about on their way home from the California School for the Deaf at Berkeley.

Danielle had become a woman at the age of ten. Alice was nearly caught off guard the day Danielle, being so young, started menstruating. Danielle was shocked to find that when she had gone to the restroom, she noticed some bleeding and quickly ran to tell her mom. Alice had anticipated this day, but not just yet. In her usual style, she patiently and thoroughly explained and showed Danielle proper hygiene and the many things she'd have to manage to take care of herself for many, many years to come. Danielle was now a woman. Danielle was not pleased.

One overcast summer day at home in Eureka, Danielle was looking out the big picture window on

Summer Street when a lady walked by. This lady had long light brown hair and was walking with four children of varying ages. Danielle saw that this lady was signing to the oldest child as she walked down the street. Danielle shot off the couch and opened the front door and ran outside after the lady. Danielle soon caught up to the lady, who had already turned to look in her direction. Danielle said to the lady with a guttural voice, "Me, deaf," as she pointed to herself. The lady looked quizzically at Danielle and then turned to the older child, the one she had been conversing with.

The child, a girl slightly older than Danielle, interpreted to the lady what Danielle had just said. The lady, noticing Danielle's body hearing aid, smiled at Danielle and had the interpreter tell Danielle that her name was Dolly. The interpreter said to Danielle, "This is my mom, her name is Dolly Mason."

Danielle didn't understand the girl's speech very well and replied, "Dawie?"

"No," the interpreter said and repeated, very slowly and with exaggerated lip movement, "D-O-L-L-Y." Dolly reached out and gave Danielle a great big hug. Danielle liked Dolly immediately. She was so excited to have finally met someone just like herself.

Hearing that Danielle had just run out the front door, Alice stood just outside the door and watched in disbelief as, about three houses down the street, Danielle tried to communicate with this older, obviously deaf, lady.

They tried talking for a little while, but soon, Danielle became frustrated. Eventually she waved good-bye to the deaf lady. The lady gave Danielle another hug before she too waved good-bye.

Danielle walked up to her house and said to her mom as she passed her, "Dat wady same deaf wike me," in her deep husky voice.

Chapter 6

Alice and Pete took Danielle down to Berkeley to attend school in the autumn of 1967. The trip from the town of Rio Dell to Berkeley, California, took eight hours of steady driving due to archaic road conditions.

Taking her precious daughter to see the deaf school was one thing, but allowing her little baby to live in a big foreign city had come to be an excruciating choice for Alice, because, like her own mother, Alice was a natural worrier.

This is not normal; this is not the way it's supposed to be. All I want to do is hold, comfort, and soothe my daughter, thought Alice, as she contemplated the direction that Danielle's life would now undergo.

Who takes care of the students? How will they teach her sign language? What do they do in case of an emergency? Who will take care of her when she's sick? These were some of the many doubts that haunted Alice as she had been asked to leave her little deaf daughter behind.

A short time after dropping Danielle off at the dormitory of the deaf school, Alice and Pete traveled to the Motel 6 in Berkeley. Their original plan was to drop Danielle off, stay a couple of days, and then go home. Alice was having a tough time of it so the days suddenly turned into a full workweek.

Every morning at 9 a.m. sharp, Alice went to the deaf school to check on their cherished little one and to see if she was afraid or sad or crying.

Alice was shocked the first time she saw Danielle playing with the other deaf kids. The joy that she picked up in Danielle's demeanor was tear-jerking. How could she not leave Danielle here? Alice thought. These other kids were exactly like her little girl. It was as though Danielle had been brought to another planet where all the people were just like her.

As Alice watched her precious little baby, playing, joking, and socializing with the other deaf kids her own age, it finally occurred to her that Danielle was exactly where she needed to be.

The deaf school was very understanding and even encouraged Pete and Alice to visit the school often throughout the year to check on Danielle's progress. "Call anytime," the kind administrator told Alice so that she might not feel so out of touch with Danielle. They also suggested that Alice and Pete call to check on Danielle's academic progress throughout the year. Alice cried all the way home.

Danielle was eleven years old and the deaf school, having tested Danielle academically, started her out in the fourth grade. The fourth grade, with deaf, age-appropriate children, made Danielle feel more established. Danielle not only learned, she bloomed.

Due to the fact that Danielle was really very bright, it took just three months for her to learn American Sign Language. She was so happy. Yes, she missed her family, but she loved many of the other kids and felt like she belonged here.

This big move to the deaf school did not go without apparent trauma. The greatest impact of this major change in Danielle's life caused her to stop menstruating. She was unaware that this body change could happen so she was hopeful that she would never, ever start again. Sadly, after Christmas vacation Danielle resumed being a woman.

Life at the deaf school was very enriching for Danielle. She was now able to do something that she had longed to do, but could not do well before. She could now truly communicate. Danielle's life felt complete.

Learning sign language also allowed an easier pathway for Danielle to improve her reading and writing. Before she learned sign language, reading and writing sometimes seemed a little senseless to Danielle because communication with other people was greatly deficient.

One day while at Marshall, it occurred to Danielle that words were the key to reading and writing and that words meant something. Shortly thereafter writing became something Danielle began to enjoy doing.

While at Berkeley, Danielle would often write long letters to her mom just to keep Alice in the loop about her many new challenging experiences, and to tell her of the things she was learning and doing at school.

Alice would always write back and put a dollar or two in the return letter so Danielle would have "spending money" to buy stamps or school supplies. Sometimes Danielle would buy school supplies, sometimes—or should I say, usually—Danielle bought chocolate.

Alice and Pete traveled to Berkeley about every three weeks. After a few months, Alice had to make the trek down to Berkeley alone, just to be with her precious little girl. Many of these trips were treacherous, triggering Alice to drive very cautiously. Winters along the northern coast of California are wet and extremely windy.

Rio Dell averages forty inches of rainfall per year with most of this rain arriving from November to April. Rivers usually fill to capacity and sometimes overflow, causing flooding and extreme weather. Another hazard, not too frequently mentioned, is widow-makers.

Widow-makers are very large redwood branches that can kill. Some of these branches can be a foot across at the base and weigh upward of a hundred pounds. The local loggers gave the aforementioned branches the name widow-makers due to the fact that when it is extremely windy or when the tree-fallers fell a very large tree, these branches may fall out of the tree before it is felled, and if not noticed, will hit and kill the logger, thus leaving the logger's wife a widow.

Sometimes, while Alice was traveling during high wind conditions, some of these heavy widow-makers fell onto the oft-traveled Highway 101. This stopped traffic while safety crews cleaned up the debris.

On several occasions Alice had to stay at an unfamiliar motel until road conditions or the weather changed. Some of the motels in 1967 were well equipped; some, not so much.

Alice would pick Danielle up at the school, usually on weekends, and the duo would rent a room at Motel 6 so they could catch up on things. Danielle was excited to spend time with her mom and to teach her many of the new signs she was learning. Danielle loved her new manual communication skills. Danielle was a quick learner and tried hard to teach Alice American Sign Language so she could tell her about the many new friends she was acquiring. Alice, now forty-four years old and already knowing two languages fluently, English and Italian, found sign language daunting, at best.

Chapter 7

The other students were obviously very excited. Danielle didn't know why.

"What's the matter?" Danielle signed to her roommate, Patty, as she tried diligently to understand why all the students were all so animated. She asked again. "Why are the kids so excited?"

Patty responded, "Don't you know what's happening today? The famous lady is coming to our school today."

"What's that sign mean?" Danielle asked, as she mimicked Patty's new word.

"Do you know what the word 'famous' means?"

"Not really," Danielle replied.

"That word means that the lady is important and a lot of people know her, like she's a special kind of person," Patty signed.

"A special kind of lady, a special person?" Danielle signed to herself.

"Hurry up and get ready. She's going to be in the auditorium in a little while. Hurry, let's go," Patty signed impatiently.

Patty waited while Danielle changed her blouse, and the two girls left their dorm room together.

On the way there, Patty began to tell Danielle that all their friends would be attending and that it was always fun when they had a special guest come to their school. Patty led Danielle to the auditorium. Danielle had not yet been in the auditorium, so she took a moment to take a good look around. It was a very large room which could probably seat the whole school at one time, and it had a stage with curtains which could be closed and opened. Patty pointed, and Danielle noticed some of the other dormies their age. Patty led the way so they could sit together with all their friends.

The lights blinked. Blinking the lights was one of the best ways to cause the deaf students to pay attention. All the kids looked up toward the stage and saw the school principal jump up onto the stage.

"Pay attention, pay attention," signed the principal with a huge smile on his face. All those young, curious eyes were centered on the principal as he proceeded. "Children, today we have a very special guest who comes to us from very far away. Many of you have seen her on TV or in magazines." Many of the students signed "yes" and nodded their heads up and down.

"Children, I wish to present to you Miss Helen Keller," signed the principal.

Danielle watched as a tall, well-kept, beautiful lady walked out from the left side of the stage holding the arm of her female interpreter. It was obvious to Danielle that this statuesque lady was blind. The interpreter walked the beautiful lady toward four chairs that were placed right in the center of the stage. Danielle noticed that Helen Keller smiled beautifully as she walked in and was very handsome in her dark dress. She also noticed just how refined and very confident she looked. The principal signed to the students that Helen Keller was born hearing and sighted, but when she was nineteen months old, she experienced a fever which left her deaf and blind.

Miss Keller's interpreter sat Miss Keller in one of the four chairs and then the interpreter sat in the chair directly next to Miss Keller's left side. The principal seated himself in another empty chair. Then he reached past the interpreter and signed directly into Miss Keller's hands.

The principal turned to the students and told them that he was going to ask Miss Keller some questions and that he would have another one of the school's own interpreters sign so they could all see the questions and know who was answering in return.

Danielle was captivated while watching Miss Keller. She had seen many blind kids before. The blind students lived in an institution that sat just above the hill overlooking the deaf school, but because the two schools seldom mingled, Danielle had never talked to any blind kids, but had seen the younger students being led around their campus holding a common rope.

Danielle noticed that Miss Keller would feel the signing from her interpreter and smiled all the while with great concentration. When Miss Keller responded she appeared to speak, but Danielle mostly watched the school's own interpreter as she told the students what Miss Keller was saying.

All the children were amazed that a person who was deaf and blind could be so educated and was able to have learned so much. Danielle thought to herself how she would never forget seeing this amazing woman and how much even a deaf/blind person could do if given the chance.

After the program was over Danielle, Patty, and some of the other dormies walked back to their rooms. All the way there the girls talked about how amazing Helen Keller was, that some of them had seen the movie *The Miracle Worker*, and how good the movie was.

Chapter 8

Life at the Berkeley school was an institutionalized life for all the deaf students. The school was run exactly like a college. Danielle loved the deaf school and made lots and lots of friends. In her early years, most of her friends were girls, but as the years passed boys soon became a presence within her inner circle of friends.

In the sixth grade Danielle's two roommates were Sherry Brown, an attractive biracial African-American girl, and Patty Riley. Patty always had a smile on her face. Patty was a joker, a fun-loving young woman with long dark brown hair and hazel eyes. These two non-hearing girls eventually came to feel more like sisters to Danielle than roommates.

During Danielle's thirteenth year, in sixth grade, it was not uncommon for most of the other girls to "go out" or go steady with one of the other deaf boys. These childish romances usually lasted days at best, but sometimes these young couples' affairs became extremely emotional and ended with a broken heart or two.

On Sunday mornings, the counselors would make sure that the young ladies who were Catholic were up in time to get ready for Mass. Danielle was a cradle Catholic and many of her classmates were Catholics as well. The girls and boys would be taken to Mass in the school van. Danielle loved going to Mass in Berkeley. Father O'Brien was a kindly priest who was fluent in sign language. He had learned sign language when he was a young man.

It is standard protocol for Catholic priests to be moved from parish to parish every five to seven years, but because Father O'Brien knew sign language, he was permanently assigned to Saint Joseph the Worker on Addison Street in downtown Berkeley. Danielle always enjoyed Father O'Brien's sermons. The priest was a very intelligent man and he was smart enough to keep his talks short and to the point.

It was very important that the girls' dormitory had many female counselors. These school counselors needed to maintain an eye on all the kids and nurture and guide them through the school year, especially the younger kids. It was not uncommon for many of these counselors to even help the kids work on their school assignments.

The boys had their own dormitory with their own male counselors. The boys' counselors not only helped them to stay out of trouble but also taught them games. Some of the more athletic counselors also assisted in coaching and playing assorted sports. Both the boys' and girls' counselors were either deaf or were hearing with exceptional signing skills, probably due to having deaf parents.

Danielle came to learn that certain counselors could be confidants and most of the girls' dormitory residents learned that they could easily go to their favorite counselor and tell their deepest, darkest secrets.

Most of Danielle's sorority sisters were kind, fun-loving, and of the same age group. California School for the Deaf at Berkeley was their home. Many of the girls thrived there. These children were educated, learned about life, and were groomed as to how they would get by in a hearing world. Not so for the girl named Kara Powers.

Kara was a bully. She was a heavy girl, about 200 pounds, with slate black hair and steel-blue eyes. If she wasn't so mean-spirited, she could be called pretty. Kara would pick on and belittle most of the other deaf girls in Danielle's dormitory, and obviously received a great sadistic joy in doing so. Due to Kara's bullying, most of the deaf girls just avoided her, which caused Kara to be more torturous. Danielle reviled Kara.

It was Saturday morning and the students were permitted to sleep in. Kara, the sneaky oppressor, snuck into Danielle's room.

Danielle was thirteen years old and sound asleep when Kara took her very ample buttocks and sat right on Danielle's face. Danielle awoke, scared to death, and started screaming. She hit and punched the pile of flesh that was smothering her. Battle as she might, Danielle could not budge the obese tonnage. Her struggling just made Kara hold fast all the harder so Danielle began beating the wall with her fist as hard as she could in hopes that her two other roommates would feel the pounding and hopefully come to her aid. Finally, after what seemed like several minutes, Patty and Sherry pulled, with all their might, the portly Kara off of Danielle. As Danielle cried and gasped for air, the cruel Kara started laughing and signing to Danielle, teasing her and calling her a baby. Sherry and Patty tried shielding Danielle from the hateful girl.

Danielle's counselor, having been alerted by another dormie, finally came into Danielle's room and wanted to know what was going on. Danielle told the counselor what Kara had done. Kara completely denied the accusation and said that it was Danielle's fault and that Danielle was making fun of her, calling her fat, and that had caused Danielle and her to start arguing.

The counselor had no other recourse but to put both students in detention. Danielle told the counselor that it wasn't fair that she had to go to detention when she was sleeping and the cruel, big fat ass Kara came in and sat on her face and tried to smother her. The counselor took Danielle aside and said that she knew Kara was a bully, but it wasn't fair to punish one girl and not the other, so punishing both of them was the only fair decision she could make. Danielle loathed Kara all the more.

In the summer of 1971, at Danielle's invitation, Sherry Brown took the opportunity to come to Rio Dell and spend a few weeks with Danielle. Sherry had never seen the redwoods and Danielle looked forward to having a deaf friend visit with her.

Danielle was so excited to have one of her roommates come up for a few weeks. She waited impatiently for the Greyhound bus to get to Rio Dell. The bus stopped directly across the street from Pete's barber shop, so Danielle waited in the shop for what seemed hours until finally the bus showed up.

Danielle watched as the bus drove off and there, standing on the sidewalk, stood Sherry Brown and a very large brown suitcase. Danielle excitedly looked both ways before crossing the street. In 1971 Wildwood Avenue was still Highway 101 and the only way to reach the north. Sherry's face lit up upon seeing Danielle running toward her. The girls embraced and Danielle grabbed Sherry's suitcase. "Follow me," Danielle signed, and the girls ran back across the highway.

It was about 2:30 in the afternoon, so there weren't a lot of customers in the barber shop. Danielle opened the door and brought Sherry into Pete's shop. The two deaf teens saw three men seated waiting for haircuts. These men stared in disbelief at Danielle and Sherry as they entered the shop. In 1971 there were no African-Americans living in Rio Dell.

Sherry waved at Pete as the girls went through the barber shop and into the backyard toward Pete and Alice's house where Danielle lived.

Giovanni and Emma Mela, Pete's father- and mother-in-law, had this barber shop built on a piece of property that they owned soon after Pete earned his hair-cutting license. The building had a suitable rental next door, as part of the same structure. It first housed a hardware store, but soon became a business called Maxwell's Toggery. Maxwell's sold men's clothes—fine-quality work pants, boots, and flannel shirts-catered to the mill worker.

For the two weeks that Sherry stayed with Danielle, townsfolk gawked when they saw the two girls walking and riding bikes through town. Danielle thought it amusing; Sherry felt quite awkward.

Chapter 9

Denny

The fall of 1971 came and Danielle started eighth grade. Danielle was smitten.

Danielle thought it weird, but for some reason, she had never really noticed Denny Jones before.

Denny was two years older than Danielle and in tenth grade. He was very handsome. He was tall, with a naturally muscular build, and had medium-length dark blond hair. Denny was an athlete, admired by both the boys and the girls. Most of the girls said he looked like Robert Redford, but Danielle didn't think so. She thought Denny was much better looking and respectful.

Since they were in different grades, the two didn't have any classes together, so Danielle made sure she and her friends sat near him and his friends at lunch time. It took about a month and finally one day one of Danielle's male friends introduced the two. In no time at all Danielle and Denny had become boyfriend and girlfriend.

Holding hands and spending lots of time together was a very natural, easy thing for the two while at school. Denny had an easygoing manner that made Danielle feel quite comfortable with him, almost like they had known each other forever. One day one of Danielle's favorite dorm counselors told her that she shouldn't have a boyfriend, especially this one, because he was older than she. Danielle signed to her, "Shut-up," then smiled facetiously.

Sometimes Denny and Danielle would sneak off campus and go to the Haight-Ashbury district to see the hippies. It was the spring of 1972 and lots of times they would see young people smoking marijuana, and many of the hippie girls wearing flowers in their hair.

As the year wore on, it became harder and harder for the counselors to keep Danielle and Denny apart.

Late one evening while Danielle was in her room visiting with a few of her friends, Gina, a sophomore and fellow dormie, signed to Danielle, out of the blue. "Have you kissed Denny yet?" she asked, half-jokingly. The question was half serious.

"No way," Danielle gesticulated. "Too many germs," she joked, as all the girls laughed.

Gina signed, "Wait a minute, wait a minute. Let me kiss him for you and I'll tell you what it is like."

All the girls laughed hysterically, even Danielle, but before falling to sleep that night Danielle pondered all that had transpired.

Summer was drawing near and the time for Danielle and Denny to part for a few months was getting closer. Denny and Danielle had gone to the park for a short, romantic walk late one afternoon, when Danielle turned to Denny and signed, "Denny, do you love me?"

Denny was caught off guard and thought before giving her an answer. The handsome, pensive Denny signed, "I like you a great deal, but I have never been in love before. I simply don't know."

"Me too," Danielle quickly signed.

American Sign Language, in its form, is not the same as the spoken word. For example, if one signs "what's the matter?" you would place the sign letter Y against your chin. This sign could mean, what's wrong, wrong, or what's the matter. ASL is a conceptual language with meanings and nuances all its own. Hence, by signing "me too," to Denny's response, Danielle was actually stating that she was not certain of her love for him either.

The school year ended and Danielle and Denny said their good-byes. Danielle was sixteen and Denny was eighteen. Before he left, Denny took Danielle aside and told her that he still wanted to be her boyfriend when school started in the fall and Danielle jokingly signed, "Let me think about it." They both laughed and then, unexpectedly, Denny slowly bent down, closed his eyes, and oh so gently, tenderly, kissed Danielle delicately on her baby-soft lips. Danielle was elated.

Danielle told Denny to write letters to her while they were on summer vacation. Denny promised he would, but sadly no letters came.

Chapter 10

The school year started again and upon seeing Denny walking toward her, making sure he had seen her, Danielle purposely turned and walked in the opposite direction. Denny chased after Danielle and grabbed her gently by the arm and turned her around, smiled at her, and gave her a big hug.

"Why didn't you write?" Danielle signed stoically and with feigned sincerity.

"I'm sorry," signed the still smiling handsome Denny. "I got busy and had to work this summer."

"Where did you work?" asked Danielle.

"Burger King," signed Denny.

"I like Burger King," signed Danielle, "but I'm still mad at you."

The school year continued and Danielle studied arithmetic, reading, and writing, but her favorite class was art.

Danielle was a natural and talented artist. While in Blue Birds, she had made many arts and crafts projects and truly enjoyed and excelled in those activities. To Danielle, art class was only an extension of the things she did when she was young. Danielle was known to be very creative and would even surprise the teachers with some of her unique designs and ideas.

Danielle's roommates, Sherry and Patty, often accompanied Danielle to downtown Berkeley where the trio could do some shopping. The young women shopped sometimes for clothes, sometimes for jewelry, and sometimes they found themselves merely window-shopping.

One day Danielle brought the girls to the hippie store that she and Denny had once visited. Sherry and Patty were a little reluctant to go into the shop, but Danielle, being the adventuresome type, convinced them that she had already been in the store once before with Denny.

The girls entered the store and Patty and Sherry were immediately surprised to see endless rows of bell bottom jeans, assorted multi-colored blouses, and lots and lots of hippie garb and shoes. Sherry and Danielle loved shoes. The girls were overwhelmed by the smell that permeated the little hippie shop. "Stinks in here," the comical Patty Riley signed by holding her nostrils shut. Both Danielle and Sherry smiled at the joke and confirmed her remark by nodding their heads up and down. The three remained in the store just looking and joking around for close to thirty minutes when one of the girls noticed a strange-looking glass object in the glass-fronted display cases.

"What do you think that is?" signed Patty to the two girls standing one on each side of her.
"I don't know," signed Danielle.

"I don't know," repeated Sherry.

The sign for "I don't know" is a very oft-used sign. It is an extended closed hand, similar to a military salute, with the flat-handed fingers touching the forehead just to the front of the temple. One then pushes the hand outward while turning at the wrist.

"Wait a minute," signed Sherry, "I'll go ask the lady." Sherry walked toward the front of the store, leaving Danielle and Patty gazing at the glass object.

This glass object was approximately twelve inches tall with a cylindrical tube going down toward its bulbous bottom. Near the bottom of one of the sides of the object, another, smaller tube protruded, slightly upward. The object looked like a vase, but the girls were confused about the purpose of the side tube.

Sherry eventually returned with a youthful-looking woman in tow. The pretty young woman was in her early twenties and was obviously a true-blooded, authentic hippie. She wore a red scarf on her head with her long brown hair flowing down her back. She had on a long, free-flowing multi-colored skirt wrapped tightly around her waist with a pink scarf-sash. Her blouse was a sheer, free-flowing white garment. Danielle and Patty were quite surprised to see that she was not even wearing a brassiere.

Sherry Brown pointed at the mysterious object and wrote on a lined piece of paper, which she had retrieved from her purse, "What's that?"

"Oh, that," said the girl as Sherry handed her the piece of paper. "That's a bong," wrote the hippie girl.

"A bong?" wrote Sherry. "What's a bong?"

The hippie girl smiled and wrote back slowly, "A bong is for smoking pot."

"Pot?" the three girls finger-spelled to each other.

Sherry signed "Thank you," to the hippie girl, then realizing that she accidentally signed to her, wrote on the paper, "Thank you."

The hippie girl lipped slowly and with exaggeration, "You're welcome," and smiled at the embarrassed girls.

Patty signed, "Let's get out of here," and the girls quickly exited the store.

The reason was never clear, but when Danielle was about sixteen, her nickname at school became the sign "Wino." Wino is signed with a W placed at the side of one's face with the pinky finger and the thumb touching the cheek. Where the pinky and thumb join together a small circular motion is then made. This nickname may have come from the fact that Danielle had a small, slightly noticeable palsy, probably due to the high fever she experienced as an infant which also left her deaf.

This palsy showed itself with small irregular jerking movements which could easily be felt if you happened to be leaning on her or holding her hand; hence the appearance of one being a little tipsy from drinking too much wine.

Danielle could have easily gotten angry when the kids called her "Wino," but instead, because she never took herself too seriously, she embraced the nickname.

On one very insignificant day Danielle was sitting at dinner with Sherry Brown. As they ate, Sherry turned to Danielle and signed, "Guess what all the kids are saying about you and Denny?"

Danielle, with a questioning look on her face, signed, "What?"

"All the kids are saying that it looks like Denny likes a lot of wine."

The two girls laughed, and Danielle was proud and a little bit scared that the other students at school knew that Denny obviously now loved Danielle.

CHAPTER 11

The year was 1973 and Danielle had just turned seventeen. Danielle and Denny were inseparable. Danielle was proud to watch Denny when he played basketball with the deaf team.

The California School for the Deaf's basketball team was on a winning streak and Denny was the star player. Danielle sat with Patty Riley and Sherry Brown while the girls watched their boyfriends play.

Patty was now going out with John Webber, a kind, handsome black guy, and Sherry was going out with David Daviton, the class president. David was an outstanding scholar, with long blond hair. David was the guy everybody went to when they had a difficult time with their homework. The three girls along with their boyfriends, usually hung out together after school. In doing so, they made up a kind of family unit.

It was a natural occurrence that many of the kids at the school for the deaf bonded together with their dormies to make this kind of "family unit." The observant school counselors were keenly aware of these minor groups and of the psychological well-being that these friendly groups provided. The attentive counselors encouraged the kids to bond to one another knowing that the human experience needed this sort of kinship. In this bonding of students, because of the institutionalized situation the children found themselves in, their relationship bonds often resembled those of siblings.

Denny was now a senior and Danielle tried very hard not to think about what would happen to her after Denny graduated from the deaf school.

Danielle was in tenth grade and still greatly enjoyed the environment of the deaf school. When she rode the bus home to Humboldt County for Christmas vacation or some other long weekend, she found herself longing for the closeness the deaf school environment provided.

While at home, Danielle would write long letters to Denny. In doing so she had to make sure that she hid the letters from her mom. Being the clever person that she was, Danielle usually wrote the letters to Denny while in the bath.

Due to the fact that Danielle was seventeen, her mom often told her that she was too young to have a boyfriend, and that she "better not have one." "If I find out from the school that you have a boyfriend, boy are you going to be in big trouble," Alice would say. "I don't have a boyfriend, Mom, don't worry," lied Danielle. Alice wanted to believe her.

Alice tried reasoning with Danielle, telling her things like, "The reason you're going to Berkeley school is so you can learn academics and possibly after high school you can go to college." Alice often tried to give Danielle positive ideas as to what things she might accomplish after high school graduation.

"If I decide to go to college, I'm going to Gallaudet, period," Danielle informed Alice one day while at home. Danielle knew that saying this would make Alice upset, since Gallaudet University for the Deaf is in Washington, D.C.

"Oh, no you're not," said Alice.

When Danielle and Alice had a conflict, Danielle would say, "Hey, Mom." Then, while Alice was looking at her, Danielle, with grandiose movements, would take off her hearing aid, causing the aid to emit a loud piercing feedback sound. Danielle would then hold the aid up into the air, sway it back and forth, and deliberately display it to Alice. This act of defiance meant, "I'm not talking to you anymore, and that's final."

It was a few months before Easter vacation. Danielle was at school visiting with her roommates when one day Patty signed to her, "Have you ever been in Denny's room before, Danielle?"

Danielle replied, with a shock, "You know the girls can't go in the boys' dormitory, or we'll get in trouble."

"I know," Patty signed, "but one time I snuck up to John's dorm room window and peeked in."

"What did you see?" asked Danielle, hoping it would be something juicy.

"Oh, nothing, nobody was there, but I sure got scared and ran away as fast as I could," signed Patty.

"Oh, you big chicken," Danielle signed back, as the girls laughed.

Danielle and Denny were on their way home from going to see the hippies one day shortly after Patty had talked with Danielle about seeing Denny's room, when Danielle turned to Denny and signed, "Denny, one day I want to come and see your dorm room."

"What?" he said with great surprise. "You know the girls can't come to the boys' dorm. You know good and well that we'll both get kicked out of school."

"I know," signed Danielle, "but I want to see it, I'm just curious, that's all."

Denny pondered Danielle's question for a long time after he dropped Danielle off at her dormitory. *I wonder if I could get Danielle in the room after everybody is sleeping,* Denny thought to himself before finally dozing off.

Finding a place where he and Danielle could talk alone with no one else around was practically impossible. Denny thought he found a secluded spot when one day he walked Danielle toward a low-drooping dogwood tree. Danielle had always admired this tree with its beautiful pink, four-petaled flowers and all its beautiful soft green leaves. The soft fruity scent of the earth undergrowth was heavy as Denny led the way. The two lovers stooped low, slowly walking under the drooping limbs, when Denny steered Danielle gently back up against the coarse-barked trunk of the stoic tree and then slowly leaned in and kissed her. Since their first kiss, Danielle always loved it when Denny kissed her.

"I think I have an idea," Denny signed to Danielle as he backed away from her slightly so Danielle could read his signs.

"What are you talking about?" signed Danielle.

"Remember you said you wanted to see my dorm room?" signed the excited Denny.

"Yes," signed Danielle.

"Well, I have a plan and I want to see what you think about it."

"Okay," signed Danielle, when all of a sudden, the two lovers turned to see one of their school counselors angrily pushing aside some of the tree limbs so he could get access to the two of them.

"What the hell do you think you're doing hiding under this tree?" signed the obviously upset counselor. "Do you want me to report the two of you to the office? Get out of here and never try to hide in here again," signed the counselor with irritated gesticulations.

"We're just talking," signed Denny with his easygoing smile that seemed to calm the fury of the counselor.

"Let's go. Get out, I mean it," signed the man again.

Denny had known this male dormitory counselor most of his life, so he wasn't too alarmed. Danielle, on the other hand, didn't know him very well at all, so she wasn't as relaxed as Denny about what had just transpired.

Danielle and Denny slowly worked their way out from under the low-hanging limbs of the dogwood tree. As the two instigators passed the interloper holding up the limbs, Denny facetiously stuck out his tongue at the counselor. The irritated counselor smiled as he watched the two lovers casually walk away holding hands. Denny quickly let go of Danielle's hand, then signed, "I'll try to find a better place next time, one that's not crowded with so many people!" The duo laughed hilariously as Denny walked Danielle back to her dormitory.

Being a senior, Denny was required by the school to turn in several papers before he was allowed to graduate. Denny was naturally a gifted student. Both of Denny's parents were deaf. Children of deaf parents almost always have a head start in school because there is no language barrier. When deaf kids from deaf parents are toddlers, deaf parents naturally sign to them so learning American Sign Language is never an obstacle.

One difficult class for Denny, English, required a five-page report on any famous American in history.

Denny loved playing baseball. When Denny was a little kid his dad signed Denny up for Little League. Once the rules of baseball are learned, having the ability to hear is not a requirement in order to play the sport. It was also very common for Denny and his father to attend the San

Francisco Giants Major League baseball games as often as they could.

Denny did not have to think very long about whom he would write about for his English assignment. He chose the famous Willie Mays for his five-page paper. To Denny, Willie Mays was a fascinating sports figure.

Willie Mays was an outstanding center fielder for the San Francisco Giants. On one memorable occasion while Denny and his father were in the left field bleachers, during pre-game warm-up, Willie Mays noticed Denny signing to his dad. As Denny looked at Willie Mays, Mr. Mays threw Denny a warm-up ball. Denny signed back to the famous number 24, "Thank you," and Mr. Mays took off his hat and bowed.

Denny's English teacher advised him to use the school library so he would not be distracted and he could eventually complete the much-needed report.

Denny went to the library. "Do you have some place where I can work without being bothered?" Denny asked the librarian. "Yes," signed the elderly woman, "follow me."

The librarian led Denny to a room that was about ten feet by ten feet with a heavy table and many chairs around it. This room's walls were glass so any passerby could see in, but because the room had a glass door, the person could be left alone. That's what Denny wanted, to be left alone. Denny signed, "Thank you very much," to the librarian, and the librarian left him.

Denny went into the library proper and looked up in the card catalog for books with information about the great Willie Mays. He was excited to find many books with lots of information about Mr. Mays. Truth be known, Denny was actually excited to write this report. He went back to the small see-through room, got all his work done, gathered his report, and returned to his dorm room so he could type his report. Denny was busy typing when all of a sudden, he had a great idea.

"I know where we can talk together without anyone bothering us," Denny signed to Danielle one day when they passed each other in the hall between classes.

"Where?" the curious Danielle asked.

"Just wait and see, I'll show you. Don't worry," said Denny with a smirk. Denny loved surprising Danielle.

"Okay," Danielle slowly signed, "but it better not have a big crowd of deaf people around."

The two laughed, Denny gently kissed Danielle's lips, and the two parted ways.

"Bring your backpack and some of your schoolwork," signed Denny as he was anxious to get Danielle to hurry up.

"Where we going?" signed the hurried Danielle as she pondered what things to bring along.

"Don't worry, just hurry up," signed Denny.

Danielle went to her room, gathered her books and backpack, and met back up with Denny.

Hand in hand, Denny and Danielle headed to the main three-story structure of the school. When Danielle realized that Denny was headed to the main office, she drew back her hand and signed, "I'm not going in there."

"Come on," signed Denny with his overpowering smile, "I won't let anything bad happen to you."

Feigning seriousness Danielle signed, "You better not."

Denny let go of Danielle's hand and opened the heavy dark green door which led into the main office. He bowed deeply as Danielle passed him as though submitting to great royalty. Danielle laughed; she always loved Denny's spontaneous sense of humor. The two continued down the hall until they reached a door located on their left side. Above the door hanging from the ceiling was a wooden sign which read "Library" in bold black letters. Denny again opened the door, bowed low, and Danielle, smiling, walked into the very large room filled with books.

Denny grabbed Danielle's hand and began guiding her through rows and rows of books. Danielle let go of Denny's hand and signed, "Why are we here, Denny?"

"Try to be patient for once, please. I want to show you something," he signed back.

"Fine," Danielle signed back, impatiently.

Denny led Danielle to a clear glass door. He opened the door and Danielle walked into the room where Denny had previously worked on his school assignment. "People can see us in here, Denny. Why did you think this is such a private place?" signed the agitated Danielle.

"Look around," signed Denny, "this library is the best kept secret. Nobody ever comes in here."

"I don't believe you," signed the doubtful girl.

"It's true. Remember last week when I told you I had a lot of homework for my English class?" signed Denny. "Well, this is where I was and nobody ever came by here the whole hour that I was in here."

"Really?" Danielle signed slowly, as she looked around.

"Yeah," signed Denny.

Denny pulled out a chair so Danielle could sit. Danielle removed her backpack and placed it on the table in front of them. She then sat down and looked around again. It was true. Danielle could see through all the walls of the small room, but try as she might, she could not find anybody watching them. The other students who used the library were obviously too involved with their own assignments to pay much attention to anyone else.

"Are you satisfied that this is a private place for us to talk?" gesticulated the ingenious Denny, with a smirk.

"Yes," signed Danielle. "It's amazing."

Denny started to tell Danielle about his plan when the librarian happened to walk by and peered into the modest room. "Are you two working on schoolwork?" the librarian signed through the glass.

"Of course," signed the proud Denny. "This is a good friend of mine," he added, pointing to Danielle. "We have an assignment we're working on together." Which, when you think about it, wasn't totally a lie.

"All right," signed the librarian. "Let me know if you require any help." The librarian walked away, looking back once at the two hardworking students.

"I told you," signed Danielle, proving to Denny that they weren't anywhere private.

Denny had a huge infectious smile on his face. "She won't bother us again. Anyway, I can see from here if she starts looking at us."

"All right," signed the still doubtful Danielle. "Tell me your big plan," she finally asked.

Denny began. "Do you know what time your night counselor checks on your room in the middle of the night?"

"I don't know," signed Danielle, "I'm always asleep."

"Well," signed Denny, "I need you to find out what time she checks on your room."

"How am I going to find out if I'm always asleep? Duh," signed Danielle.

"You're going to have to ask someone who knows," signed the smiling Denny. "Do you know any of the senior girls in your dorm?"

"Yeah, I'm pretty sure Gina, the girl with the long hair, is a senior, isn't she? You should know, she's from your class," Danielle signed.

"Yes, she is," signed Denny. "She is a senior. Ask her if she knows when the counselor checks on the rooms at night. Perhaps she knows."

Denny told Danielle his plan and Danielle eventually did find out that the night counselor checked on the students every night at midnight. Denny also wanted to know what time the counselors woke the students up every morning. He needed this information so his plan would work.

Finally, the big day came. Danielle was extremely apprehensive. If she and Denny got caught, they would both be expelled from school. Danielle even told Denny once that she was too scared and if she got kicked out of school, her mom would kill her.

"Don't worry," said the confident Denny. "We won't get caught. Anyway, I love you too much to care if anything happens. You know all I really want is to be with you."

It was a Saturday night and Danielle waited for Sherry and Patty to go to sleep. She then went to the bathroom and put her nightgown on over her clothes. She stayed in the bathroom an extra-long time. When she exited, the two roomies looked like they were already asleep. Danielle slipped into bed and turned her desk clock toward her so she could see when it was fifteen minutes after midnight.

Twelve fifteen a.m. was the predetermined time that she was supposed to cautiously sneak out of her dorm room window and then carefully slither over to Denny's room. Denny said he would be there, at the window of his room, waiting for her to arrive.

Danielle dozed off for what seemed a second and looked at the clock. The clock read 11:57 p.m. "I'm so scared," Danielle whispered to herself as she had to wait twenty more minutes. "I don't think I can do this." She began to shake. As nervous as she was, at 12:15 Danielle went to the dorm window at the foot of her bed, pushed up the window, and looked outside. The night was spectacularly beautiful. All the stars were out and the moon was a perfect crescent shape. There was a screen on the window. Danielle had never removed the screen before, so it took a few minutes for her to jimmy open the two side locks. Danielle gently pushed the window screen out and it fell to the ground.

The next thing she was supposed to do as part of the big plan was to quietly walk over to Patty Riley's desk and pick up Patty's chair. Just as Danielle grabbed for the chair, Patty changed position in bed, causing Danielle to nearly panic. When Patty finally settled down, Danielle carefully lifted Patty's chair and carried it to the window. Danielle then tried working the chair quietly out the window and down to the ground level. As Danielle looked out as to where the chair would land, she noticed that the screen had fallen directly in the way. Danielle tried desperately to push the screen askance with one of the legs of the chair. Eventually the leg of the chair finally moved the screen aside. Danielle then put the chair down, turned herself around, picked up her own desk chair, and placed it against the wall. Danielle stepped onto her chair, then slithered out the window.

Danielle, quietly as she could, slid the window gently closed behind her. Danielle remembered to put Patty's chair as far behind the outside shrub as she could. This shrub was just below and to the side of the window. Denny had told her that hiding the chair was very important and not to forget to do that.

Danielle straightened herself, looked straight ahead, and strode purposefully across the field toward the boys' dormitory. Danielle found herself walking adjacent to the sidewalk and then straight up to Denny's room's window. Denny was standing just inside his window, having already removed its screen.

"I was afraid you weren't coming," signed the shirtless Denny.

"I almost didn't," signed Danielle as Denny handed her a chair.

"I'm so glad you didn't change your mind," Denny signed.

The gentle Denny helped Danielle up and into his room. Once she was inside, Denny opened Danielle's jacket and kissed her passionately at the same time.

"Stop," Danielle signed soundlessly, "I want to see your room first."

The easygoing Denny smiled and signed glibly, "This is Josh's bed," pointing to the sound asleep figure, "and this, of course is Robbie's bed," pointing with a nod of his head.

Danielle nodded in acknowledgment, then looked up into the eyes of the handsome smiling man.

Denny, with kindness and great compassion, leaned slowly down and kissed Danielle while gently, oh so softly, he shadowed Danielle down as she laid herself peacefully upon his pillow.

"Wake up, wake up, Danielle," signed the scared Denny as he had just noticed that the clock read nearly 3:00 a.m. Danielle woke with a start and hastily gathered her clothes and put on her jacket.

"Please be careful," the gentle man signed as he helped Danielle out of his window and down to the waiting chair. Danielle turned to him before she left and kissed him passionately one more time.

As she headed back to her room, she turned and saw him giving her the "I love you!" sign. Danielle returned the sign and hurried back to her dormitory window.

In the morning Danielle opened her eyes and smiled. *We did it,* she thought to herself and got up to use the restroom. When Danielle walked past the window, she remembered that she had forgotten to replace the window screen. She opened the window and saw that the screen was still on the ground outside.

Danielle hurriedly put on her shoes and walked down the hall and out the back door of the dormitory. She walked over to the screen, reached down, and picked it up. As she turned, she realized that a dormitory counselor had followed her out.

"What are you doing out here, Danielle?" signed the curious counselor.

"Me?" asked Danielle. "Oh, I'm only putting back the screen in the window."

"The screen? Why did you take the screen off the window in the first place?" the counselor asked with annoyance.

"Oh, um, I was joking with Patty Riley, she farted this morning and I told her I couldn't breathe so I opened the window and put my head out and the screen fell off. We all laughed so hard. I'm sorry, it won't happen again, I promise."

"It better not," signed the cranky counselor. She watched Danielle replace the screen to the window and the two walked back into the dormitory together.

CHAPTER 12

Danielle was always melancholy when spring break came around. She recognized that she wouldn't be seeing Denny for what seemed like a long time, and the long bus drive back to Humboldt County seemed daunting.

"I won't be able to see you for two whole weeks," Danielle signed slowly and with a frown to Denny as they sat together facing each other cross-legged on the lawn.

"I know," signed Denny, returning the frown. "Look at the bright side. It's only two weeks, and we'll get to have a nice Easter with our families and hopefully we'll get lots and lots of chocolate." he signed with a comforting smile. "You'll get to see your cousins and your grandparents," he continued as he tried to cheer her gloominess.

"You're right," signed the mopey Danielle, "but that doesn't make me feel any better."

Danielle looked a little out of sorts to Denny as he ran to meet her as soon as he saw her after their spring break. "What's wrong?" signed the curious Denny.

"Oh, nothing," signed Danielle.

"Did you have a nice visit with your family?" asked the concerned man.

"Yeah," Danielle signed. "Me and Dana stayed with my Nonna for a few days and ate a lot of delicious Italian food. Dana is learning a bunch of signs now."

Hand in hand, the two walked slowly back to the girls' dormitory without much conversation. Denny turned and kissed Danielle and signed, "Are you going to sit with me at dinner tonight in the cafeteria?"

Danielle did not answer, then signed, "Denny, it's getting close to graduation and I'll never see you again." She started to weep.

"Oh, Wino," Denny signed, patting Danielle on the back as they embraced. "Now I know why you're looking so sad. I get it. We're both growing up." He signed optimistically, "Aren't you excited that I got accepted to Gallaudet?"

"Yes, but that doesn't change how bad I feel about it."

"I know," signed the troubled man. "It will get better soon though. You'll see," Denny added as he tried to be comforting.

It was the end of April 1973 when Denny walked up to Danielle, and she signed to him, "I have to talk to you alone. It's important."

Denny made a face and signed, "Um, okay, where should we go? Do you want to go back to the library?"

"No," signed the restless Danielle. "I want to go to the park."

Denny was very worried; he had never seen Danielle so agitated before.

It was a beautiful Saturday morning and Denny had told Danielle that he would come by her dorm at 10 a.m. so they could walk to the park together. Danielle came out of the dormitory and into the arms of the waiting Denny. Denny could tell that Danielle had been crying. "What's wrong, Danielle?" signed Denny as Danielle began to sob.

"Let's go," she impatiently signed as the two began their walk. Danielle was so upset that she had a hard time thinking of anything she wanted to say. The lovers slowly made their way to the park.

Danielle purposefully picked a seat on the park bench that the two had often, joyfully, sat on before. Danielle turned to Denny, looked around cautiously to make sure they were totally alone, and slowly, with great struggle, signed to Denny. "Denny, I missed my period!"

There was a long, awkward pause. Denny was in complete shock. Life had changed. Denny signed back, ever so slowly, as if needing to digest the words, "You missed your period?" The kind and gentle Denny, slowly and with great love, wrapped his strong arms around his beloved Danielle, as he too, began to weep.

CHAPTER 13

"Nana, how will I know the girl I'm supposed to marry?" I asked my Mexican grandmother back when I was nine years old. We had been speaking to each other while she was making flour tortillas as an accompaniment to the chili verde that she was making for dinner.

"Hijo," my nana said, "when you meet the girl God has already picked for you to marry, hijo, your heart will skip a beat." *Hijo* means "my son" in Spanish.

"My heart will skip a beat?" I repeated this strange response to myself slowly as though my brain needed to contemplate.

It had taken me more than twelve hours by car to make it to College of the Redwoods in Humboldt County. Having worked for three years after high school graduation, with the help of my mom and dad, I started the forestry program at C/R in the fall of 1975.

Although I was born in Long Beach, California, in 1954, I was never a city boy. When my best friend Richard and I were thirteen, we'd go with his dad, Rollo, to where there were acres and acres of endless dirt roads. Looking back, these dirt roads must have belonged to some of the many cities that make up Los Angeles County.

It sounds crazy now, but Richard and I used to sit on the front wheel wells of Rollo's 1950 Oldsmobile 88 as he ventured over the vastness. I loved it. Rollo's car shocks were strong, the car was heavy, and the terrain massive. We'd just ride around sometimes for what seemed like hours, all the while Rollo was enjoying himself, drinking beer in the car.

After I finished high school at Phineas Banning High School in Wilmington, California, I started working in an airplane parts place in Long Beach. Due to the fact that I have a birthday in October, I was young for my high school graduating class, graduating at just seventeen.

I worked in the airplane parts place and saved enough to buy a car. I managed to crash my first car, a 1969 Chevrolet Impala. My second car was a brand new green 1973 Volkswagen Super Beetle. This green Bug was what I had when I moved to Humboldt County.

I was in the men's dormitory at College of the Redwoods and my roommate's name was Steve. Steve was a good-looking guy and we hit it off right away. I was twenty and Steve was eighteen. Steve was about my height with thick dark wavy brown hair growing to his shoulders. He was thin and had a great smile.

When we first began rooming together, Steve and I would make sure we first met up and then we could go to the cafeteria together and eat. As time wore on and our circle of friends grew, we would just sit together if we happened to be down at the cafeteria at the same time.

Steve and I had a great relationship. I was kind of the big brother. I was pretty popular around the dorms, mainly because I had a car.

"Jack, could you let me know when you're going to Eureka next time? I need to pick up some groceries," Steve asked.

"Sure, I've got a few things to do right now. Do you have a class at six or seven tonight?" I responded. If the two of us went to Eureka, we always took the time to visit McDonald's.

The weeks and months passed by, and because Steve was my roomie and already had his license, it was just easier for me to let Steve use my Bug. Learning to drive a stick-shift can be difficult, but Steve rode a motorcycle at home so it was easy to teach him how to shift. He was always very responsible.

My fall schedule was chock-full of various classes. I was a forestry major so I had a few classes that I thought I would love. It turned out that Forestry and Natural Resources, the two main classes you must pass if forestry is your major, were somewhat disappointing to me. To my surprise, the class that I most enjoyed was English. I had scored very low in my English college placement exam, likely due to my "not so great" education in the Los Angeles school system.

I started out at C/R in what was then called bonehead English. I had an amazing teacher, Miss Meachum. Miss Meachum could teach anybody with half a brain the purpose of English and its utilization. Once I eventually realized how and why the comma is used, English became a fun but challenging class.

I passed my first semester of junior college with a 2.8 grade point average. I was proud of this because I possessed such a rudimentary high school course of study. It appeared I had the sort of mentality that didn't retain much if I didn't get up early and review before a big test. I ultimately learned how to study, but taking notes has always been extremely difficult.

Classes for spring semester 1976 were picked, and I made sure I had twelve units so I'd be a full-time student. One of the electives that I was really looking forward to was drama class. I was looking for something that would be fun, so why not drama class.

My first drama class was scheduled to start at 2 p.m., and I got there a little early. I was chatting with a few of the dormies when I suddenly looked toward the room entrance. I caught my breath; my heart skipped a beat. There, that girl, the one who had just come into the room, within my soul, I knew she was going to be my wife.

Oh, my goodness, she was so beautiful! I just couldn't take my eyes off of her. She had dark brown if not black hair, beautiful, flawless skin, and her eyes were a vivid coffee-bean brown. I didn't want her to catch me staring at her so I kind of tried to look around the room a little bit. I quickly made up my mind that I had to ask her out on a date before I lost sight of her when the class ended.

I thought she'd say she had a boyfriend or maybe she was busy. But I was determined. I had to ask her out. Where would I take her? I thought. What would we do? I just didn't care. I had to ask.

The instructor gave us our first assignment, a short paper on what we hoped to learn from this drama class, and sent us on our way. "See you next week," said the instructor.

Before she had a chance to leave, I quickly made my way over to the most beautiful girl I'd ever seen. She happened to notice me walking toward her and she smiled at me. "Hi," I said, before she could make her exit, "my name is Jack. Would you like to go roller-skating with me sometime to Rohner Park?" She looked at me and smiled, so for a moment I thought she might be interested, but before I knew it, she turned and walked away.

That's it, the love of my life, the girl I'm supposed to marry. She just smiled and turned away. I was devastated, cut to the quick. I couldn't help it. I was hurt, hurt deeply.

"God," I said to myself, "Nana said my heart would skip a beat. It did. I felt it. I know it did. Now what am I supposed to do?"

It was time for our second drama class and so naturally, I went there early so I could find out if that girl came back, or if I frightened her away.

There she was. She walked in again, and my heart felt like it stopped. Again, I caught my breath. I smiled at her when she looked my way. She must not have seen me; she turned her head away. What else could it possibly be? She's supposed to be my wife; she just doesn't know me yet. "Hello, beautiful girl, I'm going to marry you, you just don't know it yet," I wanted to yell.

The teacher entered the room. Our instructor was named Jane Hill. Jane had a cup of coffee in her hand as she walked into the room with all her instructor stuff. She placed the coffee and her stuff on the desktop and turned around. Jane then motioned for that girl, the one that I asked to go roller skating, to come up to stand beside her. "Class," Jane said, "this is Danielle Silbernagel. I forgot to introduce her to the class last week. But class, Danielle is deaf. If you want to talk to her, make sure she can read your lips."

No wonder. "Thank you, God." I couldn't make up my mind whether to walk over to her right then or wait for our break in an hour. I ruminated on this thought and then decided to wait until the break. But this time I'd make sure she knew I was asking her out on a date.

I grabbed one of my lined pieces of paper. On the paper I wrote, "Hi, my name is Jack. Will you go roller skating with me to Rohner Park in Fortuna sometime?" There, I had a plan. Now all I had to do was make sure to give her the paper before she left after class.

Once again, I was completely prepared to head her off before she exited the room. Once the instructor dismissed the class, boom, there I was standing in front of Danielle. Once more, she looked at me and smiled, but this time was different. While I was nervous and much afraid that Danielle would say no, I smiled at her and handed her the lined paper with my introduction.

Danielle gently reached for my paper as I stood staring at her beauty up close. *God, please have her say yes!* As I waited for her reply, I held my breath. She read my paper, looked up into my blue-hazel eyes, and answered in a completely throaty guttural voice, "Ai hab to axe my mom." She then handed me the paper back.

I held up both my hands as to say, "Wait a minute, wait a minute. Can we talk?" I mouthed with very conscientious articulation. She looked at me askance as I gently reached for the paper. On the paper I wrote, "Can we talk?" She nodded her head up and down. YES! She said we could talk. We walked together, and as I arrived at the classroom door first, I stood to the side of the door, stooped low, as if she were royalty, and motioned outside. She smiled as though she was amused.

"Where do you live?" I asked as we sat on the first plant border we came across. It appeared that most of the vegetation planted around the campus of College of the Redwoods had a convenient redwood plank sitting structure around them. Once more, she gave me that quizzical look and then I reached for the lined paper. "Where do you live?" I wrote.

She quickly grabbed the paper from me and wrote, "Rio Dell." She handed me the paper and I nodded in acknowledgment. Danielle grabbed the paper from me. "Where you live?" she wrote in return.

"I live in the dorms," I replied, turning the paper toward her so she could read it. She then did something very unfamiliar to me. She pointed her finger upward in front of herself and shook it from side to side. When I made a face, she grabbed the paper from me and wrote, "Where?"

Oh, I thought while pointing to the direction of the boys' dormitory. Danielle nodded. I didn't know what else to say so I said, "Do you want to see my dorm room?" Oh, I thought and once again grabbed the paper. I had barely finished writing and as I looked up, she was already nodding. She had obviously read the paper as I was writing. I instantly stood up and gestured with my left hand. "Come, walk with me, I'll do anything you want." I probably didn't say all that with my hand-waving motion, but that's what I wanted to say.

Danielle and I walked slowly to my dorm room. I was keenly aware she could not hear so I waited for her to look at me before I mouthed bigly, "Do you have a car or do you ride the bus?" She looked at me strangely, then I motioned with my two hands as though I was driving a car. Danielle smiled and nodded. "Where's your car?" I mouthed as I made a quizzical look on my face and raised my hands with the palms up and shook them around. Danielle pointed down toward the front of the school where all the parking places were. Yoo-hoo, she understood my speech! We reached my dorm room. I knocked, making sure Steve was decent. Good, no answer. I unlocked it and pushed the door open. We walked in, Danielle leading the way.

My dormitory room was approximately ten feet wide by sixteen feet deep. My bed and desk were nearest the door. Steve's bed was against the back wall with his desk and mine being back to back angling toward the middle of the room. Having the desks set up this way gave each of us some privacy.

Danielle looked around, then walked to Steve's side of the room where our sink and vanity were located. She looked in the mirror, looked at the sink, then put her hand to her chin, shook her head up and down pretending she was a building inspector. She took her finger and swiped it along the countertop as though checking for dust. She made a face as though it passed her approval.

"Do you want to sit down?" I said as I pointed to my desk chair. Danielle shook her head no. She signed something as she motioned toward the doorway. "Oh, you have to go now?" I mouthed. She nodded as though she understood my meaning. "Will I see you again?" I said, being careful to articulate my words well. She nodded again and I hoped she understood me. She walked through the open door as I waved a greatly exaggerated good-bye. Danielle waved back and I watched her as she walked away.

It was 8:35 in the morning. "Who could be knocking at my door so early? Did Steve forget his key again?" I thought Steve had a class at 8 o'clock this morning. Steve liked early classes; I preferred 10 a.m. or later.

"Who is it?" I sleepily grumbled out loud, not moving my head from my pillow. No answer came. "Who is it?" I called out louder, thinking the perpetrator had not heard me grumbling. I reluctantly got up in my boxers, grabbed my glasses, and opened the door.

Before the door fully opened, I grouchily said, "What?" There she was, the most beautiful girl ever. "Hi," I sheepishly said. Danielle signed something that I didn't understand, but I motioned toward the inside of the room, meaning, "Do you want to come in?" She shook her head no but she handed me a small 3x5-inch card. I blinked a lot, hoping my eyes weren't deceiving me and the most beautiful girl in the world was really right here standing in front of me. I reached for the card and looked at it. AMERICAN SIGN LANGUAGE MANUAL ALPHABET, read the card across the top. "For me?" I asked as I pointed to my chest. What an idiot, of course it was for me, but I was totally flustered and embarrassed that I was still clad only in my boxers.

Danielle gestured as though to say "I'm leaving now." I nodded, then gestured, "Wait! Wait!" holding up my open hands. Danielle stared at me and gestured with her head with a slight up and down nod as though she understood. I turned away, leaving the door open, and reached for a piece of paper out of my notebook. "Did you ask your mom if you could go roller-skating with me?" I hurriedly wrote. I handed Danielle the paper. I watched her read it and she nodded. I smiled hugely. She handed me back the paper and turned and walked away.

"Thank you, God, thank you, thank you." I was elated, I was excited, I was overjoyed. Within my head, I saw Snoopy doing his happy dance.

I climbed back into bed, put my head back on my pillow and read the card. I had seen this manual alphabet before, but never took the time to read each individual letter. It's difficult to express but learning the manual alphabet was never tedious. I now had the chance to find out how to communicate with the most beautiful young lady in the universe.

I put everything else aside. It took me one day to learn the manual alphabet. I just practiced and practiced and practiced. I spelled everything I passed by as I walked to the cafeteria for brunch. I never ate breakfast, but I always ate two hamburgers for lunch.

Hamburger. H-A-M-B-U-R-G-E-R I spelled slowly with my fingers. It got easier and easier the more I practiced. I needed to look at the card several times, but I was bound and determined to learn how to spell with my fingers.

It was drama class day. I walked to class and when I was almost there, I saw Danielle sitting on the planter box structure that we had first sat on the other day. "Hey," I said as I smiled and walked quickly to where she was seated. She returned the smile and stood up. I motioned toward the classroom. We walked in and took a seat next to each other. That's when I saw Danielle glance up at another girl who had come into the room. Danielle started signing to her.

The girl was of medium stature, long strawberry blonde hair, and a little pudgy. "Hi," she said to me, "my name's Rachel. I'm Danielle's sign language interpreter," she said with keen satisfaction.

Danielle started signing to Rachel and then Rachel turned to me and said, "Danielle wants me to tell you that you have to meet her mom before you can go on a date together." I nodded, but was kinda bent out of shape that I had to have this stranger explain to me what Danielle was saying.

I looked at Danielle and said, "Where do you want me to meet your mom?"

The interpreter signed to Danielle for me and Danielle signed back to her. Rachel started talking to me as though it was from Danielle and said, "Come to my house for dinner and you can meet my mom."

"Okay, sure, no problem… What's your address?... What day?... When?"

All the incidentals were hashed out and before I knew it, I was driving down to Rio Dell to meet Danielle's mom. Would she like me? I would try hard to make a good first impression and to be on my best behavior.

It wasn't difficult to find Danielle's house. "Green house with flowers in front, behind the barber shop," was what she had written under the address when she handed me the paper with the directions.

I was anxious as I got out of my green Bug and walked up to the door. I had even worn shoes so I could make a good impression. At home in Los Angeles, as long as I wasn't at work, I never wore shoes. The undersides of my feet were like well-worn, thick leather and impervious to the cold hard ground.

I opened the screen door and knocked. Danielle's mom must have seen me drive up because I didn't have to knock a second time. "Hello," I said as the lady whom I assumed was Danielle's mom cautiously opened the door. "My name's Jack."

"Hello," said the woman, as she eyed my person. "My name's Alice."

"Alice," I said. "My mom's name is Alice."

"Come in," she said as she opened the door.

Alice hadn't smiled yet so I got the impression that she wasn't impressed that I had worn shoes.

Danielle was seated at the dining room table. She got up, grabbed my hand, and led me to another chair at the table.

"Where are you from?" Where do you live?" "How old are you?" I answered what seemed to be pre-rehearsed questions from Alice. She seemed unimpressed, but I wasn't planning on marrying her, I was planning on marrying Danielle!

After I answered hundreds of questions, she said that Danielle had helped her make dinner. Alice finished up a few things, then said that she would be going to her room. "Good night," I said.

What! I was ecstatic. I was delighted. I was hungry. I spelled to Danielle slowly and with much difficulty with my unreliable fingers. T-H-E D-I-N-N-E-R S-M-E-L-L-S D-E-L-I-C-I-O-U-S.

She smiled and got up and started dishing up spaghetti with a dark red sauce. This red sauce was very acidic, but in a delightful, well-seasoned way. Danielle also served garlic bread. I later found out that Alice was Italian and that Danielle's family only ate homemade spaghetti sauce.

After dinner, Danielle brought out what looked like a small white electric typewriter. The machine was about nine inches from top to bottom, about three inches thick, and about twelve inches wide. "My TTY machine," she said. I repeated, "Your TTY machine." She nodded.

I found out later that the TTY machine was used by the deaf to call each other on the telephone. The handpiece portion of the telephone is placed on top of the TTY, which has two circular receptacles where the phone's handpiece is placed. The person on this end then calls another person by dialing the phone in the standard way. When the phone rings on the other end of the call, the deaf person knows a call is coming in because a light connected to the TTY blinks. When the person on the other TTY answers the phone, they usually start typing so the other deaf person knows that they have answered. The red LED letters start running across a small LED display where the deaf person can read what the other person is saying.

Danielle had ingeniously thought of another way for her and I to use this TTY. Since I am hearing and she is deaf, communication between the two of us was awkward, at best.

Danielle placed the TTY on the kitchen table and typed. The red LED letters ran by on the small display. I read, "This machine my TTY. I use for phone call." Danielle then slid the machine toward me as though she wanted me to type back. I immediately typed, "Amazing," as I made sure she could read what I was writing. "I have never seen a TTY before." That was it, we were hooked; we instantly had a way to communicate.

I was always a good typist. I started learning typing in the seventh grade at my father's insistence. "You'll use it your whole life and you'll never be sorry you learned," he told me. My dad was so right.

"What's your nationality?" I typed to Danielle.

Danielle looked at me quizzically and typed out "What?"

"Oh," I wrote, "are you Mexican, or Spanish or what?"

"Oh," she wrote back. "Me Italian and German."

"Wow," I said. "I thought you were like me."

"What you," Danielle wrote.

"I am Mexican and Irish," I typed.

"Nice," was all that appeared on the LED screen.

Danielle and I typed for what seemed like hours when she got up and got the two of us a piece of chocolate cake. "You want drink milk?" she asked in her guttural throaty voice.

I nodded, then said, "Just a little bit." And with my thumb and forefinger I signed to her and gestured with a little place between my thumb and index finger. I realized this hand gesture also was the manual alphabet letter G.

The chocolate cake was moist and rich. As I took a bite, I was surprised to find that I could easily taste cherry flavor. Yum, cherry and chocolate really taste great together. "I can taste cherry in the chocolate cake," I typed on the TTY.

Grabbing the machine from me, Danielle wrote, "Yes, my mom put cherry jello."

"Delicious," I wrote.

I stayed at Danielle's until 10 p.m. I told her, on the TTY, that I better leave and she smiled and nodded. Alice never did come back out of her room. Danielle's dad never came out to meet me, but I did hear when he came in the back door, took a shower, and must have gone to bed.

I asked Danielle on the TTY, "Can I see you tomorrow?"

"Sure," was all she said.

"See you tomorrow," I lipped as I walked out the front door and got into my Bug. I waved; Danielle waved back.

Thank God for TTYs. Danielle and I were never seen without it. We'd hang out any time we could between classes, before classes, after classes. I just loved being around her.

Our second week together, Danielle typed, "Do you want learn sign language?"

"Yes." I nodded.

"My best friend Rene teach sign language."

"Really? Where," I typed.

"Here," Danielle typed.

"You mean at C/R?"

"Yes," she typed as she smiled at me.

"When can I take the class?" I asked.

"Now?" was her answer.

"Sure," I typed.

Danielle typed again. "I ask Rene when you meet with her."

"Great," I stated.

The following day Danielle arranged for me to meet Rene. Rene was currently teaching beginning sign language at C/R.

"You can just add the class," Rene said to me. "You're already learning fingerspelling."

Fingerspelling. So that's what they call spelling with your fingers, fingerspelling. Who'd have guessed?

Rene was just wonderful. She was in her late twenties with light brown hair, a beautiful smile, and a baby on her back.

It was great to finally see a baby again. Having grown up with a lot of relatives I loved babies.

S-A-M-U-E-L, Rene fingerspelled to me very slowly.

"Who's Samuel?" I asked, after I read Rene's fingerspelling.

"My baby," she said. "My baby's name is Samuel."

I added the sign language class to my schedule. In 1976 Signing Exact English was at odds with American Sign Language. Due to the fact that the deaf do not sign word for word as in the spoken word, but sign conceptually, the educators at the time thought teaching deaf students Signing Exact English would help them when writing English.

    I loved Signing Exact English. I was like someone who hungered, I wanted more and more. At our first class I realized Danielle was Rene's teacher's aide. I got to see Danielle at class time and after class we would often go to my dorm room. There we would use her TTY, but the more we hung out the better I got at sign language.

Chapter 14

It was sometime in early February and I had just finished dinner in the cafeteria. I was walking back to my room thinking, *Wasn't Danielle supposed to meet up with me this evening?*

Danielle had an impressive way of being able to find me while I was at school. I had given her my class schedule and I had a fairly disciplined routine. She usually found me if I was somewhere on campus.

From the cafeteria to the dorms took about five minutes to walk so I walked, taking my time, savoring the beautiful Humboldt County evening. If I looked to the left, I'd see a forest of majestic redwood trees; if I looked to the right, I'd view a green pasture with white-faced brown beef cattle grazing.

Where is Danielle anyway? I hope she can make it this evening, I thought to myself. Just then a strange realization came from my inner being. *Do I love her because she's beautiful or is she beautiful because I love her? I LOVE HER. I do. I—LOVE—DANIELLE!* I realized.

As I reached my dorm room, I was still scanning the dorm parking lot where Danielle often parked when I noticed that my dorm room door was not fully shut. "That Steve," I said to myself, "in a hurry again, probably late to class."

I gently pushed the door open and I felt a slight resistance. I looked at about shoulder level when I noticed fingers wrapping around the end of the door. I wondered who might be in my room playing around. I started to poke my head in as the door slowly gave way, and I stepped in. There she was, the love of my life—nothing else mattered more than she.

Danielle waited until I got fully inside. She then took the items I had been carrying from my hands and purposefully placed them on my bed. There, behind the brown door, the door that I had closed and opened a million times, Danielle looked up into my blue-hazel eyes as I leaned down and gently, and with more love than I had ever known, kissed her.

After our first kiss, kissing was something which to Danielle and I always seemed to possess a purity about it. It was something that Danielle and I rarely displayed openly when others were about. Kissing was our private expression of love, something that was sacred and not to be shared openly.

Danielle and I loved being together. Sometimes she'd teach me new signs. Sometimes we'd lovingly tease each other and most of the time, while we were walking, Danielle would hold on to my elbow.

At first, I thought it strange. I'd see other couples holding hands, but I soon realized if Danielle and I held hands, I involuntarily stopped her from communicating with me. Her hands were her words. Gestures were her speech. Her eyes were the crux of the world around her.

Danielle, I soon realized, could see things that other people left unnoticed. One day, while we were walking back to the dorms. Danielle pointed to a couple seated on a planter box. Danielle could tell by their body language that they were arguing. I was completely oblivious to it. "How do you know they're arguing?" I half-signed, half-fingerspelled.

"Look, arms crossed, that mean she angry. She angry. He not," she spoke as she signed.

Danielle wore a hearing aid in her left ear. This aid did not become so apparent to me until we got to the stage in our relationship where we did a lot of hugging. If I embraced her on the hearing aid side the aid would let out a squeal. This squeal, I later found out, was feedback, the same kind of feedback that a speaker will emit if the microphone is held too close to it.

One day, Danielle and I were in the College of the Redwoods library. I had a paper that was due in English 1A, Reading and Composition. I was writing about euthanasia and was collecting information and facts to affirm my view. Danielle was reading some magazines.

As she pulled up a chair and sat next to me, I glanced up at her, smiled, and noticed her hearing aid. I never really noticed the small, behind the ear hearing aid before because of its tinyness. I noticed it this time because her hair had been accidently tucked in behind her ear, probably when she put the aid in that morning. I had a thought. "Hey, Danielle, can I see your hearing aid?" I signed and spelled.

I have always been of a curious nature. I love to learn. Danielle signed, "Sure," grabbed the small hearing aid, took it off of her ear, and handed it to me.

All of a sudden everybody in the library looked at the two of us. This super tiny, inconspicuous hearing aid let out the loudest, ear-piercing squeal as she handed me the attention-seeking culprit. I made an alarmed face as I desperately pointed to the hearing aid, trying to tell Danielle that the aid was making a deafening sound.

"Too loud?" Danielle asked in her now more exaggerated, guttural voice.

"Yes." I nodded urgently as I now began to hear many accusations of "SHUSH!" from the other people in the library.

I handed the squealing device back to Danielle, who turned the hearing aid off with a switch that I now noticed was on the back of the aid. Danielle then re-handed me the now silent offender.

I grimaced as I addressed the other sixty or so patrons who were in the library for some peace and quiet and studying. "I'm sorry, I'm sorry, I'm sorry," I mouthed, silently. Most of the library-goers smiled back, acknowledging this was obviously something quite unexpected, but some of them looked back, how shall I say? Pissed.

I was learning a lot about sign language and my life was changing. If I wasn't with Danielle, I was thinking about her. When I was with her, my life was completely and totally full.

Danielle showed up at my dorm room one morning. The door was open and I had my stereo on playing Steely Dan. Steely Dan was always my favorite music group. While I worked at my desk, my back to the front door, Danielle snuck in. I must have seen a shadow, because I turned and there stood the most beautiful girl in the world. I stood up to kiss her hello. Then she turned up her hearing aid until it squealed, turned it down a little, and signed, "Let's dance. I love to dance."

Danielle obviously could either feel the beat or hear something or both. It was very apparent that she had great rhythm. We danced around the small room to the song "Dr. Wu" by Steely Dan. It's not fast, it's not slow, so I grabbed her and held her close as we did a modified slow dance in which I believed she could feel my rhythm. We danced and danced and then danced some more. The scent of her hair, the feel of her breath on my skin, was intoxicating. When the song ended, she raised her head, looked into my eyes, and I slowly leaned down to kiss her tender lips.

I ventured down to Rio Dell every night. Danielle's mom and dad would go to bed about eight p.m., which gave Danielle and me time to use the TTY, use sign language, and enjoy each other's company.

One day one of my dormies, Sarojni, told me that she and some of our other roommates were going to the free clinic in Eureka to get checked up and to get some birth control. Sarojni wanted to know if Danielle and I wanted to go with them and if we had any room in my car. Sure, I said. I had no idea what to expect at the free clinic.

All my dorm friends were always inclusive toward Danielle. Maybe they couldn't understand everything she said, but if I wasn't around, they would be kind enough to write on a piece of paper and Danielle would respond in kind.

We all arrived at the free clinic in downtown Eureka and walked in. When Danielle and I walked into the clinic I immediately could smell some type of cleaning agent.

The reception room was clean and well kept. The receptionist said, with a grin on her face, "Are all of you together?"

"Yes," responded Sarojni. Sarojni was always very outgoing and unafraid.

"Please take a seat and I'll let the doctor know you're all here."

We seated ourselves. It was early afternoon and there was another lady there with a baby in a stroller. She smiled at us. We were four girls and four boys. Danielle, Sarojni, Barbara, and Denise were the girls. Peter, Joe, Russell, and I made up the boys. A nurse came out and called a name and the lady with the baby went in. While we waited, some of the guys read magazines while the girls just talked.

The nurse came back and one by one called on each of the girls. One by one the girls came back. Sarojni came back carrying a bag, Barbara came out with nothing. Denise went in and came out carrying a really big bag. When the nurse came out and called Danielle's name Sarojni motioned to Danielle that it was her turn. Danielle went in for about ten minutes and she too came out carrying a bag.

"Jack," the nurse called as I stood up and followed her down the hall.

The nurse was kind. She asked, "Are you sexually active?"

I was kind of caught off guard. "Yes," was my mumbled response.

"The doctor will be in to see you shortly."

"Thank you," I mumbled.

The doctor soon walked in and said, "Hello, Jack, my name is Dr. Sherrin." Dr. Sherrin was about fifty years old with shoulder-length dark blonde hair. She had expressive blue eyes and was wearing a white lab coat. "I see you're here for a checkup and to get some birth control?" she stated as she read my chart. I smiled and shook my head yes.

Dr. Sherrin put on a pair of blue gloves, never a good sign, and took a seat on a small roll-around swivel chair. She then said, "Okay, please stand up." I did what I was told. "And drop your pants." I did what I was told. Dr. Sherrin then pulled out with her right hand a small flashlight from her coat pocket and turned it on. She then grabbed Mr. Happy with her left hand, swung him right, examined, swung him left, and examined. Dr. Sherrin then reached for the boys, manipulated lefty between her thumb and forefinger as I grimaced, manipulated righty between her thumb and forefinger, and I grimaced again. The doctor said, "Everything looks fine, you can pull up your pants now." I smiled. I felt manhandled. I pulled up my pants and buttoned the fly of my Levi's as the doctor turned to where all her medical supplies were stored. "Here you go," she said, handing me a paper bag. I said, "Thank you," and opened the door, then quickly exited the room.

I heard the nurse call Peter's name while I sat down next to Russell. Russell immediately leaned to me and asked in a whisper near my ear, "What did they do?"

I leaned into him and whispered back in his ear, "The doctor asked me if I was sexually active and then checked me to see if I had VD."

Russell whispered in my ear, "What's VD?"

"Venereal disease," I whispered back, into his ear.

"Oh," whispered Russell. Russell then leaned back to me. "What's venereal disease?"

I replied in a whisper, "You know, crabs, gonorrhea, syphilis, stuff like that."

"Oh." A few seconds of silence went by, and then Russell leaned back to me and whispered in my ear, "What's gonorrhea?"

I leaned back to him and said, "I don't know." We turned to each other and smiled.

After everyone had a chance to see the doctor, we all exited the clinic. The girls all walked out of the clinic together as the guys all walked out behind them, leaving the clinic with the feeling of being manhandled.

Chapter 15

Weeks passed and I had gone to Danielle's one evening hoping that we could go for a ride and maybe for a hike.

I got to her house, got out of my car, and knocked at the door. Alice opened the door, greeted me, and asked me to come in. "Sit over there," she stated, indicating to the dining room table. "I sent Danielle to the store. I wanted to talk to you anyway."

Me? I thought. Maybe she wanted to know where I was planning on taking Danielle for the evening.

While I was seated at the dinner table, I grabbed the *Times-Standard*, our local newspaper, to read up on the local news. Alice came through the kitchen, walked toward me, then purposefully slapped down on the dining room table something that truly grabbed me by surprise.

"What's this?" she asked while I evaluated the familiar object. It was two inches square with the word "TROJAN" written on it.

"Um, that's a condom." I said, trying hard not to sound like a smart-aleck.

"I know it's a condom," she mocked back, shaking her head with her response. "What does it mean?" she asked sternly.

I gathered my thoughts before I calmly said, "It means I love Danielle."

"Do you plan on marrying her?" she asked.

"I want to get married," I responded.

"Does Danielle want to get married?" Alice asked.

"She's just not there yet," I answered.

"What if she gets pregnant?" Alice asked.

"I want to get married." I responded, with determination this time.

Alice retrieved the tattletale object just as she heard Danielle come through the front door.

Danielle could see from our body language that Alice and I had just finished having a serious conversation. Alice quickly left the room, then Danielle signed to me, "What's wrong?"

I signed back slowly and with great concentration, "Your mom found a condom. Didn't you hide them from her?"

"She must have looked in my purse," she signed back.

"Your purse?" I replied. "Oh well," I continued, "the big secret is out, we don't have to hide what we've been doing anymore."

The tension with Alice was palpable as I went to pick up Danielle the next day. I wanted to take Danielle for a ride so we could go somewhere to be alone without any disruption. We drove to the park. Danielle always held my hand while I drove.

I parked my Bug, turned to Danielle and signed, "Do you want to get married to me?" I asked the question with all seriousness and genuine concern. It was surprising how Danielle could tell just by the look on my face if I was serious or just playing around.

Danielle thought a while and signed back, "I don't know! I wanted to go to Gallaudet College."

"I know," I signed back, "but if you want to get married, I really want to marry you."

"We'll see," was all she said.

I took Danielle home, kissed her good night, and she went into her house.

It must have snowed during the night because the next morning, while I was sound asleep, Danielle snuck into my dorm room. She silently walked over to my bed, quickly drew down my covers, and threw freezing snow on my back.

"No, stop, that's freezing," I signed as I quickly jumped out of bed with a start.

Danielle was so delighted with herself that she was able to catch me off guard. I tried grabbing for the bag of snow that she was holding and desperately tried to put some of the snow down the back of her jacket. "Stop it, stop it," she kept signing. We laughed, I grabbed her, and then we kissed.

One evening while I was visiting Danielle, Alice said that she and Pete were planning a trip down to the city and wanted to know if I would like to come along.

"Sure," I answered. "What's on the itinerary?"

"Danielle wants you to visit the California School for the Deaf," was her only reply.

"That would be awesome," I said.

The trip down to Berkeley was fun. We drove down the Avenue of the Giants for a few miles when I mentioned to Pete that I had to use the facilities. I think Pete had taken a liking to me. Pete stopped the camper-truck. I got out and ran behind a giant redwood, and Pete ran to the other side as we quickly passed our water.

When we got back into the truck Danielle smiled at me. The four of us were seated on one long bench seat. We were seated Pete driving, then Alice next to him, Danielle next to Alice, then me. Danielle and I always held hands. This holding hands of ours was as though I was always able to tell her, silently, "I'm here, I love you, you are my splendor."

We arrived at the Berkeley school and Danielle was obviously very excited to go to the main office. She and I went into the impressive concrete building.

Pulling me by the hand, she took me to the office door. We walked in and the receptionist immediately noticed Danielle and I standing on the other side of the counter. The lady gestured to Danielle and boom, hands a-flyin' all over the place. The lady came from out behind the counter and gave Danielle a great big hug. Hands a-flyin', hands a-flyin'.

"Hello, my name is Barbara," the receptionist spoke plainly to me.

"Oh," I said, "my name is Jack."

"Very nice to meet you."

Hands again were flyin' as Danielle signed and the lady signed back to Danielle. The receptionist went into another room and brought out other people. Each of these other people came past the counter and hugged Danielle and again hands were flyin' in all directions. Each of these new encounters ended with an introduction to me.

Each new person signed to me as they spoke. I in kind signed back, slowly, as I introduced myself and nervously signed and fingerspelled my name. Knowing I was hearing, all of the people were kind enough to speak as they introduced themselves. Some of these people could speak well because they were hearing, but most of them spoke as deaf.

Danielle was able to show me the dormitory buildings on the California School for the Deaf campus as well as the cafeteria and other outbuildings. She told me that we were not allowed to go into a classroom because classes were now in session. As we passed a classroom, I, being of a curious nature, quickly looked in and saw the teacher signing to the class. The class was responding in kind. These classes were eerily silent as we passed.

Danielle and I walked the campus for roughly twenty minutes. Danielle was very animated in showing me the school. I could easily tell how much just being here visiting meant to her.

This place, this school, these grounds had been her home for many years, and it showed.

We went back to the camper-truck where Pete and Alice were still waiting. "Did you have a good time?" Alice asked Danielle.

"Yeah, I see lot of friends," Danielle spoke in reply. I was getting used to hearing Danielle's voice.

Pete and I had a room at the Motel 6 in San Francisco and Danielle and Alice had the room next door.

Pete always made me feel comfortable while he and I were together. "You do much fishin'?" Pete asked me as we hit the hay.

"I don't own a pole yet," I answered, "but I wouldn't mind going with you next time you go."

"How 'bout abalone? You ever abalone?" Pete asked.

"Not yet, but I'd love to try it with you sometime," I responded and didn't remember falling asleep.

A couple of weeks after our trip to Berkeley, Danielle and I had to go to the free clinic. Danielle took a blood test. We had a lot to talk about. We stopped at the park. I then drove her home.

Danielle and I walked into the house; Alice was sitting on her couch watching television. "Can I speak to you a minute?" I asked, politely.

"Sure," she said as she got up to turn the television off. "What's the matter?" Alice asked me.

I was already seated at one of the dining room chairs while Danielle took a seat across from me. I reached across the table with both hands and Danielle placed both her hands in mine. "Danielle's pregnant," I said to Alice.

"PREGNANT?" Alice responded, aghast. Alice pondered this surprising news then said, with conviction. "Are you guys planning on getting married?"

"I want to get married," I said. "Danielle says she wants to think about it."

I got home and the following day I called Alice from the pay phone at the residence hall. "Did you get a chance to talk to Danielle?" I asked her.

"Pete and I had a long talk with her last night. Why don't you come by tonight after school?"

"All right," I said. "See you tonight."

I went to Danielle's after my classes were over. As soon as I got there Danielle opened the door and led me by the hand to her bedroom. She closed the bedroom door and signed, "Okay, we can get married." I kissed her longingly.

Alice made all the necessary arrangements. "You have a meeting with the priest at St. Bernard's on Thursday," said Alice. "He'll tell you everything you will need to do."

We met with the priest. I also called my mom and dad and told them that we were getting married and if they could please come up for the wedding.

Chapter 16

Danielle had asked Rene, our sign language teacher, to be her matron of honor. I asked my dormie Peter to be my best man.

It was strange how all the arrangements for the wedding came together so well. I invited each and every dormie I could find. After living on campus for nine months one becomes good friends with a lot of people. The word was quickly spreading. "Saint Bernard's Catholic Church in downtown Eureka, Monday at five thirty p.m.," was always my response when asked where the wedding would be held.

My mom and dad came to Humboldt County three days before the planned marriage. Alice and my mom became fast friends and Pete and my dad found out that they had both served their country in World War II and that their birthdays were only one day apart.

It was Saturday morning and I asked my dad to go with me to Eureka. My mom stayed behind with Alice for the day, as they had a lot to talk about.

I had saved up for this particular purchase, so my dad wasn't surprised when I parked in front of Ten

Window Williams, our local quality jeweler. I had saved seventy-seven dollars and hoped that this would be enough.

"Good morning," I said as the saleslady smiled and walked up to me.

"Can I help you gentlemen?" she asked.

"I'm getting married and my fiancée and I would like two very simple gold rings," I answered.

"Congratulations," she said. "When are you getting married?"

"Monday," I proudly answered.

She jerked back slightly as if surprised. "Do you know her ring size?" she asked hesitantly with a smile."

"Yes, size eight," I responded.

"And yours?" she said.

"I think I'm a ten, but I'm not quite sure," I answered.

The saleslady went into the back of the store and brought out two beautiful, simple, matching shiny golden rings.

"Perfect," I said under my breath as she handed them to me. I put the larger ring on my left ring finger and was pleased to find out that it fit. I then gave both rings back to her as she returned to the back of the store. My dad and I looked around the jewelry store while the saleslady took the rings to box them up and to write up the purchase.

"That will be eighty-five dollars and thirty-seven cents," she said to me upon her return.

I was completely mortified. I didn't have enough money to buy our wedding rings. I pondered my choices. Maybe I wouldn't need a ring? Perhaps we could find something cheaper somewhere else? I looked at my dad reluctantly.

"How much do you need, son?" he asked me.

"Ten?" I replied meekly. He immediately reached into his right rear pocket, pulled out his well-worn black leather wallet, and handed me a crisp twenty-dollar bill. "Thank you," I said.

We left the store. "I'll pay you back somehow," I told my dad on our way home.

"Don't worry son," he said, "that's what dads do when they love their children."

I had to look away as the tears rolled down my cheeks. After driving my dad back to Alice and Pete's home, I went back to the dorms.

Danielle and I had decided to follow the long-standing tradition of not seeing each other the day of our wedding. I awoke early in my dorm room the day of our wedding. All day long I missed her, but suddenly realized that after today, we would be staying together every day and night forever from today on. I was perfectly content.

I went to Saint Bernard's early. Fr. Stanburry had asked Peter and me to come early so we could go over the ceremony and figure out all the details. I threw a wrench into the system when I asked Father, "How is Danielle going to see the interpreter if the interpreter is standing right next to her?"

It took Father a second, then he said, "The matron of honor will stand next to you, Jack, and your best man will be standing next to Danielle." I smiled; how clever was that!

Our ceremony was to begin at 5:30 p.m.

Fr. Paul Stanburry, a young, handsome priest, was kind and of a gentle nature. Fr. Paul's looks reminded Danielle and me of John Denver, the famous singer/songwriter. He looked like he was my age, twenty-one, but was more likely in his early thirties.

While many of the dormies were coming in and seating themselves, Rene, Danielle's matron of honor, came down to the main altar when Fr. Paul was talking to Peter and me. I smiled at Rene and told her how beautiful she looked. Rene had a very fair complexion. Her cheeks always had a rosy glow as though she were on the verge of embarrassment. Father explained to Rene that she would be standing next to me during the ceremony so she could sign to Danielle, and Rene too thought that a very clever idea. "I was wondering how we were going to do that," she replied.

"How does Danielle look?" I asked Rene anxiously.

"You'll see," was all that she said.

Rene left, walking to the back of the church and closing the vestibule doors behind her.

Fr. Paul, Peter, and I walked past the altar and into a small side room. It was apparent that the priest got dressed in his magnificent robes in this side dressing room. Peter and I looked on with fascination as Fr. Paul said special prayers as he donned each piece of vesture. I had no idea that priests recited special prayers when they dressed up. I was already a bundle of excitement and I found myself tearing up as I watched Father don this special attire.

Father said to Peter and me, "Let's join our hands together in prayer." While Peter, Father, and I held hands, Father Paul prayed in his gentle, kind voice, "Oh, Holy Spirit, come down upon this young couple and make their marriage a great example of your boundless love and unity. Oh, and Lord," he added, as though an afterthought, "please bless their precious baby with abundance, let them know that this baby is truly a sign of your great love in our lives. In Jesus' name we pray, AMEN."

Well, if I wasn't already crying, praying for our new baby put me over the edge. I looked around the small room and asked Father if he had any Kleenex. He pointed to a box just behind me and I wiped my eyes and blew my nose. Peter smiled at me; he too had tears in his eyes.

The three of us then walked from this side room, out past the sacred altar, and down three stairs to find ourselves standing in the middle aisle, waiting for Danielle to come to me.

With Peter, my best man, standing next to me, I looked around the church. It looked as though the guests had naturally seated themselves, the bride's friends and family on the right and the groom's friends and family to the left. I counted about a hundred people gathered.

Every eye in church was on Peter, Fr. Paul, and me. "Hello," I said out loud to those assembled. They all laughed.

At long last, the time had come. I looked toward the back of the church. I would soon have a bride. *Oh, how I love her,* I thought.

The double doors then opened and I could see Rene. She walked down the aisle toward us very slowly and with purpose. She was holding a bouquet of beautiful pink carnations.

Rene took her place to the right of Father Paul, and I again looked to the back of the church.

There she stood. The love of my life. I caught my breath; my heart skipped a beat. I recalled the first time I had seen her. Deep within my soul, I knew she was going to be my wife! Tears immediately came to my eyes.

Pete, Danielle's dad, stood to her left and Danielle was holding on to Pete's right elbow.

The amber, setting sun's light was radiant behind the pair as they slowly and resolutely walked to me.

Danielle looked resplendent. She wore a dusty white, crumpled, free-flowing dress. In her right hand, she clutched a pink and white floral bouquet. On her head she wore a simple yet elegant wide-brimmed white hat. Her smile was radiant.

As the pair got closer to me, I could see that Pete was crying. I thought I had better not look at him for too long or I'd start tearing up again.

"Who gives this woman to this man in holy matrimony?" Father Paul announced, as the two got to their place.

"Her mother and I do," was Pete's response. Pete, a man with great compassion, then kissed Danielle on the cheek. Pete looked at me and I took three steps toward them as Danielle reached for my left elbow.

Danielle and I took our places. I looked at Danielle as we faced each other. Her smile was breathtaking. I smiled back at her. Danielle was to the right of Father Paul. I stood to the Father's left. Peter, my best man, stood on Danielle's right and Rene stood to my left. Father Paul began.

"Ladies and gentlemen, we have here before us a young couple in love. As you can probably see, Danielle's matron of honor is standing next to the groom. Likewise, the best man is standing next to the bride. This is a small accommodation that we had to make because Danielle's words are seen rather than heard. As you can see, Rene, the matron of honor, is signing everything that I am saying. Fascinating," he said under his breath.

"Let us begin." Father continued. "Jack and Danielle, have you come here to enter into a marriage without coercion, freely and wholeheartedly?"

"We have."

"Do you promise to love and honor each other as long as you both shall live?"

"We do."

"Are you prepared to accept children lovingly from God and to bring them up according to the law of Christ and his Church?"

"We are."

"Since it is your intention to enter the covenant of Holy Matrimony, please join your right hands." I reached for Danielle's hand, passing mine in front of Father's, and Danielle grabbed it and held on.

Father continued. "Jack, repeat after me."

"I, Jack…….take you, Danielle,……to be my wife,……I promise to be true to you,……in good times and in bad,……in sickness and in health,……to love you and to honor you,……all the days of my life."

The priest then turned to face Danielle as Rene signed. "Repeat after me," the priest said. "I, Danielle…"

Danielle now only voiced our vows without signing. "I, Danielle……. take you, Jack,……to be my husband,……I promise to be true to you,……in good times and in bad,……in sickness and in health,……to love you and to honor you,……all the days of my life."

Father said, "May the Lord in his kindness strengthen the consent you declare before the Church and graciously bring to fulfillment his blessings within you. What God has joined, let no man put asunder. May the God of Abraham, the God of Isaac, the God of Jacob, the God who joined together our first parents in paradise, strengthen and bless in Christ the consent you have declared before the Church, so that what God joins together, no one may put asunder."

Father turned to Peter and said with a grin, "Do you have the rings?" Peter smiled hugely and presented the two golden bands that I had given to him for safekeeping. He showed them to the priest, who prayed, "Bless and sanctify your servants in their love, O Lord, and let these rings, a sign of their faithfulness, remind them of their love for one another. Through Christ our Lord."

We all responded, "AMEN."

Father sprinkled the rings with holy water as Peter held them up to him. Father told me to take Danielle's ring and Peter handed Danielle my ring.

"Jack, place Danielle's ring on her finger," the priest said, as I slid Danielle's ring on her left ring finger. "Repeat after me," Father said. "Danielle, receive this ring as a sign of my fidelity." I repeated. Father then said, "In the name of the Father and of the Son, and of the Holy Spirit." I echoed.

Father gestured for Danielle to place the ring on my finger, "Danielle, repeat after me."

"Jack, receive this ring as a sign of my fidelity." Danielle voiced, while the tears rolled down my cheeks. "In the name of the Father and of the Son and of the Holy Spirit." After everybody said, "AMEN," Danielle then reached, with her right thumb, in front of Father Paul, and wiped the tears gently from my cheeks.

Father then said to Danielle and me, "I now pronounce you man and wife. You may kiss your bride." Danielle then took a step toward me, and I to her. We kissed each other gently on the lips.

"Ladies and gentlemen," the priest announced, "I am pleased to present to you, Jack and Danielle Saffell, husband and wife."

I beamed, as tears of joy again flooded my eyes and rolled down my cheeks.

Chapter 17

    After the wedding ceremony, Danielle and I, both of our parents, and many of the dormies packed into O.H.'s steakhouse on 5th Street in Eureka. O.H.'s was the kind of steakhouse where you could walk in and pick your lobster from a tank. Alice had made reservations for twenty-five people, so our wedding reception was held in a private room in the back.

    We were all having a great time eating and drinking, drinking and eating. The kind waitress served wine to everyone who was over twenty-one. "Are you over twenty-one" she would ask each dormie. "No," was the reply from most of my friends. If they were not twenty-one, they were then served Martinelli's apple cider instead. I had turned twenty-one the previous October so I was served white wine. Danielle, on the other hand, was just twenty. The kind waitress said to Danielle, "Are you twenty-one?" Danielle did not understand the question and looked to me. I responded to the waitress, "She's twenty." The waitress purposefully filled Danielle's glass with apple cider. I said, "Thank you," and she left the filled room.

Everyone was joking around and having a good time as Peter, my best man, stood. "I'd like to propose a toast to the newlyweds," he announced. I looked around and noticed everyone's eyes were on Peter.

Alice was sitting next to Danielle. I quickly reached across Danielle and exchanged Danielle's glass of cider with Alice's glass of wine. No one noticed what I did except Danielle. I sat back in my chair and looked at my bride. She was wearing her radiant smile.

Peter continued. "Everyone quiet down, please." All eyes were still fixed on Peter. His cheeks flushed as he slowly lifted his glass of cider and pronounced, purposefully and with his strong, deep voice, "Let us raise our glasses in a toast to this young couple." He paused. "May their life always be filled with an overflowing of marriage's three L's."

"HEAR, HEAR!" was the joyful, heartfelt response by all. Everyone tapped their glasses together and took a sip of their drinks. There was a long pause, then one of the dormies yelled out loud, "What exactly are the three L's of marriage, Peter?"

Peter smiled his amazing smile, knowing that he had just pulled a fast one. "The three L's?" he said. "You don't know what the three L's of marriage are?" He then said wittily, "Well, let me then tell you. The three L's of marriage are LOVE, LUST, and LOYALTY."

Everyone laughed out loud as I could feel my face growing redder and more flushed.

Danielle signed, "Why is everybody laughing?"

I signed to her what Peter had just proposed in his toast to us and added, "Peter said he wishes that our life together is always filled with love, lust and loyalty.

Danielle smiled warmly at Peter, then turned back to me and signed, "What's that mean, lust?"

I signed back to her, "Lust? Lust is, um…" I had to think about this one. "Lust means when you're horny."

Danielle made a face and signed, "That's weird," as she took another long drink of her white wine.

After a long night of eating and drinking and having a good time, Danielle and I finally drove home to Rio Dell.

Pete and Alice had rentals. Pete had a small one-bedroom studio apartment next to and behind the barber shop. The house next to the barber shop happened to be the house that Alice's dad, Giovanni, had built, where Alice, her sister Flora, and brother Albert grew up there living with their parents, Giovanni and Emma. The house was converted by Pete into a double unit. This studio apartment was where Danielle and I lived for the first two years of our life together.

I went to the employment office on K Street in Eureka and told them I was looking for work. The people there were kind to me, asked me about my skills, and found a job that might work for me at Lazio's fish market down on the docks in Eureka. I filled out an application, got the job, and started working there for $3.25 an hour, forty hours a week. The only problem was that I had to work the swing shift, 5 p.m. to 2:30 a.m.

Arriving home around three fifteen in the morning was a hard thing to get used to. Like any normal person, Danielle, it seemed, was naturally ready to get up around 7 or 8 a.m.

Clangs, pounds, and squeaks were what my tired body would hear in the wee hours of the morning. Granted, 8 a.m. is not the wee hours of the morning for most people, but to a body still wanting to sleep, I beg to differ.

"Danielle," I grumbled, as I got up and peeked into the living room–kitchen area, "you're making a lot of noise and I can't sleep."

"Sorry," she signed with a smile.

I smiled back and signed "I love you."

She signed back, "I love you more," and I went back to sleep.

It was the Fourth of July and I bought fireworks at the Red Devil firework stand in Rio Dell. I invited Pete and Alice, who happened to live a hundred feet from us, to come out as soon as it got dark so we could watch the fireworks.

As I judged that it was time for the big show, I set up two sawhorses that belonged to Pete and started the magnificent fireworks show. This show was going to be spectacular due solely to the fact that I had spent a lot of money, the $39.95 special box, and I was totally into it.

Finally, the show began. I lit the smaller things first, on to the medium-sized cylinders, and then the giant one, the Big Daddy. After ten minutes, I was done.

I smiled at the attentive audience, Danielle, Pete, and Alice. Danielle said, "Is that all?" I meekly signed, "Yes." *TADA!* was what I wanted to say, but all that I could think about was, *what a stupid waste of money. I'll just have to get a bigger box next year,* I thought.

By now Danielle was twelve weeks along. She was experiencing bad morning sickness and the smell of certain foods made her sick.

I looked in the phone book and called a few obstetricians, asking if they would take my beautiful bride and stating that we had Medi-Cal. As I found out, most of the doctors didn't take Medi-Cal because it was a lot of paperwork and they didn't get paid very much for their services. Medi-Cal was California's medical insurance for low-income people.

Finally, I called Dr. Goss's office.

"Hello, Eureka Obstetrics. How may I help you!" said the voice of the receptionist.

"Good morning," I said. "I am calling for my wife. Her name is Danielle Saffell, she's twenty years old, about three months pregnant, and she is deaf. We are hoping that Dr. Goss could be her doctor? I've called around," I continued, "but none of the other doctors want to take her because we are on Medi-Cal. I was hoping that you might be able to squeeze us in?"

"Please hold," was the receptionist's response. I stayed on the phone hoping this doctor would be the one. "Sir," the receptionist said as she came back on the phone, "how will we communicate with her if she is deaf?"

"I'll take the time off work and come in with her every time, if that's okay," I said.

"Just a minute," she responded. "Sir," she said as she came back, "I have an opening in about two weeks. Has she been seen by another doctor yet?"

"Not yet," I responded. "We did take a pregnancy test at the free clinic. That's how we found out."

"Okay then," she said. We set a date and time and I promised I'd have Danielle there.

We had to be at the office thirty minutes early so we could fill out all the paperwork. I worked on filling out all the pertinent information. The questionnaire asked age, date of your last period, have you had a child before? Stuff like that.

They called Danielle and me in and we met the doctor. Dr. Goss was about fifty years old and graying at the temples. "How do you feel today, Danielle?" asked the doctor.

Danielle smiled at him, then looked at me. I interpreted, "How do you feel today, Danielle?"

"I get sick in the morning," was her reply.

"Very common," was his response. "Is this your first baby?"

When I replied in the affirmative, the doctor said, "Okay, let's take a look."

The doctor had Danielle lie down on the examining table. He held out a tape measure and measured something.

"What is he doing?" Danielle asked me.

"Dr. Goss, Danielle was wondering what you are doing," I said.

"Oh." The doctor looked at Danielle. "I'm measuring your uterus to determine how far along you are. The uterus grows as the infant grows and this assists us to make certain everything is okay with you and the baby. Let's see if we can hear the heartbeat, shall we?"

"The baby's heartbeat?" I asked, somewhat surprised.

"Yes," he replied with a grin.

Dr. Goss then pulled out a big, white teardrop-shaped instrument. "This will be cold," the doctor said to Danielle and squirted a large amount of a clear gel over her lower stomach. He placed the monitor on her stomach and slid it around, up and down, side to side, with no results. "Sometimes at this stage, it's hard for the monitor to pick up the heartbeat. We'll hear it next time," he said.

The doctor cleaned off Danielle's stomach, reached for her arm, and helped her get up. "Thank you, Doctor," I said. Danielle read my lips and signed, "Thank you, Doctor," and we left the room and set our next appointment.

My mom called one day and asked if Danielle and I could go to Los Angeles and visit because she wanted to have a wedding reception for Danielle with hopes that all my relatives would come.

Danielle was totally excited to go on this trip. She told her mom, "Mom we're going on a trip to Los Angeles to visit Jack's family." Alice was completely against it. "Mom," Danielle said, "we're just going for one week. Jack knows what he's doing. Don't worry."

Apparently, that didn't calm down the naturally worrisome Alice. "You'd better call the doctor and ask him if she can travel," Alice demanded of me.

"Okay, I'm pretty sure she'll be fine, but I'll call tomorrow," I promised her.

I called Alice from our little studio apartment. "No travel restrictions is what the doctor's office told me when I called and asked if we could take a short trip. Don't worry, Alice. I'll take good care of her. I always do," I said.

"I'm not worried," she retorted, "I'm simply being safe."

I went to work and told my boss that my family was going to give my wife and me a wedding reception. I told him that they had been planning this for a while and asked if I could please have a week off.

My boss seemed perturbed by my question. "You just started working here a little while ago," he said, gruffly, but he ultimately relented and let me leave. "Just for one week, no more."

We took my green Volkswagen to Los Angeles, the city of Carson to be exact, and stayed in my old bedroom in my parents' house.

The reception was planned for the following Saturday after we arrived in the big city. It was to be held at my aunt's house in San Pedro. Several of my close relatives came to the reception. My first cousins, my aunts and uncles, my nina (godmother), my nino (godfather), and even my great grandmother (abuelita) and grandmother (nana) were there.

I was very excited when I noticed that my great-grandmother had arrived. She was tiny and had her white hair pulled up into a bun.

When I was young, I loved listening to her tell stories with her raspy voice about her life growing up in Mexico. My abuelita spoke only Spanish, so if I got lost in the conversation or didn't understand, my nana would always translate for me by filling in the facts. Abuelita stood 4' 9"; she was eighty-three years old and weighed about ninety pounds. Her face was a rich nut-brown color and was filled with thousands of tiny wrinkles, likely due to her simple but difficult life in Mexico. She was assisted by her daughter, my grandmother. Nana took my abuelita and gently sat her on the sofa.

Danielle looked around at the crowd and was intrigued that I had so many relatives. In all I think there were probably forty or so of my closest relatives present.

I looked at my abuelita and grabbed Danielle's hand and we walked over to the couch. *"Hola, Abuelita,"* I said. Hi, Grandmother. I then placed Danielle's hand into hers and said in my very broken Spanish, *"Esta es mi esposa, Danielle. Abuelita, Danielle es sorda."* This is my wife, Danielle. Grandmother, Danielle is deaf.

"Esta sorda? Ah porbrecita." She's deaf? Oh, poor thing, was her heartfelt response. My abuelita reached for Danielle and tenderly felt the soft, rich contours of her lovely face. This face that I had totally fallen in love with. *"Hijo, tu esposa es muy hermosa."* Son, your wife is very beautiful, said my great grandmother.

Danielle stared into my abuelita's eyes and signed, "How long has she been blind?"

"Four or five years," I signed back.

"Poor thing," Danielle signed.

Danielle and I then walked around my aunt Titi's house to meet all the new relatives. My aunt Titi's given name was Bertha but her family always called her Tita. It was a nickname that was given to her at a young age because my grandmother was also named Bertha. My two brothers and I never referred to her as Tita; to us she was simply Titi.

Titi's house was well set up for entertaining. Near the breakfast bar Titi had set up a small table and on the table was a wedding sheet cake for me and Danielle.

I kissed Titi's cheek and told her, "Thank you for this beautiful reception."

"You know that I love you," was her smiling reply.

I had been practicing a special something for Danielle and I asked Titi if she had a record player on which I could play a song. Titi looked at me strangely, but had my uncle John, her husband, get their small portable record player for me. I set the record player on the reception table next to the cake, and plugged it in. I looked at my mom, who brought from her purse a 45-RPM single record that I had earlier given to her to bring.

I took Danielle by the hand and sat her next to my mom and dad, who were seated at a table in the middle of the room. I then turned to all my relatives. "If I could have everyone's attention," I stated aloud. "I have been practicing this song as a gift to my beautiful bride. I hope you all like it," I said and signed.

I put the record on and as it began to play, I signed this song to Danielle.

When I'm gray will you stay by my side
Till darkness comes over my eyes?
And when I'm sick, will you lick my wounds over
And feed me with your loving smile.

Will you still love me tomorrow?
Or will you be changing your mind,
Will you deceive me
Or will you believe that I'm loving you all of the time.

If I should die just before I awaken
To see the light shine in your eyes
Have no fear please, I'll be here when you need me
To feed you with love, all the while.

Will you still love me tomorrow?
Or will you be changing your mind.
Will you deceive me
Or will you believe that I'm loving you all of the time.

        – "Will you still love me" by Ian Thomas

    I was really concentrating on the words as I signed this song to my beautiful bride. After the song ended, I walked over to the record player, lifted the needle, removed my record, and turned around as everyone began to clap. I didn't know what I was expecting, but as I turned to face Danielle and everybody else, they were all crying.

    "That was beautiful, so poetic," Titi said.

"Oh, hijo, it made me cry," said my nana.

Everyone looked to Danielle as she signed to me, "Thank you, I love you!"

"I love you more," I signed back.

The next day I had another surprise for Danielle. We drove to Disneyland.

The drive to Disneyland from my mom and dad's home is approximately forty minutes, depending on traffic. It occurred to me that in Humboldt County, we didn't have to worry about traffic.

Danielle loved surprises and I loved thinking about ways I could surprise her. It had been nearly four years since the last time I had been to Disneyland.

We parked our car and rode the people tram to the main gate. Danielle loved all the excitement as we strolled around and looked at all the rides. I tried to coerce Danielle on rides like the Mr. Toad's Wild ride or the Tea Cup ride, but she would have none of it.

"I'm pregnant and I don't think I should be going on rides like that. Too rough," she signed to me. I kept that in mind as we started looking for tamer rides. We ended up riding Sleeping Beauty, the Haunted Mansion, and the Jungle Cruise.

Danielle pointed. "Deaf," she signed as a group of young children passed us by. As some of the children were in deep conversation with their peers, one of the boys looked Danielle's way. So, Danielle naturally signed, "Deaf, me."

The little boy's eyes grew large as he tapped the friend he was walking with, and pointed and signed "Deaf." Both of the little boys smiled hugely and waved at Danielle. "You have good time?" one of the little boys signed. They were about eight or nine years old. Seeing such little children sign was amazing.

Danielle signed back, "Real good time, me." The two boys waved good-bye as Danielle looked at me. "When I start Berkeley School, I remember see many kids their age. They so cute," she signed.

We left Disneyland about 7 p.m., as Danielle was beginning to become worn down after such a long day. We went back to my Mom and Dad's house. My mom had made Chili Colorado, beans, and rice. Red Chili, as we always called it, is one of my favorite dinners. Thankfully, my mom made Red Chili often. Danielle signed, "Delicious," upon tasting it for the first time and we both ate it all.

I had one more surprise for Danielle before we left Los Angeles. I checked the *Los Angeles Times* pet section for Danielle's surprise, every day while we were visiting.

"Where is Cucamonga?" I asked my mom the following morning after I called one of the pets for sale listings in the paper.

"That's far away, almost to San Bernardino. It would take you about three or four hours to go and come back," she stated.

I called a couple of other listings and finally found what I was looking for.

"What you looking for?" Danielle signed to me.

"Oh, just a surprise for you," I signed.

"What kind of surprise?"

"Oh, something you will like," I replied.

My mom had a big street atlas of cities of Los Angeles County. As a florist, she was very familiar with many of the cities in the Los Angeles area. After the two phone calls I made, I wrote down the addresses and found them in the atlas. Danielle and I got in my green Bug and took off.

My first stop was Thousand Oaks. Having grown up in Los Angeles County, I was used to all the traffic and rushing about to get a task done. To Danielle this was daunting. "So many people," she signed to me, as we traveled the freeway.

"I know," I signed back, "just like ants."

"True," Danielle signed.

When we got to our destination, a very well-kept ranch-style home, I took Danielle by the hand and we knocked at the door. We were met, behind a security door, by a lady about fifty-five years old. "May I help you?" she said.

"Hello, my name is Jack. I called you about your male Siamese kitten."

"Oh yes, please come in," she said softly. The lady left the room and came back with a nine-week-old male seal point kitten. Danielle just beamed.

Our second stop was Santa Monica. We drove not on the freeway, but kept to the side streets. I arrived at my destination and looked at Danielle holding our young male kitten. "I'm going to that house over there," I signed. "Do you want to go or stay in the car with the kitten?"

"I'll stay in the car," she said.

I went to an attractive blue and white stucco house and knocked. I was invited in, got what I came for, and hid the small surprise under my T-shirt.

As I reached my Bug, I pulled out, from under my T-shirt, a beautiful seven-week-old blue point female Siamese kitten. Danielle was overjoyed.

We were finally headed back home to Humboldt. "What are we going to name the kittens?" I asked Danielle on the ride home. We had both of the small kittens in a cat carrier in the back seat.

"I want call girl cat Baby Blue," she signed.

"I like that name," I signed.

"You name boy cat," signed Danielle.

"You sure?" I said. "Okay, let me think about it."

Tupo. Tupo was a name I had heard once while watching a basketball game at our local Carson Park when I was about eleven years old. The name kind of stuck with me. I thought it a pretty cool and unusual name. I told Danielle, "You like the name Tupo?"

"What?" she replied." "TUPO?" she said slowly. "Okay," she said and signed. "I don't know what that means," she said, "but I told you that you could name the boy cat. Tupo is fine with me."

We got home, got into a regular, everyday routine, and life moved on.

Due to the fact that we lived so far away from Pete and Alice, a hundred feet, Alice quickly fell in love with Danielle's two Siamese cats. "Where did you find those beautiful kittens?" Alice asked me. I told her that Los Angeles is huge and if you're willing to travel around a little bit you could get just about anything you wanted.

"Are you ready yet?" I yelled to Danielle. I don't know why, but I always talked to Danielle as though she could hear me well. Due to the fact that Danielle wore a hearing aid, I was keenly aware that she could hear something, but exactly what she could hear was always a mystery.

We arrived at Dr. Goss's office for our second visit and were greeted by the receptionist. "Jack and Danielle Saffell to see Dr. Goss," I said.

"Please have a seat. The doctor will see you in a moment."

"How do you feel today?" I asked Danielle, groggily, as I had to have her here at the doctor appointment at the crack of dawn, eleven a.m.

"Are you still tired?" she asked me, noticing my still puffy eyes.

"Yes," I said. "Can I take a nap on your shoulder?" I jokingly signed.

"Forget it," was her response as she leaned over and kissed my lips.

The nurse came to the door and called Danielle's name. We got up and followed her into the examining room. "Let's first get your weight," the nurse told Danielle. Danielle didn't need an interpreter because it was plain to her what the nurse wanted her to do. "Good," stated the nurse as she smiled at Danielle. "You gained five pounds since your last visit."

Danielle looked at me as I signed, "You gained five pounds since last month."

"Really?" Danielle signed. She made a face. "Ask her if that's good or bad."

"Danielle wants to know if that's good or bad that she gained five pounds."

"That's very normal," said the ogling nurse. "We want Danielle to gain about thirty to thirty-five pounds throughout her whole pregnancy."

"Oh, okay," I said. Danielle signed to me, "Say, say" which means, "What did she say?" I told Danielle what the nurse told me and she looked content.

"Good morning," the doctor said as he came into the room. "Hello, Danielle, how are you feeling?" He motioned for her to come sit on the examining table.

"I get sick almost every morning," Danielle told him.

"That's very normal. Your body is changing very rapidly," he said. "If you eat crackers and a sip of ginger ale before you get out of bed in the morning, that should help settle your stomach."

Danielle looked at me. "Say, say," she again signed. I signed what the good doctor had just said and she nodded.

"Lie down, Danielle," the doctor said as he touched the examining table. Danielle lay down, and the doctor pulled her blouse up a little and also pushed her pants down a little. Danielle was by now having to wear maternity pants. He then brought out his tape measure and again carefully measured her uterus.

"Do you feel the baby moving yet?" the doctor asked Danielle. I was shocked. I had no idea that Danielle might already feel the baby move. Danielle must have read the doctor's lips because she shook her head no.

Dr. Goss brought out the teardrop-shaped electronic stethoscope and first squirted some gel over Danielle's lower tummy. The doctor then slid the gel around. Danielle said, "Cold."

The doctor smiled and then, after some manipulation of the stethoscope, said, "Hear that?" as he looked at me. Thump, thump, thump was what I was hearing.

"Is that the baby?" I gasped as he looked at me.

"Yep."

"Why does it sound so fast?" I asked curiously.

"Must be a girl," he countered with a sly smile. "Danielle, can you hear that?" The doctor looked at Danielle.

Danielle turned her hearing aid up as loud as she could. The aid squealed as Danielle tried hard to listen and said, "I don't hear anything."

"Maybe next time," the kind doctor replied.

"We heard the heartbeat," I told Alice as we arrived home. "I need a nap," I added and went to our bedroom in our tiny one-bedroom studio apartment.

Alice stayed and visited with Danielle as I napped. Alice could fingerspell when she communicated with Danielle. Most of the time, Danielle read Alice's lips and if Danielle said, "I don't understand you," then Alice would fingerspell the word. Communication had always been difficult for Danielle when talking with hearing people.

One day at about noon, Danielle came and woke me up and said, "Jack look at this!" She held in her hands the *Times-Standard* newspaper. She had been patiently waiting for me to wake up, but she was so excited at what she found that she decided noon was long enough for me to be sleeping.

"Deaf Club meeting," she signed and said to me as she brought the newspaper to my sleepy head.

I signed with my face still in the pillow, "Deaf Club?"

"Yeah," she said. "I want to go."

I slowly got up and rubbed my sleepy face. "What's deaf club, let me see," I said and signed.

"DEAF CLUB MEETING. ALICE BIRNEY SCHOOL 7PM. AUG 7th," read the notice in the paper. It was going to be on a Saturday night, so I signed to Danielle, "Sure." Danielle was absolutely elated.

Hands were a-flyin'. Danielle could hardly contain herself. She was so excited to see so many deaf people at the meeting. It appeared to be about thirty people in attendance, but some of the people were hearing family members who had accompanied the deaf person.

Danielle introduced me to Dolly Mason, the lady she had met when she was eleven. Dolly moved her lips as she spoke to me, and signed, but did not use her voice. Most of the deaf were older adults. Danielle then led me to a person I had not yet met, and said to me out loud and with sign, "This Janey Quinn, my old friend. We went school together," she stated proudly. Danielle then turned to Janey and signed, "This my husband, Jack. He hearing." I reached for Janey's hand and shook it. "Handsome," was all Janey signed to Danielle, as though I was invisible.

I was still learning how to sign, so most of the deaf folks were very patient with me. They really slowed down their signing when asking me a question.

"You deaf?"

"No, hearing."

"Where work?" an older deaf man named Ed Schieberl asked me.

"I work at Lazio's fish company," I responded. "Near the bay," I added.

"You like smell your work?" he signed and smiled at me.

"No," I replied. "Stinks," as I held my nose shut.

"Yes," he signed as he laughed out loud.

Janey and Danielle exchanged phone numbers, which for a second, I thought was strange. Danielle reminded me on the way home that she had the little TTY. "Oh, I forgot," I signed.

It was our third visit to Dr. Goss'. Danielle again tried to hear the baby's heartbeat, but was again disappointed. Dr. Goss assured Danielle that the baby was doing fine. "Do you feel the baby moving now?" asked the kind doctor.

"Yes, I think so. Feels like butterfly flying around inside."

"Yes, you're absolutely right. That's your baby."

"Amazing," Danielle said and signed as my eyes filled with tears.

At night when I'd climbed into bed, Danielle would spoon me. Sometimes, early on, I thought I'd feel the baby moving around with my bottom against Danielle's sleepy tummy.

Danielle was in her seventh month when I talked to her about the Lamaze Natural Childbirth Class. "Yes, that's what I want to do," was Danielle's response. Both Danielle and I were more inclined toward the natural when it came to certain decisions concerning the baby.

"Have you thought about if you want to circumcise the baby if it's a boy?" I asked Danielle one day as we drove to Eureka to buy groceries.

"What's that mean?" Danielle spoke and signed.

"Circumcise means cutting off the foreskin of a baby boy."

"NO WAY," she replied.

"I agree," I signed. "We'll keep him more natural."

I called St. Joseph's Hospital and inquired when the Lamaze class was going to start. The class was going to be on Thursdays at 7 p.m. I had to ask my boss to let me have a couple of hours off on Thursday nights. He told me that he'd let me go and we'd call it my lunch plus one hour off for personal time.

Danielle and I loved Lamaze class. Our instructor's name was Jackie McShane. There were six couples, most of them our age. There was one couple in their forties and they were always very kind to Danielle. We were considered by most people in 1976 as kind of crazy not wanting to use any drugs during the birthing process.

One of my most uncomfortable conversations was when guys from work asked me if I was really going to stay with my wife during the delivery.

"Of course," was invariably my reply.

"You're weird," most of the men said.

"I wouldn't miss it for the world," I answered.

Danielle was beginning to experience a lot of Braxton Hicks contractions. We were able to utilize these false labor pain contractions to practice the breathing techniques we had so carefully learned in Lamaze class.

We'd be in bed and Danielle would take a strong "cleansing" breath, which would be my sign for "I'm having a contraction." I would turn and face her and with my hand, I would count with my fingers, tapping her arm, one, two, three, four… until she once again took a strong "cleansing" breath, confirming that the contraction had stopped.

Danielle was thirty-eight weeks and we were in with Dr. Goss. He told me that he was going to check Danielle and see if she was dilating. "She's at about two centimeters now," said the doctor. "Any day now."

"So painful," Danielle told me one night after I came home from work.

"Did your water break?" I asked.

"No, so painful," was all she'd say.

Danielle couldn't tolerate the pain by the time 7 a.m. came around.

"I'm taking Danielle to the hospital to see what's going on," I told Alice when I phoned her.

"Keep me informed."

It took us thirty minutes to get to the hospital, and all the while Danielle would take her cleansing breaths. I thought birth was imminent.

The hospital admitted Danielle and got her a room. The nurse put a monitor around her abdomen to monitor her contractions. "Yeah, she's having contractions, but those are Braxton Hicks," said the nurse. "Those don't really help the cervix dilate. Danielle is still two centimeters dilated, just go back home and come back when she can't tolerate the pain again."

We went home, I took a nap, and got up to get ready for work.

"How are you feeling?" I signed to Danielle.

"Hurts," was her reply.

"Do you want to go to the hospital?" I asked.

"I don't know," she signed to me.

I went to work. At midnight, I asked my boss if he cared if I went home a little early. "My wife is getting close to having our baby," I told him. He must have been in a good mood because he told me to go ahead.

When I got home, Danielle was in excruciating pain. "Why didn't you tell your mom to call me at work?"

"I don't know," she signed.

I took Danielle back to the hospital. They admitted her and put the monitor around her belly again. The contractions were still irregular but her cervix was beginning to soften.

The nurses called the doctor at home. "Let's put her on Pitocin," Dr. Goss said. "That should help her contractions become more regular."

The nurses started Danielle on Pitocin, but slowly at first. Every couple of hours the nurse would check Danielle to see if she was dilating, and then would crank up the Pitocin.

"Everything's coming along fine," Dr. Goss said as he stopped by to see Danielle before he went to the office.

It was getting to be late in the afternoon. Danielle would have a contraction and then wait a minute and then another contraction would come. Her uterus would wait five minutes, then begin another two contractions one minute apart. Danielle's body kept up this rhythm until 4:45 p.m.

"I have to push," Danielle told me.

"NURSE," I shouted down the hallway. The nurse came quickly to the room. "Danielle has to push," I told her.

"Tell her not to push," said the nurse as she gloved her hand. I heard Danielle take a strong cleansing breath as another contraction began. The nurse checked Danielle's progress. "She's at eight, tell her not to push," she demanded.

"Don't push, Danielle," I begged her several times. After three more massive contractions Danielle began to push. She could hold back no longer. I could feel the distress that it took for her not to push. "Go ahead," I finally told her, "do what your body is telling you to do," I signed, as tears streamed down my face.

She grunted a massive grunt and pushed with all her might and finally took a breath. "It's so painful," Danielle signed to me.

Just then Dr. Goss walked in. He started quickly giving orders to all the nurses and told me, "Get on your scrubs, the baby is coming NOW!"

I quickly put on my paper scrubs and booties. I washed my hands and came back to stand at Danielle's head. "I need to push," Danielle signed.

"Push," I said. "Push." I was so filled with emotion that I couldn't help but feel the anguish Danielle must be going through.

Danielle grabbed my hands and squeezed with all her might. She then pushed as hard as she could until her faced turned bright red. I looked toward the doctor as he grabbed the baby as Danielle was finally able to push the baby out. I could see that the baby was red and had dark hair. Dr. Goss placed the baby on Danielle's belly as Danielle grabbed for the baby and cried, out loud, "MY BABY, MY BABY!" My eyes then erupted with emotion.

Danielle looked at me and reached for my cheeks, then gently wiped away my tears.

Chapter 18

Danielle had never been around babies before. I, on the other hand, being the oldest grandson over twelve other cousins, had been a constant source of free babysitting.

Danielle and I had talked a lot about what we would name our baby long before it was born. I came home from the hospital for a couple of hours after our baby was born, so I could shave and shower. I got back to the hospital later in the evening.

Danielle was holding our baby and fingerspelling to her the name we had chosen for her as though she could read it. A-L-E-A-C-E. I watched Danielle fingerspell, as the new baby's eyes were wide open just looking at her mom. Again, my eyes filled with tears just watching Danielle talk to her baby in her own language, the language of the deaf. Amazing!

Aleace came home from the hospital on Christmas Day 1976.

Danielle and I had decided that she would nurse our baby. We both felt that this was going to be the easiest and best thing for our new baby. Alice disagreed. "How do you know how much the baby is getting? What if the baby doesn't grow?" These were some of the questions that plagued Alice. All the while Danielle was determined to nurse our newborn.

It seemed like a great idea at the time, but Danielle, the baby, and I moved into Danielle's old bedroom at Pete and Alice's house. We had set up a bassinet in Danielle's old bedroom. Every time the baby cried during the night, I would wake up, give the baby to Danielle, and she would nurse her. I overemphasized to Danielle how important burping the baby was after each feeding. I had witnessed firsthand how painful colic was for a newborn, having helped my best friend from high school and his girlfriend with a colicky infant; not a fun experience.

Danielle was a natural. She'd feed the baby, burp the baby, and loved just cuddling her newborn baby girl.

Two weeks passed by and poor Danielle started complaining of breast pain. I called the doctor's office and they wanted to see Danielle right away. Breastfeeding was not common during the 1970s. Danielle had mastitis, a very painful inflammation of the mammary glands. Dr. Goss advised Danielle to stop breastfeeding. "Some women just can't nurse their babies," said the concerned doctor.

We started Aleace on SMA formula. We had to buy bottles, formula, a sterilizer, and several other items that we hadn't planned on purchasing. I was definitely not a happy camper. The one solace about bottle feeding was that I could now assist with the feedings and it was no longer just Danielle's responsibility; now all of us could chip in.

We ultimately went back to our studio apartment around a month after Aleace was born. I had purchased a crib and it fit, barely, in our single bedroom.

Danielle began to form a routine. She'd get up about 7:30 in the morning and get Aleace ready for the day. When I'd wake up at noon, I'd take a bath and Danielle would give me the baby so I could get her all lathered up and squeaky clean, then hand her to Danielle, who would towel her off and get her dressed.

Aleace was so stinkin' cute! Danielle would often sign and speak to her while rocking her in our rocking chair. Danielle would add gibberish words and sometimes I'd hear a real word thrown in from time to time.

We took Aleace to a pediatrician in Fortuna for a checkup. Dr. Mogel gave the month-old baby a clean bill of health.

Aleace was born with one abnormality—a purplish-blue baseball-sized mark at the small of her back. The pediatrician at General Hospital where Aleace was born had called it a Mongolian Blue Spot. The doctor told us that babies born of dark-complexioned people have been known to have these spots. Yes, I am half Mexican but of very fair complexion and blue-hazel eyes. Danielle was half Italian, but she was lighter than me. Perhaps Aleace would be of a beautiful mocha complexion.

Soon after waking, I would often put on some records to listen to. I love music. I'd frequently turn the stereo on in the living-room-kitchen and turn the bass up rather high. Danielle could then feel the music better and would often walk up to me while holding Aleace and we would slow dance together while holding the baby lovingly between us. These were times of great happiness in our marriage, Mommy, baby, and Papa in a loving embrace.

It was about six weeks after Aleace was born when we heard the terrible news on the local 6 p.m. news. Our obstetrician, Dr. Goss, was found dead at the little airport near Eureka, apparently from a suicide.

Danielle was very sad. "Why he do that?" she asked me, voicing and signing, when I told her what was being said on the television.

"I have no idea," I signed back. "Maybe he had money problems, who knows."

I called the new obstetrician in Fortuna a few weeks later. It was time for Danielle to get checked before we could resume our marital embrace. We talked about having more children, but Danielle signed, "Later." I readily agreed.

"Dr. Johansson and Anderson's office," the receptionist responded on the phone.

"Hello, my name is Jack Saffell and my wife is named Danielle. Danielle is deaf and we just had a baby two months ago and we were hoping to get Danielle a checkup."

"What type of insurance do you carry?" was the first question.

"I don't have insurance, but Danielle has Medi-Cal."

"Please hold." I waited about three minutes when the receptionist said, "Dr. Johansson said that he will see your wife. How will we communicate with her?"

"I will come with her if that will be okay," I said.

Our appointment was made. It was going to be two more weeks before we could see Dr. Johansson. I trusted we could both be patient while we waited.

We arrived at Dr. Johannsson's office. Danielle walked by my side while I held Aleace in a light blue baby carrier. I opened the door and tried to bow, as I often did, teasing Danielle as though she was a princess, but now I was holding a precious bundle and my bow was not very elegant. Danielle said, "DA," with a smile on her face.

Danielle, because of her hearing loss, made noises that hearing people do not. If Danielle was caught off guard by some antic that I was acting out, she would say, "DA," very quickly. I loved to hear her say, "DA." I then knew that I had caught her off guard, thus making the joke fun.

I had to fill out about fifty pages of paperwork; well, maybe it was only three, but it seemed like fifty pages of information about our insurance, who was the responsible party, and all the other pertinent information.

"Danielle Saffell," the receptionist called from the doorway. I touched Danielle and she got up. I grabbed the sleeping Aleace and the three of us walked through the door.

"Hi, I'm Donna," the nurse said to us, and I introduced my bride and myself. "Follow me, Danielle." Donna motioned to Danielle as they walked down the hall. "Get on the scale." Donna motioned to the tall silver doctor's scale and Danielle removed her shoes, handed me her jacket, and got on the scale.

Donna then took us into the room. She turned to me and asked, "What's the reason for your visit today?"

I smiled and said, "It's been almost nine weeks since the baby was born and I was told that we should see an obstetrician so Danielle could get checked out and we could talk about birth control."

"Danielle, I need you to remove your pants and undergarments, then have a seat on the table," Donna said. "Here is a paper drape to cover yourself with." She wrote down some notes, smiled at us, and said, "Dr. Johannsson will be here in a few minutes."

"Say, say," Danielle signed to me when Donna left.

"She wanted to know why we were here today," I signed.

"Oh," Danielle said. She thought about it. "What did you tell her?"

"I told her we wanted to get you checked out and that we needed some birth control so you don't get pregnant."

"Yes," was all she signed.

"You need to take off your pants and underwear and then cover yourself with this paper," I told her. I helped Danielle onto the paper-covered table once she was ready.

A very tall, handsome, blond doctor opened the door and walked into the room. "Hi, I'm Dr. Johannsson. I am very glad to meet you." He warmly took Danielle's hand in his and shook it. I stood and Dr. Johannsson shook my hand as I said, "I'm Jack."

"How old is the baby?" the doctor asked.

"Almost nine weeks," I said.

"Have you guys started having sex yet?"

"Not so far," I answered. "We didn't want to get pregnant so soon."

"I'm proud of you," said the kind doctor. "Danielle, I'm going to have you lie down." Dr. Johannsson grabbed Danielle's hand and helped her lie down. He then pushed down on Danielle's tummy with both hands and asked, "Does that hurt?"

"No," Danielle responded. The doctor grabbed Danielle's hand, then helped her sit up.

"What kind of birth control were you guys thinking of using?" the doctor asked Danielle.

"Say, say," Danielle signed to me.

"Dr. Johannsson wants to know what kind of birth control you wanted to use."

"I don't know," Danielle signed to me.

"What kind would you recommend?" I asked the doctor.

"I would suggest an IUD. It's simple to put in and it should last a few years," he said.

I signed to Danielle what the doctor said.

"WHAT?" Danielle said, rather loudly. Dr. Johannsson laughed. "I don't know what that is," Danielle said.

"Me either," I said.

"I'll be right back," the doctor said. He left the room and quickly returned.

"This is an IUD," he said while holding up a piece of plastic with some copper wire wrapped around it and a long string attached. I didn't want to seem too stupid, so I said, "How does it work?" To tell the truth, I wasn't really sure where exactly the doctor would put the IUD.

"I'll insert it into the uterus and it keeps Danielle from getting pregnant," he stated.

"WHERE?" Danielle said and signed as I interpreted what Dr. Johannsson had said. "I don't know," signed Danielle.

"I'll leave you two alone and you can talk about it. Just push this button once after you figure out what you want to do. Okay?" said the doctor.

"Thank you," I said.

The doctor left the room. "What do you want to do?" I signed to Danielle.

"I don't know," she responded. Then she asked, "Does it hurt?"

"I have no idea," I said. "If it doesn't hurt, do you want to try it for a while?"

She thought for a bit, then said, "Okay, let's try it."

I pushed the button. Donna knocked on the door and poked her head in. "Donna, Danielle said we could try the IUD."

"OK, I'll let the doctor know."

Dr. Johannsson came back in with Donna in tow. "Good choice," Dr Johannsson said. He and Donna set out all the things they would need and put them on a silver roll-around table that held a cloth covering it. This was obviously going to be an invasive procedure with all the doodads and instruments on the silver table.

Donna helped Danielle lie back down on the examining table while Dr. Johannsson placed Danielle's feet into two metal foot holders. The doctor then placed a strap around his head that had a very strong flashlight attached. He peeked under the paper drape that Danielle was wearing, grabbed from the silver table a couple of mysterious-looking tools, and voila, he was finished.

Dr. Johannsson then took off the flashlight strap, reached for Danielle's hand, and helped her sit back up.

"Is that it?" I asked incredulously.

"Yep, a fairly simple procedure, really," said the physician.

"Um," I said out loud, "um, Doctor?" I tried to form a sentence in my brain. "Doctor, will I feel the string?" I finally asked.

"Not at all," he responded, looking at me with a big smile on his face.

The three of us left the office and went home.

Danielle received a telephone call on her TTY one morning while I was still in bed.

"Who was on the phone?" I asked her when I finally got up around noon.

"You heard the phone ring?" she asked me.

"Yep."

"It was Rhonda, the sign language teacher from Humboldt State. She wants to know if I can come to her class," signed Danielle.

"Do you want to go?" I asked my bride.

"Sure," she signed. "When do they want you to go?" I signed.

"She will call me back. I told her I would talk to you about it first to make sure we could make it," Danielle signed.

"Okay with me, but let me know what day," I signed.

We got to Humboldt State about one in the afternoon. The class was at one o'clock, we were running late, and I had no idea where we were going. Thank God Danielle knew exactly where she was going. I just followed her while I carried Aleace inside the baby carrier. We entered a classroom that reminded me of the classrooms I had passed by while we were at California School for the Deaf, eerily quiet.

Danielle walked into the classroom as though she owned the place. I meekly followed, smiling as I looked about the classroom for a secluded seat Aleace and I could occupy.

Danielle, having been motioned to by Rhonda, walked to stand next to the teacher at the front of the class.

Rhonda, not saying a word, motioned for the class to pay attention. "Class," she signed without speaking, "this is a good friend of mine, Danielle Silbernagel."

"No," signed the smiling Danielle, "me new name, Danielle Saffell."

"Oh," smiled Rhonda, "yes, this is now Danielle Saffell. Sorry, I forgot," she signed, laughing.

Danielle then signed to Rhonda and the class, pointing to me and Aleace, "This my husband, Jack, and my baby daughter, Aleace."

"Oh, how wonderful. Congratulations!" Rhonda signed.

All the attention was on Danielle. It was always surprising to me that Danielle really loved helping classes with sign language. She never seemed nervous. Rhonda would ask the class in sign language if they had any questions for Danielle. Danielle was always happy to answer.

Aleace was now seven months old. She was awake and in a good mood, so I had her standing up on my lap trying to keep her entertained while her mom was up in front of the class helping out. While standing on my lap Aleace would bounce while I held her up by holding her under her arms.

The class was silent, and Aleace started babbling, "Dah, dah, dah, dah, dah, dah."

Oh, how cute, I thought. One could really hear the baby making noises since the class was signing and everything was absolutely silent.

All of a sudden, while I was holding Aleace and letting her bounce with her feet on the desktop, Aleace continued saying, "Dah, dah, dah," and then from her bottom came an explosive sound. *FART... FART... FART!* Aleace smiled at me, like she had just told a good joke. The whole class began to laugh out loud. I was utterly and completely mortified.

Danielle looked at me and signed, "What's wrong?"

"Your daughter just had the loudest farts I have ever heard," I signed to Danielle with one arm.

"Farts?" Danielle signed.

"Yes," I responded. "Super loud, too."

"Doesn't matter," signed Danielle. "That's natural," she signed to me while I continued to blush.

Chapter 19

"Jack!" Danielle yelled for me from the bathroom, and I could tell by the desperation in her voice that something bad had happened.

"What?" I said as I urgently opened the door. There, on the throne, with her pants half down, sat my beautiful bride holding a white plastic number 7 wrapped with copper with a string attached. "Where did that come from?" I asked, stupidly. I knew what it was, I just couldn't figure out how Danielle happened to be holding one.

"It just came out," she said.

"It just came out?" I signed. I was pretty stunned. I had to think a bit. "Did you pull on it?" I asked.

"No, it just came out," signed my bride.

Nearly two years had passed since Danielle had the IUD implanted. "I'll call Dr. Johannsson's office and tell them what happened."

"Don't have sex," the helpful receptionist warned me as she got us an appointment for the following week.

"They gave you an appointment for next week," I told Danielle. "They told me we couldn't have sex until we see the doctor."

Danielle jokingly crossed her two pointer fingers as though she was holding up a crucifix to a vampire and pointed it at me. I smiled at the joke, then my smile turned to a sad face as I realized the great sacrifice this would entail.

"I could give you another IUD or this could be God's sign to you guys that it's time for another baby," said the joyful Dr. Johannsson.

I had to ponder this. "Doctor, could you give us a minute? Please!" I pleaded.

"Just push the button on the wall when you're ready," he said.

Danielle and I discussed, in great length, if she wanted to have another baby or not. I have always loved babies.

"What did you guys decide?" said the kind doctor as he walked back into the room.

Danielle looked at Dr. Johannsson and told him with her speech, "We want another baby."

"That's wonderful. Go home and call me when you're pregnant," said the smiling Dr. Johannsson.

Aleace had her second birthday. We celebrated with Pete, Alice, Aunt Flora, and one of Danielle's closest cousins, Dana. We brought out a homemade cake that Alice had made, and put two candles on it. Once the candles were extinguished, we let Aleace grab the whole thing and try to shove it in her mouth. She got it all over her face and everybody laughed and had such a good time.

"Hello, Dr. Johannsson's office," the kind voice on the other end of the line said.

"Hello, this is Jack Saffell calling for my wife, Danielle."

"Hello, Jack. How are you and Danielle doing?" she asked.

"Fine, thank you. Do you think we could make an appointment for Danielle to see Dr. Johannsson, please?"

"How does April first sound?"

"Is that a joke?" I asked.

"No, it's not, but it sure sounds like it should be," she laughed.

"Okay," I said. "See you on April Fool's Day."

"That didn't take any time at all now, did it?" Dr. Johannsson said as he walked into our room. "Danielle, hop up here on the table so I can check you. You're about nine weeks along," said the doctor.

"Really?" signed Danielle. Dr. Johannsson looked at me for the interpretation.

"Really?" I said.

Our second child was due on October 31, 1979. Wow, I thought maybe the baby would be born on my birthday, October 26.

Once again, Danielle got morning sickness. Crackers and ginger ale, I remembered from our first pregnancy. We were overjoyed at the prospect of having our second child.

That spring, Aunt Flora informed me that they were looking for warm bodies to sing for Easter at church. I like to sing and I'm a baptized Catholic. *Sure,* I thought. I asked Danielle about me singing at church and she said, "Whatever you want."

I met Linda Doebel while sitting on the steps of St. Patrick's Church in Scotia. "Hello," I said as a smiling woman walked up the steps toward me. "I'm Jack. Are you Linda?"

"I sure am," she said. Linda was carrying a guitar in a case.

The choir practiced several times before Easter came around and Linda and I became fast friends. "You need to learn the guitar," Linda told me one day.

"Don't you think I'm too old to learn?" I heard my twenty-four-year-old mouth say.

"No way," she said. "I was about your age when I started."

I found a beautiful guitar that fit right in my price range, twenty-five dollars. It was a steel string country-looking guitar. I found out I could take guitar lessons at the Nazarene Church in Fortuna on Thursdays. I was hooked.

Danielle's pregnancy proceeded without any problems. Her morning sickness seemed to subside at about five months along. This time Danielle knew right away when she began to feel the baby move. I loved when we would spoon. I soon began to feel this new baby as it pushed on my bottom, another gift from God, I thought.

By this time in our lives I was working at Garcia's Mexican Kitchen in Arcata. The boss at my previous job, Lazio's Fish Company, was dogging me all the time and for the sake of my well-being, I quit. I really hated to do it, but sometimes one is just pushed into a corner.

I was an excellent cook. Due to the fact that my grandmother and mom had taught me how to cook, I was a natural.

"Can you make flour tortillas?" Joe Garcia, the owner, asked me the day I walked into the restaurant and asked for a job.

"Yes, sir," I proudly replied. He peered at me with those dark brown eyes. *He must think I'm a gavacho* [white boy]," I thought.

"You can make flour tortillas?" he again asked.

"Yes, sir," I responded.

"All right," he stated slowly. "Make me some."

He pointed to the different areas of the kitchen when I asked, "Where's the flour?" "Where's the salt?" "Where's the manteca [lard]?" Again, he looked at me as though I was a pariah.

It took me about twenty minutes, but after I started cooking the tortillas on the grill, I developed a routine where I'd place each cooked tortilla on a dish towel, cover it, then proceed to make the next one.

While I was still cooking the tortillas, Joe walked up to my pile of tastiness, took a tortilla off the pile, and put some butter on it. He folded the perfectly made tortilla, closed his eyes, and took a big bite. He then smiled a great big smile and said with disbelief, "Who taught you how to make flour tortillas?"

"My nana," I said.

"You're Mexican?" he asked quizzically.

"My mom." He then said something I frequently heard from strangers. "You're the whitest Mexican I've ever seen. You're hired."

Danielle and I began to attend St. Patrick's Church regularly. I became so intrigued by my faith and really began to learn about Catholicism from an adult's perspective.

I took the Right of Christian Initiation of Adults while Danielle was pregnant. Aleace was growing and signing and learning new words all the time.

My mother-in-law, Alice, often took Aleace to Fireman's Park in Rio Dell. She was always an outstanding grandmother and mom, helping Danielle and teaching her all kinds of tricks about raising kids and motherhood.

I was earning $3.65 an hour at Garcia's Mexican Kitchen but I recognized the local sawmills paid around $5 an hour. During the daytime I'd call Pacific Lumber Company in Scotia.

"We're not hiring," said the aloof voice on the other end of the telephone. The gentleman's name that I talked to each week was Gary Cook. Mr. Cook was probably trying to deter me from calling so often. My nana had a saying in Spanish that she would often recite to me: "*Hijo, la única diferencia entre tú y un burro es que el burro tiene hermosos ojos marrones.*" Son, the only difference between you and a donkey is that the donkey has beautiful brown eyes. When it came to persistence, Mr. Cook didn't know it yet, but he had met his match.

I also made it a habit of calling Carlotta Lumber Company in Carlotta proper. Carlotta Lumber Company was tiny compared to the massive Pacific Lumber Co. Carlotta had about eighty employees, Pacific Lumber about eight hundred.

One day in September I called Carlotta Lumber Company.

"Hello Jack," said Barbara's familiar voice. "Good news, we are hiring and Bill wants you to come in for an interview."

What? An interview?

"Sure," I responded, "what time should I come in?"

I drove to Carlotta the next day and had my interview with Bill. "Can you drive a forklift?" Bill asked.

"Yes, I can," I answered.

"What kind of schooling have you had?" he asked.

"I went to C/R a couple of years ago, but my wife and I got married and started having kids."

"How many kids do you have?" he asked.

"I have a beautiful brown-eyed two-year-old daughter and another baby on the way," I responded.

"When can you start?" he asked.

When can I start, I got the job, are you kidding me? said my inner self "I should give my present employer a two weeks' notice, out of courtesy," I heard my mouth say.

"I wouldn't want it any other way," said Bill. "Call Barbara when you get a chance, so she can get you an appointment with Dr. Jutila in Fortuna for a physical."

"Bill, thank you very much for the job, I promise I will never disappoint you. Good-bye," I said, as I shook his hand.

"Five twenty-five an hour," Joe Garcia said when I went to work that night and told him about my interview with Carlotta Lumber. "I wish I could pay you more, Jack. You're easily one of the best cooks I've ever had."

"Thank you, Joe," I said. "I love cooking."

"And it shows" he said.

After the two weeks were up, I said my good-byes to everyone. The final night I worked everybody stayed after work and gave me a little going-away party.

Carlotta Lumber Company hired me as a planer-chain puller. A planer-chain puller slides assorted sizes of fir and redwood boards off a sorting table as the lumber rides down the force-driven chain. As with any job, there is an art to perfecting the job. As a chain puller one wears a thick leather apron. These aprons could be purchased at the hardware store in Scotia. The apron protects the lower body from the hips down from slivers and also allows one to push and pull the boards so that they land on the unit of lumber. Another very important piece of clothing is heavy-duty gloves. It was not uncommon to go through three or four pairs of gloves a month. Chain pulling was an arduous job. But I learned, and best of all, I got paid $5.25 an hour and had health insurance for the first time.

"The front apartment will be available starting October first," Alice told me one evening after I came home from Carlotta.

"Awesome," I replied. "When can I see it?"

"Joe should be out in a couple of weeks," said Alice.

Danielle was excited. "It's bigger than this place," she said. When I finally got to see it, it was perfect for us. I used to pay Pete $250 for the back apartment, but now our rent was going to skyrocket to $350 a month.

We started moving into the new apartment at the end of September. It looked like the previous tenants were getting a divorce and both had already gotten new places to live.

"Don't carry that, Danielle," Alice would shout. "You're eight months pregnant. Just watch Aleace and let me help Jack do that."

"Fine," Danielle retorted. "I want to help too," said my beautiful beach ball.

"We'll get it, punkin," I said endearingly.

"You only call be punkin because I'm fat," she said, smiling.

"No way," I responded. "I call you punkin because I love you so much." We then kissed and Alice looked uncomfortable.

Danielle went into labor early. She was supposed to have the baby at the end of October and her labor started October 16. After a few hours of active labor Danielle's water broke.

"Jack," I heard an alarmed voice from the bathroom. I ran to the bathroom and Danielle said, "My water broke."

I called Dr. Johannsson's call center and finally spoke with him.

"Is she in active labor, Jack?" asked Dr. Johannsson.

"Doctor, it seems to be the same rhythm of contractions as she had with our daughter. Two contractions then several minutes pass, then two more contractions," I reported.

"Go ahead and bring her to the hospital. They'll get you settled in and the hospital will call me if the baby's birth is imminent."

It was midnight when I called Alice. "Danielle's in labor and I'm bringing her to the hospital," I said.

"Okay, I'll come over now and then bring Aleace to my house in the morning," said Alice.

When we got to the hospital, they admitted Danielle and checked her to find out what her progress was. "She's between two and three centimeters," the nurse reported.

"Thank you," I said.

"Say, say," Danielle signed.

"The nurse says you're between two and three centimeters dilated."

"That's all?" Danielle said out loud, showing her obvious disappointment.

The nurse told us that we wouldn't be going home without a baby because Danielle's water had already broken and it was their policy not to let the mom go home after that happened. I was happy.

Dr. Johannsson came to see Danielle at the crack of dawn. "Let's check you out and see what's going on," said the ever-optimistic doctor. Danielle really liked Dr. Johannsson because of his professionalism and outstanding personality. It was obvious to Danielle that Dr. Johannsson really cared about her. "You're at about three centimeters now," the doctor told Danielle.

Danielle was learning how to read Dr. Johannsson's lips. "Okay," sighed Danielle.

"Why don't we hook you up to Pitocin so you can have this baby today?" the doctor said.

Danielle remembered how hard the contractions were with Aleace once they connected Danielle up to the machine. Danielle grimaced, but soon relented and said, "Okay, let's do it."

The time was a little after 8 a.m. when the Pitocin was started. "So painful," Danielle would sign. We again used the Lamaze technique of natural childbirth, having taken a refresher class by a nurse named Trieste at Redwood Memorial Hospital in Fortuna. Trieste was a very good nurse and up to date with the newest procedures.

It was 10:30 a.m. when Trieste came to visit with Danielle and me. "How are you doing Danielle?" Trieste asked as she stood at the head of Danielle's bed.

"So painful." Danielle signed, then Trieste turned to me for the interpretation. "So painful." I said.

"Danielle," Trieste said. "Try moving around when you're not having a contraction. Try getting on your knees and rock back and forth with your pelvis. See if this helps."

It was amazing, but Danielle once again had the same pattern in labor as she had with Aleace. Two contractions a minute apart and a five-minute interval and two more contractions a minute apart and so on. Dr. Johannsson had been in once about noon. He checked Danielle and said she was a little past four centimeters dilated.

Throughout the day Danielle tried varying positions and different breathing techniques, and we did a lot of walking up and down the hall. Just about 4 p.m., while Danielle and I were walking the hall, a massive double contraction just about made Danielle collapse.

"Let's get back to the room," I implored Danielle.

She motioned "hold on" by holding one hand up while continuing to hold the handrail, waiting for the second contraction to subside.

Danielle took my elbow as we slowly walked back to the room. She settled back into bed. "Give me some ice," she said. I heard the cleansing breath and she now was turning red as she breathed through the contractions. "Give me your hand," she demanded. She squeezed my hand until there was no color left, but I continued breathing with her through the contraction. She took a cleansing breath, meaning the contraction was over.

The clock read 4:44 p.m. Cleansing breath. She had my complete attention as it was time for a double contraction. As the contraction intensified, she signed, "I HAVE TO PUSH!"

"Go ahead," I signed. I remembered how unnatural it was the last time she was in labor to tell Danielle not to push. "Nurse!" I called down the hallway as the contraction subsided. "Danielle's pushing now!" I said as I went back to be with my wife.

"So painful," Danielle signed as the second contraction began. This time, after her cleansing breath, she closed her eyes and started pushing again.

"Tell her not to push," said the kind nurse. "We're waiting for Dr. Johannsson." Danielle's eyes were closed so I just let her push.

Dr. Johannsson walked in, gloved his right hand, and walked over to Danielle's right side. Danielle opened her eyes and saw the doctor there. "I'm going to check your progress next time you have a contraction," he said.

Cleansing breath. Dr. Johannsson checked Danielle and said eight, almost nine, to the nurses and Dr. Johannsson looked at me and said, "Get your scrubs on."

I turned from Danielle and quickly suited up. I could hear more cleansing breaths and patterned breathing in between the pushes.

Dr. Johannsson placed a sterile blue paper drape under Danielle and told her, "Go ahead and push with the next contraction, the baby is right there."

I looked at my beautiful bride and she signed, "Say, say."

"Dr. Johannsson said the baby is right there."

Cleansing breath; Danielle pushed. The clock read 5:02 p.m.

"Here it comes," said the excited doctor. "Good, good, stop pushing." Dr. Johannsson placed the baby on Danielle's tummy.

"MY BABY, MY BABY!" Danielle said as she reached for our precious daughter. I began to cry.

The baby's cord was cut and Dr. Johannsson continued to suck out mucus from the baby's nose and mouth. I looked over the baby as the doctor and nurses spoke. Her color didn't seem right and she was not yet breathing.

"Doctor, I'm giving her an Apgar score of three," said the head nurse.

"I agree," Dr. Johannsson said. "Danielle, the nurse is going to take the baby to the nursery to wash her up and make sure everything is okay," said the patient doctor. The nurse quickly wrapped the new baby in a blue paper blanket and whisked her off.

Danielle grabbed my face, making me look at her, and signed, "STAY WITH MY BABY!" It was uncanny how perceptive Danielle was when it came to body language.

"But I feel I should stay here with you," I signed.

"NO, STAY WITH MY BABY," she demanded.

I signed, "I love you."

Danielle signed back, "I love you more. GO, HURRY!"

Just as I left Danielle's room, I saw the nurse turn into the nursery carrying our baby. I walked up to the viewing window and watched as nurse Laura put the baby in a bassinet and hurriedly began sucking the mucus from our daughter using a bulb. Nurse Laura turned the baby to her side, rubbed her back quite harshly, and began cleaning the vernix off of her body.

I was familiar with what newborns should look like and it was obvious that our new baby was in distress. I kept watching nurse Laura through the window as she continually tried to get the baby to breathe. I watched our newborn baby begin to turn blue. It is very hard to describe the color, but purple and blue together just about describes the color of our baby. Nurse Laura was now desperate. She looked up from the newborn, glared through the viewing window, right into my eyes, and mouthed, "GET ME A NURSE!" It was then that I realized that our baby was dying.

I really didn't know where to find another nurse but I just ran down the hall in the opposite direction from where I was. "Nurse," I said as I happened upon another nurse. "Laura needs you, now," I said with great desperation in my voice.

"Where is she?" the nurse asked.

I motioned for the nurse to follow me and together we ran down the hall to where Laura was still fighting to save my daughter's life.

The nurse that I found quickly ran to Laura's side. The two nurses together worked like a well-practiced team. Laura would say something, then the other nurse would respond. The other nurse would say something and then Laura would respond. The nurse that I found down the hall pulled up a pump with a small tube connected and began sucking more and more mucus from our newborn. Laura then picked up the wall phone and called someone. While the two nurses continued to fight for the life of my baby, Dr. Mogel walked toward me then into the nursery. I watched the doctor take over for the nurses and he continued to work at getting the baby to breathe. Slowly, extremely slowly, the baby's color began to become pinker. I could tell by the keenly serious look on the doctor's face that they were having a difficult time.

The doctor who came to the aid of our daughter was named Dr. Mogel. Danielle and I had taken Aleace to see Dr. Mogel for her checkups and routine shots.

"Jack," Dr. Mogel said as he exited the nursery.

"Yes," I replied.

"The baby is having difficulty breathing on her own," said the doctor. "We're going to run some tests and try to find out what's going on. It looks to us as though she is a preemie. Her weight is normal for a newborn, but she has some other signs that make us think she's not full term. It seems that her lungs aren't fully developed and she also has underdeveloped fingerprints."

It took me several minutes to digest everything Dr. Mogel told me. "Thank you for everything," I told the doctor.

"Jack." The doctor hesitated. "This baby is very sick; I've lost newborns who've looked better."

I went back to the room and told Danielle that the baby was having a difficult time breathing. Dr. Johannsson was just finishing up. Danielle required a few stitches.

"What are they going to do?" Danielle asked.

"They're going to do tests on her," I signed.

"Oh, my baby," Danielle signed. "Go back and keep an eye on her," Danielle told me.

"I'll come back and check on you in a little bit," I said.

Danielle signed, "GO!"

Dr. Mogel ran a series of tests on our new baby. I was shocked when I watched him give the newborn a spinal tap. "Help her, Lord," I begged. Just then Danielle walked up beside me and grabbed my elbow. She could see that I was crying and reached up and wiped my tears away. "Shouldn't you be in bed?" I said to her, shocked that she was already walking.

"I don't care," Danielle signed. "My baby is more important."

They placed the baby in an incubator and turned up the oxygen in hopes that this would assist the baby while she continued her labored breathing. It scared me watching as the baby labored, trying to breathe so hard that her whole abdomen would rise and fall.

I took Danielle back to her room. "Danielle, I'm going to the chapel. Is that okay with you?"

"Go," she signed, "I'm okay. I love you."

"I love you more," I responded.

Redwood Memorial is a Catholic hospital. I knew exactly where the chapel was. I had to walk to the other side of the hospital, near the entrance. I reached for the door and walked in. Serenity. Serenity was what I found as I looked up to the Crucifix. I knelt down. I made the sign of the cross and took a deep breath. I again looked at the Crucifix.

I began to sob. "Oh, my Jesus. I love you; I love you; I love you," I prayed. "You oh Lord, Master of the Universe, I implore you. Let my baby live. Let my baby live. I promise you, oh Lord, right here, right now, that I will do anything you ask of me. I give you my life, oh Lord, please, let my baby live. I love you."

I stayed in the chapel for another fifteen minutes or so spending time with my Jesus. He didn't even care that I was crying.

I went back to check on the baby and she was still fighting for her life. I went to see Danielle and she told me to go home and take a shower and shave. I came back about an hour later.

Dr. Mogel was looking at my baby through the viewing window. I walked up to him. "Hi, Doctor," I said.

"Hi, Jack," he replied.

"How's the baby?" I asked with urgency.

"To tell you the truth," he said, "I'm bewildered. Your baby is doing fine now."

"She is?" I was absolutely flabbergasted.

"Yes, she's breathing on her own and her color is perfect," he stated.

"How did that happen?" I asked, a bit dumbfounded.

Dr. Mogel looked right into my eyes and said very slowly, "It was a miracle. I simply can't explain it."

Chapter 20

"Joy," Danielle said and signed when the nurse asked her the name of the new baby.

"Oh, how perfect," replied the competent nurse.

Danielle waved me over and signed, "Hold the baby."

I reached for the newborn and as I snuggled her head against my cheek, rich fragrances overcame my being. Daphne, rain, sunshine, and lavender enveloped me when I held the little one for the first time. I was flooded with sheer emotion as tears again spilled down my cheeks. Danielle smiled and gestured for me to lean close as she wiped my tears.

Danielle informed me that this baby was going to use Pampers and not cloth diapers as we did with Aleace. "If you nurse the baby, then maybe we could afford the Pampers," I told her.

"I will," was Danielle's promise.

Danielle was a natural. Nursing the baby was obviously something that Danielle received great pleasure in doing. She, Aleace, and the baby developed a great routine. Aleace was such a big helper. Danielle would dress the two girls in the morning and when Danielle changed the diapers, since Aleace was now almost three years old, she was old enough to help Danielle and to throw them away in the garbage.

Two weeks passed by. One day as I came home from work, Danielle was crying. "What's the matter?" I signed as I walked in the back door.

"My breast hurts so much. It's the same thing that happened with Aleace when I tried to nurse her," signed Danielle.

"I'll call the doctor," I said.

"Bring her in tomorrow morning," Dr. Johannsson's office told me on the phone. I called work and told them that my wife had a doctor's appointment and they understood.

"Nothing to be too concerned about," said the gentle, smiling doctor. "Only a little mastitis," he stated. "Lay back, Danielle. This is going to hurt a little, but I'll be as gentle as I can."

Dr. Johannsson gently squeezed out what looked like a cheesy substance from Danielle's right breast. Danielle grimaced as the doctor manipulated her.

"Okay, go home and take it easy on the right side. Feed the baby from the left side for a couple of days until the right side feels better. I'll prescribe some antibiotics for you," said the competent doctor.

"How will I know when to use it again?" Danielle spoke.

"Your body will let you know," mouthed the patient doctor.

Just as the doctor had said, Danielle was able to start nursing on the right breast again after a few days. Danielle never had another bout of mastitis after that. It made me wonder if they could have done the very same thing when we were trying to nurse Aleace.

Our family of four seemed complete.

"Are you having more kids?" Alice asked me about a month after Joy was born.

"I don't believe so," I replied. I hadn't really talked to Danielle about it, but I was pretty sure I was going to get a vasectomy so Danielle wouldn't be burdened with a lot of babies.

"What's that?" Danielle asked one afternoon after I told her I was going to get fixed.

"A vasectomy will make it so we don't have any more children," I said.

"But I'm not sure! What if I want another baby?" she said.

"You can see how hard it is raising two kids already. I don't think it's a good idea to have any more," I said. I was convinced I was doing the right thing.

"Whatever," was Danielle's answer.

The procedure was rather simple. Notice I didn't say painless. The procedure, although touted as being painless, was very painful.

Alice watched the kids while Danielle and I drove to the urologist in Eureka. The surgery was performed in the doctor's office because the hospital was a Catholic institution and their protocol does not allow sterilization. I had the vasectomy on Thursday and that gave me three days off from work to heal.

I should have taken the whole week off. I was able to work, but the guys at work were aware of what was done to me. Although they harassed me a bit, they helped me out more than usual.

"Is your voice higher now?" my co-worker James asked.

"No, not at all," I answered, feigning a falsetto voice.

James got a big kick out of it, telling the other guys, "Ask Jack if he has any side effects because of his recent surgery." Each time they did, I dutifully replied, "Oh no, not at all," in a squeaky female voice.

Danielle was not pleased. "I'm angry at you," she told me one day.

"Why now?" I asked.

"You didn't even think about me when you got the surgery," she said.

"I got the surgery because I WAS thinking about you," I snapped back.

"Not true," she signed.

"Well, it's too late now!" I signed back angrily.

"Leave me alone!" Danielle signed and said loudly.

"Fine, C YA," I signed and said louder as I walked out the back door. I needed to let off some steam so I went for a walk.

This time in our lives Danielle and I were becoming very involved with our Catholic faith. All I could think about while I prayed on my walk was how selfish Danielle was being even after I was the one who went through all the pain so we wouldn't have to think about having any more kids.

By the time I got back home, it had been about thirty minutes. I was calmed down so I went and sat next to Danielle.

"Get away from me," she said and pushed me away. I just moved closer to her as she was feeding Joy. Danielle pretended to ignore me.

After about ten minutes I put my head on her shoulder. "I love you," I signed. No response. "I'm sorry," I signed. Still no response. "Do you forgive me?"

"No," Danielle quickly answered.

"That's okay. I will always love you even if you get mad at me," I signed. I then slowly and gently turned her face toward me and kissed her soft, beautiful lips.

"Let's go to Ettersburg," Pete said to me one summer's day. "Can you get the time off from work?"

"I'm due two weeks' vacation, so I'll just tell them I need some time off," I said.

I told Danielle that a trip to Ettersburg was in the making. "I love Ettersburg," she said and signed.

We took a family-sized tent with us and drove our own car and followed Pete and Alice in their camper as we drove to the King's Range in southern Humboldt. As we descended the hill into Ettersburg proper, I fell in love. I'm not exactly sure, but it would be hard to find a more beautiful, breathtaking place on earth than Ettersburg.

Spread out before me was a valley rich with plant life and fauna. The trees surrounding us were stately green and commanding. Centrally located was an ancient apple orchard as the gentle Mattole River meandered calmly through this homestead as it reached for the great Pacific Ocean. Danielle said, "Look," as a doe scampered away with her fawn. The fawn had those vivid white spots on it's flanks as though God himself had hand-painted them as we neared the large, white two-story house.

We stopped in front of the Frenches' home and Pete went in and talked with them. Mr. French and his wife came out and said hello to Alice and also to meet my family and me. The Frenches were ranchers. Mr. French was a rugged man who had the look of someone who worked hard all his life. Mrs. French, on the other hand, was his complete opposite, delicate and gentle.

Mrs. French greeted Aleace and Joy with a beautiful smile. "Oh, how precious," she said. She then reached out her hand gently toward Danielle and said, "How have you been, Danielle? It's been years since I've seen you. You're all grown up now. Don't you look radiant."

The Frenches raised sheep and were operators of a mature world-renowned apple orchard. Many, many years ago this orchard was loaded with apple trees that had been hybridized by Mr. Walt Etter. The Frenches gave us directions to a pasture about two miles away and said that it ran right up against the river bar of the Mattole. We all waved and said our good-byes.

Danielle took Aleace and Joy to Alice's camper while I set up our tent. Danielle was a lot more meticulous than I was, when it came to the set-up and incidentals of our tent.

"Didn't you think to lay plastic down before you put the tent on the ground?" signed Danielle when she finally came out of the camper.

"No, actually," I said. "Your Highness, while you were having your afternoon 'high tea' with your mommy in the camper, I was putting up the tent and you were nowhere to be found." My voice dripped sarcasm.

"Good, next time put plastic down first," she stated.

"Yes, Your majesty. Anything you say, Your Majesty," I signed. Danielle grinned back at me.

"Could you watch Aleace while Danielle and I go for a walk?" I asked Alice. Joy was taking a nap and I promised we'd be back in about an hour.

Danielle and I walked hand in hand up the Mattole. The day had started out warm and sunny. By now it was nearing eighty-five degrees. The day was so warm I could smell the humidity emitting from the great Mattole as we strolled. The King's Range is extremely remote. The Mattole River flows right through the heart of it. Danielle and I had walked for around twenty minutes when we sat down on the river bar and Danielle grabbed my elbow. We sat there soaking up the scenery; the peace was palpable.

"I used to swim right here with my cousins when I was a little kid," Danielle spoke softly.

I looked around, stood up, and started taking off my clothes. I am not a big exhibitionist but the only person for miles around was my beautiful bride.

"Are you going swimming?" Danielle asked as she noticed what I was doing.

"No way," I signed sarcastically, "I have a sudden urge to do the laundry." I threw my underwear at her and ran into the beckoning emerald blue swimming hole on the Mattole.

The air was keenly warm and the water felt splendid as I splashed and dived deep into the water. As I came to the surface, I looked to the river bar and signed for Danielle to come in.

"No way, smart-aleck," she signed."

"Chicken liver," I signed back to her. She smiled and looked askance as if to say "You're crazy, and I'm not going to look at you." I dove down again and came up for air.

I swam around leisurely and as I looked back to the river bar, Danielle was already walking into the water. "Feels amazing, huh?" I signed as Danielle swam to me.

Danielle was a great swimmer. She could easily swim circles around me. I then got a face full of water as Danielle splashed me when I came back up from a deep dive. I dove down again and tried grabbing at her feet while she swam. Danielle has always had tender feet and I knew it. "Don't touch me," she signed, joking.

This impromptu swim of ours would become, for me, a place of tranquility and repose. A place I would return to in my mind, time after time after time.

We came out and before we put our clothes back on, I attempted to whisk the water off of our bodies with my hands like a squeegee. It was such a warm day that we dried out quickly. By the time we came back to camp, even our hair was dry. Alice looked at us without saying a word. I got the impression that we hadn't pulled the wool over Alice's eyes, but we never did fess up about going skinny dipping that day.

For Danielle and me this day was ours. It was our special day.

Chapter 21

I can't think of a more exciting and monumental moment for a family than when their eldest starts kindergarten.

Aleace started kindergarten at Rio Dell Elementary School. Her teacher was named Mrs. Whitchurch. Mrs. Whitchurch was kind, patient, and a great book reader.

It appeared that Aleace was going to be very tall for her age. It came as a surprise to Danielle and me that because of Aleace's height, more age-inappropriate things were expected of her. I often had to comment to other parents, "She's only four years old." Most of the parents were shocked and said, "Oh, I'm sorry, I thought she was six." Aleace was very intelligent and she loved books.

Danielle loved getting involved with Aleace at school. One can only imagine how much Danielle missed due to her great hearing loss, but that never kept her from being the best mom.

It was a given that because I was hearing, I worked with Danielle every time I heard her articulate a word wrong.

"Why do you make me talk?" Danielle signed to me one day.

I thought for a moment before I answered and signed, "With the children starting school, what if you have to tell the kindergarten teacher that Aleace needs to take some medicine?"

"I don't know," Danielle signed.

"What if the teacher asks you a question about when Aleace ate some grapes?" In my attempt to think of something off the cuff, that was the best I could manage for the moment. "It could be almost anything," I said. "I want you to be able to tell the teacher something and the teacher will understand your speech."

"Oh, I see. I understand," she signed.

On Aleace's fifth birthday, Danielle organized a birthday party and it seemed that the whole kindergarten class was there.

"Jack, can you help me with Aleace's birthday party?" Danielle asked me a week before the event.

"What do you want me to do?" I asked, somewhat cautiously.

"I want you to do the piñata," she signed.

"I can do piñatas. Hello, I'm half Mexican, I can do piñatas."

It was the big day and Aleace had never had such a big birthday party before. Gramma Alice kept a keen eye on two-year-old Joy while Danielle and I worked on Aleace's party.

I found a blue donkey piñata that I bought in Eureka at the only Mexican store we had in Humboldt at the time. I filled the piñata with a couple hundred pounds of candy. Well, maybe it was only a few bags, but it seemed like a lot of candy.

The kids arrived along with their moms. Everyone was so happy and excited. Danielle always did so well. She focused so intensely at the other moms when they asked her questions. Most of the time she had to look to me for a translation, but once in a while she understood or the moms thought she understood. I was just so proud of her.

Danielle was busy and one of the moms said to me, because she could see me sign to Danielle, "Tell Danielle that she did such a great job at setting the table." The mom and I were across the room from Danielle.

"I'm going to get Danielle's attention. Would you say that to her instead?" I asked.

"Certainly, the kind lady said.

POUND. I thumped the floor with my foot hard enough for Danielle to feel the vibration. This pounding on the floor is common in many deaf households. Danielle looked at me, then I pointed to the kind mom, and the lady said, "You did such a great job at setting the table for the birthday party and I love your homemade cake. Did you make it?"

Now she's done it! She didn't repeat exactly what she told me to tell Danielle so I knew, because the mom had said so many words together, that Danielle would look at me for the translation. "She wants you to know you did such a great job at setting the table for the party. Also, she wants to know did you make that homemade cake." Whew. If I knew the lady was going to say so much I would have answered instead.

Danielle was learning to read the lips of the other moms, but she understood better if they kept the questions short. I'd often set myself in Danielle's shoes. If the moms kept talking it would begin to look like a bunch of gibberish.

Rene, our matron of honor, had taken many classes at Oregon State related to the deaf and hard of hearing. She'd told me once, "I'll give you an example of how difficult lip reading is. The lip movement for the words GREEN, RED, and WHITE are all the same." Can you imagine if someone said to Danielle, "I live in the green house on the corner"? Danielle would drive around for hours looking for the red house or maybe even the white house on the corner.

I took everybody outside and brought them under the huge fig tree that grew in our backyard. This fig tree was planted by Danielle's grandfather Giovanni Mela. This variety of fig tree, known as the King Fig, is capable of producing figs here in Humboldt County's coastal climate. Danielle always loved when it was time to pick figs.

I asked all the moms to have their children make a big circle and make sure to keep their child from getting too close to the cut-off broom handle that I made just for the occasion. In my lifetime I had seen way too many kids hit by the swinging piñata stick. I threw a long rope coiled over a large fig limb and the blue piñata was carefully tethered to the rope.

Danielle told me she wanted Aleace to go first because it was her birthday. I blindfolded my beautiful little daughter and reminded all the kids to stay way back so they wouldn't get hit by the stick.

"Let's count," I told all the people as I proceeded to turn Aleace. "One, two, three." Danielle moved in to hold Aleace still once I got her turned around. "All right, let her go," I signed to Danielle.

Danielle moved back and I yelled to Aleace, "Swing, mija." Aleace swung as I dutifully pulled up on the rope, keeping the candy-filled donkey just out of reach. I told all the kids, "You get three swings to hit the donkey, so do your best."

One by one the children were blindfolded, turned three times, and given the chance to hit the donkey. One of Aleace's school chums obviously had a plan. I could tell Alex, a stout kid from Aleace's class, had been thinking and watching exactly what I was doing as each child approached the sweet treat–filled donkey. As soon as I blindfolded him, one, two, three, Danielle held him while I grabbed the rope. I shouted out, "Swing." He immediately swung high, knowing I was going to pull the donkey up and out of reach.

Good thing I have pretty good reaction time because I was just barely able to pull that chunky donkey extra high as one of the donkey's blue legs got hit pretty hard. All the kids yelled and screamed, thinking Alex was going to be the liberator and smash that massive candy-filled delight. Not so fast.

"Good job, Alex," I told the little boy.

I hate to boast, but I am an excellent piñata rope puller. This is not a widely known fact but I'm faster than you might expect when it comes to having amazing piñata rope puller coordination.

"Next," I said.

I was bound and determined to make this piñata take up most of the party time because we only had two activities planned, mutilate the piñata and pin the tail on the donkey.

Aleace came up to bat for the second time. This time I turned the kids around only twice. "Okay, hit it," I yelled to Aleace as I pulled on the rope. I let her hit the piñata dead on. I was expecting a huge explosion, but it appeared that the obese piñata was too loaded with candy, which gave it extra rigidity. I let each subsequent child hit the piñata from then on, hoping they'd weaken it enough to finally burst.

Eventually, when Alex got up to bat, I told him, "Give it a good hit," as I backed away.

I kept that blue confection-filled animal right at his eye level and he clobbered that overweight piñata so hard that the back half of the donkey went flying and the other half stayed with the rope.

That wonky donkey was so full of candy that the front half spilled its guts right down from the rope. I told Alex, "Take off your blindfold and grab a bunch of candy." All the kids in kind dove for their share of the junk food overkill.

"How much candy did you put in that cute little blue donkey?" one of the moms asked me on our way back into the house.

I answered carefully, "I was thinking when I filled it that I wanted each kid to take home a lot of candy. Fun, right? Probably about twenty pounds."

Chapter 22

It was 1984 and Joy had started kindergarten.

"The telephone rang this morning and I answered the phone, but it wasn't the TTY," Danielle told me one day. (She could see the light blink with each ring.)

I had to think of something so I wouldn't miss an important phone call. One of the guys at work said, "Why don't you just buy an answering machine and be done with it."

"How much do they cost?" I asked.

"Not too much," he answered, "maybe forty bucks."

Well, to him forty bucks was not too much. But for me, Papa Penny Pincher, forty bucks could buy a lot of school clothes. I went to Radio Shack to price answering machines.

"It just came on sale," the kind gentleman said.

"This one?" I asked.

"Yes," he replied. "Twenty-nine ninety-five." I splurged and purchased the much-needed answering machine.

I took the new fandangled machine home and proudly set it up. I called my mother-in-law and asked her to call and leave a message.

"What's leave a message mean?" she asked.

"When the phone answers it will say, 'Hello, you have reached 764-6758. Please leave a message.' Then you just say this is your mother-in-law, and then you tell me what a great son-in-law I am."

"Oh," she said.

Alice called back and I waited and watched the answering machine work. "Hello, this is 764-6758. Please leave a message." I watched as the cassette tape turned around on its spool.

"Hello, hello," I heard Alice say.

I immediately picked up the phone. "You're supposed to leave a message," I said again.

"No one said anything," she responded.

"That's the point," I answered back. "If I'm working and Danielle is home, then the machine will answer and people will leave a message."

"Why does everything always need to be so complicated?" said Alice.

I got home from work one day and noticed the blinking light on the message machine. "Hello, Jack, this is Gary Cook," the message said. "I'm looking for a hard worker and I think I finally got something for you. Could you please call me?"

GARY COOK. Gary Cook was the gentleman that I had called every week for the last four and a half years. I just couldn't believe it.

"Danielle, Danielle, Gary Cook called me," I said, beaming.

"Well, call him at home," Danielle said.

"I can't call him at home. I'll call him tomorrow at break time," I said, and that's what I did.

"Hello, Gary, this is Jack Saffell."

"Hello, Jack," Gary replied. "I've got a job opening. It's not an easy job, but I'm sure you could do it."

"What is it?" I asked. "Green chain puller," he responded.

Yikes. Pulling green chain is probably one of the most difficult jobs in a lumber mill. As the boards are cut and sized, they are then sent out onto a chained table to be sorted. I had pulled planer chain here at Carlotta Lumber, but green chain was a little bit harder due to the weight of some of the green lumber. Many of the 2"x12"x20'-long redwood boards could weigh in excess of one hundred pounds.

I answered without hesitation, "I'll take it." I then said, "Gary, you will never know how much this means to me and my family. I promise I will not disappoint you."

The first two weeks of my new job were almost more than my body could take. I'd come home for lunch each day, eat three bologna and cheese sandwiches, chips, and sweetened iced tea. Even though I upped my caloric intake, I still lost ten pounds that first two weeks of work.

"I don't know if I will ever learn this job," I said to myself. "Please help me, Lord, I want to be able to support my family."

Slowly but surely, I began to retain the work that was given to me.

I had worked there the ninety-day trial period and thought things were hunky-dory when I got a slip from the main office. My supervisor told me to report to Gary Cook. I was scared. I had put my heart and soul into learning this chain puller job. I could only hope that it was enough.

"How are things going?" Gary asked me after I had waited in the hall for my turn to speak with him.

"Fine," I responded.

"It is protocol for us to evaluate each new hire after his first ninety days of work," Gary said. "Your supervisor is pleased with your work and has asked me to give you a raise."

"Praise the Lord," I shouted inside. "Thank you," I calmly responded.

I had prayed and thought about a surprise for Danielle ever since taking the green chain job at the Pacific Lumber Company. It was going to require me to secretly save a lot of money, but I'm pretty sneaky when it comes to surprises.

I was now earning over a hundred dollars a day, but it seemed the more money I made the more taxes were taken out. This sneaky surprise was going to take longer than I had hoped.

"I have a doctor's appointment on Tuesday," I told Danielle.

"What for?" she asked.

"I need to get a small surgery to fix something," was all I told her.

"Fix what?" she asked.

"I need to fix something that only happens to men. Women don't get it," I calmly remarked.

"Whatever," said my beautiful bride.

My surgery date was set and I needed to take off at least a week from work, preferably two, said the experienced Dr. Schmidt.

The day of the surgery approached and Danielle drove me to the hospital. "I'm going to be in surgery about three hours," I told Danielle. "Please wait in the waiting room for me so when I get out you can take me home."

When Danielle dropped me off, I kissed her and signed, "I love you." She signed back, "I love you more."

I was given a local anesthesia and Dr. Schmidt proceeded with the much-anticipated surgery. The experienced surgeon said that only about sixty percent of men who have this surgery receive a positive outcome. I told him that was good enough for me.

I got out of surgery and Danielle was nowhere to be found. It was impossible for me to get out of bed for the first three hours so I just waited and fumed, waited and fumed.

Finally, Danielle showed up. "WHERE HAVE YOU BEEN?" I signed and said angrily.

She could see from my face just how angry I was. "I couldn't stay around," she signed.

"WHAT? I'm your husband. You need to stay with me," I said not calmly.

"I'm sorry," Danielle said. "I just couldn't do it."

On our way home, I was so upset that my face was red and I couldn't think of anything I wanted to say that wasn't mean and hateful. I carefully walked into the house and got on the couch and got some ice packs and put them on the surgery site.

"Danielle," I eventually said after calming down. "This surgery was supposed to be a surprise for you."

"What do you mean a surprise for me?" she asked.

"Remember when I got fixed so we wouldn't have any more babies?" I asked her.

"Yes," she replied.

"Well, I got the operation changed back today. If God wants us to have more babies now, he can send them to us," I said.

"You mean, maybe I can have another baby?" she asked excitedly.

"Yes," I said. "If the surgery I had today worked; you can have more babies."

Danielle began to cry. "You don't know how much this means to me," she said.

"I think I do," I responded.

I rested the whole week with hopes of being well enough to get back to work without any problems. Fortunately, I was able to do my job without any complications. It was necessary for me to ice up every evening, but things finally got back to normal after a month or so.

Danielle was so excited. She asked me to get a pregnancy test two months after my surgery. The stick test came back positive. She was pregnant. Danielle started crying after she took the test.

"Why are you crying?" I said as tears came to my eyes.

"Remember when I told you I couldn't stay in the hospital when you had your surgery?" she asked me.

"Yes," I responded.

"Well," she paused, "I'm afraid to tell you."

"Danielle," I signed. "I love you; you can tell me anything. Nothing you can say will ever make me stop loving you."

"When I was seventeen, my baby died," she finally signed.

"WHAT?" I responded.

"The hospital where you had your surgery reminded me of the place where I had to go." She started crying harder and tried signing as she wept. "I went to a place like that and my baby died," she signed with great remorse and embarrassment.

"DANIELLE. I love you, please don't be angry with yourself," I signed and said.

"I can't help it," she signed. "God will never forgive me."

I got up and held her close. Danielle sobbed.

"Danielle?" I signed after releasing her a little so she could see me sign. "Please, please know I will always, always love you."

"I know," she signed, "but it hurts so bad when I think of my little baby."

Together we cried for the soul of that poor little baby.

I had already made the doctor's appointment for Danielle to see Dr. Johannsson when Danielle started bleeding.

Danielle miscarried at eleven and a half weeks' gestation. She retrieved the baby from the toilet and wrapped it lovingly in a paper towel and put it in a small box. Danielle had me bury that poor baby in the back yard.

She cried for two weeks. I took her to see Dr. Johannsson on our regular appointment day and he said that these things happen quite often and not to be worried and that she would be pregnant again in no time.

"You're due April fourteenth," Dr. Johannsson told Danielle.

Danielle got pregnant a little more than a month after her miscarriage. She was beaming. She was aware that she could miscarry again, but at least she could be hopeful.

Our beautiful daughter Lamay was born April 8, 1986. This gift from God was born when Halley's Comet was closest to the earth. I later learned that Samuel Langhorne Clemens—Mark Twain—was also born with the comet. Only God knows what a great gift of inner healing the birth of this beautiful child brought to the soul of my precious, beautiful, deaf wife.

Lamay weighed 8 pounds 8½ ounces and was 20 inches long. It was such a quick labor for Danielle that we were all taken by surprise. We stayed home for a couple of hours while Danielle was in labor.

"Maybe we better go to the hospital," Danielle mentioned.

Alice came to the house and stayed with the kids while Danielle and I moseyed over to the hospital. Good thing we moseyed quickly because Lamay was born two hours after we got checked into the hospital.

I left the hospital to go home and shower and shave. Danielle was ecstatic when I got back to the hospital with Aleace and Joy in tow. "Look," Danielle showed the girls, proudly.

As I watched Aleace and Joy lovingly touch their new baby sister, tears of joy and contentment filled my eyes. Danielle reached over and wiped the tears from my cheeks. Our little family was growing. What a wonderful blessing! God is good.

Chapter 23

I walked into the house through the back door after work one day. Lamay was about eighteen months old and Danielle was nursing her. I always loved watching Danielle nurse the babies. When she finished feeding them, she always handed them to me so I could burp them and hold them and love on them. I love the smell of babies.

On this particular day, once Danielle's hands were free, she signed, "I think I'm pregnant."

"That's a good one." I laughed at her joke. "You're so funny, that's a good joke," I signed. Her expression was completely stoic. "You're laughing inside, right?" I signed. "Are you teasing me?"

I have been known to tease Danielle once in a while. I thought this whopper was a great joke. But Danielle's facial expression did not change.

"What are you talking about?" She'd cut me to the quick. "You can't be pregnant," I signed in disbelief. "You haven't even started your period since Lamay was born, how can you be pregnant?" I added nervously.

"I don't know," she signed, "but I think I felt the baby move today."

"Felt the baby move today? What are you talking about, felt the baby move today?" I signed with skepticism. "No way," I signed. "I'll prove you wrong and on payday I'll buy you a pregnancy test and show you who's right."

"You're due April first," Dr. Johannsson told Danielle.

Is this a joke? I thought to myself. *April first. Jesus, you know I love you, but please help us with these four beautiful babies, these beautiful gifts.*

This pregnancy meant, for me, that I'd have to be extra careful in the future, like separate bedrooms or something.

Dr. Johannsson told Danielle that it was okay for her to keep nursing Lamay but to stop about one month before the new baby was due. Danielle stopped nursing Lamay March 4. Imagine that. Danielle was growing a baby inside, nursing Lamay, and was still able to keep herself healthy by eating right. Amazing.

Christian was born March 25, 1988. He weighed 9 pounds 12 ounces and was 20½ inches long. Danielle was so proud that she bore a son. I was pretty proud too.

"Are you going to circumcise him?" the nurse asked Danielle.

"No way," she signed.

"Danielle said no way," I told the nurse as I interpreted for my beautiful bride. Danielle and I had held this conversation many years earlier when she was pregnant with Aleace.

Danielle and I both believed that keeping things the way God built them was probably the best choice to make for a baby boy. I jokingly told the nurse, "If God wanted baby boys to have a foreskin, then wouldn't they be born with one?" I actually don't believe she realized that I was being sarcastic.

Linda Doebel, one of our best friends, bought a place out Holmes Flat way. Linda and Ron, her husband, had lived in Scotia, a company-owned town, for many years. Linda and Ron bought twenty acres with a two-story farm home on it.

I had asked to have our name put on the housing list in Scotia ever since I got hired there. It was our hope to find a larger home.

"Ask Gary Cook if you could have our house after we move out," Linda told me.

I went into Gary's office after work one day and asked him if we could move into the Doebels' home after they moved out. "We'll see," he said.

After they moved out, the Pacific Lumber carpenters spent several months fixing and repairing

Linda's house in Scotia. When the carpenters had finished all their work, the painters got in there and painted the whole thing.

Gary phoned me one day. "You can have the Doebels' house," he said.

We moved into the Doebels' house when Christian was just a baby. The house had four bedrooms and two bathrooms. We were so glad to be there.

"Jack, Jack!" Danielle called to me.

I carefully opened my sleepy eyes to find that it was still dark. "What?" I asked.

"Jack, Jack!" Danielle said again.

I realized that Danielle must not have put on her hearing aid. "What?" I signed into her hands.

"My baby."

I got up and turned on the light. "What are you talking about? It's five o'clock in the morning," I signed.

"My baby," she said and signed. "I forgot my baby."

"What baby?" I signed back.

"My baby at our old house. I forgot my little baby," she said nervously.

"You want me to go get the baby right now?" I signed questioningly.

"Whenever you want but I want you to go get my baby," she said and signed.

"I'll go get the baby when the sun comes up, okay?"

"But I don't want you to forget," she signed.

"I promise, Punky, I'll go get your baby," I said as I kissed her softly. I turned off the light. "Goodnight," I signed into her hands.

I went back to our old house and exhumed the poor little thing. I brought the little baby and its box to the new house and had Danielle and the other kids come out. As Danielle held Christian, we all held hands and prayed the Our Father as I reburied our beautiful baby. I lovingly planted flowers over the baby's grave, which I watched bloom year after year after year.

When we lived in Pete's two-bedroom apartment our gas and electric bill was about fifty dollars a month. This new place had a brand-new forced air system. We just loved it. It kept the house so warm and comfy and cozy. Then came the gas bill—$247. What? $247? Are you kidding me? There was no way we could afford that every month.

I quickly brought out lots of blankets. We soon learned that due to the fact that Scotia provides their own electricity, using an electric appliance is much more inexpensive than using natural gas. I purchased an electric stand-alone heater for the front room and held the rest of the house at a temperate sixty-three degrees. Sometimes, not all the time, we could see our breath in the bedrooms.

 Danielle was sitting on the couch one Saturday morning, holding Christian, when the song, "Rikki, Don't Lose That Number," by Steely Dan came on the radio. Danielle, it seemed, was able to feel the bass in certain songs and this song was full of deep bass. I reached for Danielle, and she got up while holding the baby and we started dancing. Christian was between us and Danielle's smile was radiant.

 Lamay, seeing us dancing, came to us. I picked her up. Just then Joy walked into the living room, came up to us, stood on my and Danielle's feet, and reached around us to hold on. I called out, "Aleace." Aleace came running into the front room, saw what we were doing, came and stood on the other side of Danielle and me, and climbed onto our feet.

 There, in that joyful living room, all five of the people I loved the most, danced around and around, smiling and laughing, all the while the music played on. Thank you, Lord, thank you! This is a wonderful life!

 I found out from Linda Doebel that I could put a chest freezer in the garage and that the electricity to the garages wasn't monitored because Pacific Lumber made their own electricity.

 Danielle and I went to Eel Valley Appliance in Fortuna and bought the biggest chest freezer they sold. This chest freezer was such a great addition to our household. We learned to save a lot of money by purchasing meat in bulk, and when possible freezing fresh corn and other vegetables.

Scotia was a company-owned town. The town had a school, gymnasium, theater, hardware store, pharmacy, bank, Hoby's Market, and the world-renowned Scotia Inn. There were approximately 250 houses in Scotia, all of which were extremely well maintained.

Just like they did in our case, if a family happened to move out, then the town carpenters went in, fixed it up, and repaired any damages. After the carpenters were done with their repairs, the town painters went in and painted. To aid in its care and upkeep of the town, Scotia even maintained its own plumber and garden departments.

I asked to be transferred to the shipping department a couple of years after Christian was born. I recognized that I'd get compensated a little less money, but it would be worth it in the long run. The wear and tear on my body was very noticeable the four years I was on the green chain.

I had worked in the shipping department for a couple of years when one day a job posting was pinned on the cork bulletin board.

TOWN-GARDENER, it read. *The worker will be under the supervision of Don Bryant. Duties shall be to mow, trim and maintain lawns and trees throughout Scotia. Starting pay negotiable.*

I finally had the opportunity to read the job posting while we were on break. I turned to the guys and said, "I'm going to apply for that job."

Everybody laughed at me. "You'll never get it," chuckled Cecil Williams, one of the tally men who worked along with the rest of us. "You're not even related to anybody in town," he remarked.

"I don't care," I shot back. "I'm going to give them the opportunity to say no," and I left it at that.

I walked into the Human Resources Department and asked if I could apply for the gardener job.

"There's quite a stack over there," Debbie, the Human Resources secretary said as she pointed to a pile of papers about seven inches thick on Don Bryant's desk.

"That's okay. I'd still like to apply, if I may," I said with a big smile on my face.

Debbie gave me a simple fill-in-the-blank in-house job application. The application wanted to know how long I worked for P.L., how much I made an hour, and where I lived.

Dave Kaplan and I had worked together on the green chain. Dave had been a gardener for only two years after working on the green chain for about five years. Dave was a great guy and one of the hardest workers I'd ever worked with. He was a Seventh Day Adventist, a good Christian man, so he and I got along great. Dave had gotten an electrician's job down south, so he was the reason the Scotia gardener job was now open.

I prayed and asked the Lord for the gardener job. Danielle and I were now very involved with the Catholic Charismatic Renewal, and praying was something I was learning about. Danielle and I prayed together and left the rest up to the Lord.

A month went by before I was approached by my shipping supervisor, Ken Taylor. Ken handed me a slip of paper and walked away. The paper read, "Call Don Bryant at your earliest convenience."

I called Don Bryant at break time.

"Could you come into my office and see me?" he asked. "I'd like to talk to you about the gardener job."

"What time would you like me there?" I asked.

"Could you come in tomorrow about ten a.m.?"

"Great," I said, "see you at ten tomorrow."

The next day I walked into Don Bryant's office and saw that he was busy. I stood back in the hall until the man he was talking with came out and walked past me.

"Jack, come in," Don said.

I introduced myself and answered all the questions that Don asked me. "Is there anything you want to ask me?" Don said.

"Yes," I said. "Do we ever work Saturdays or overtime?"

"No, it's pretty much a seven thirty a.m. to four thirty p.m. Monday through Friday job," he responded. I shook his hand and thanked him for the job interview.

Ken Taylor came up to me on Monday morning. "Looks like you got the gardener job. We have to wait until after the Fourth of July so we can get someone to fill your vacancy."

I later learned that Don Bryant walked up to my house in Scotia, peered over the back-yard fence, and looked in to see if I was maintaining my own yard. I think he liked what he saw. God is good, I thought, with great affection.

Chapter 24

On many occasions while going to Eureka, with me driving and the whole family in the van, Danielle would turn around and scold the kids for being so noisy. It constantly surprised me, but Danielle could hear their commotion. The extent of just how much she could really hear was always a mystery.

When we went to bed, Danielle would always take out her hearing aid. If the baby would wake up during the night, it was strange, but I could feel Danielle begin to stir. By the time the baby was really crying, because she was breastfeeding, all I had to do was give Danielle a little tap with my elbow, and she knew the baby needed her.

Both Scotia and the neighboring town across the Eel River, Rio Dell, were protected by volunteer fire departments. When the firefighters were needed in Scotia an extremely loud whistle would blow. Likewise, in Rio Dell, if their firemen were needed, a very loud siren would sound. Amazingly Danielle could hear neither Scotia's loud whistle nor Rio Dell's blaring sirens.

Incredibly, Danielle could hear a dog barking or certain people's voices. Sadly, she could not understand speech, so talking with individuals was always problematic.

Technology was now improving very rapidly. One day I needed time away from work to take Danielle to see Dr. Jarvis, her audiologist in Eureka. We had been seeing Dr. Jarvis ever since Danielle and I were first married.

"These new digital hearing aids seem to be more precise now," Dr. Jarvis told me at Danielle's latest hearing test. "I think it's time for Danielle to get a new, more advanced aid."

The new hearing aid was one which Dr. Jarvis could adjust for Danielle to get the most benefit by tuning it to her specific hearing loss. I was so excited because from what Dr. Jarvis had said, he was extremely hopeful that Danielle might understand some spoken words, especially from a man's voice. I had always known that if it was just Danielle and me in the bedroom and she asked me a question, if I spoke and signed, she seemed like she could understand some of my words.

Danielle was fitted with the new aid. Along the way home, an ambulance with sirens blaring, quickly passed us by. I looked over at Danielle. "Did you hear that?" I asked.

"Yes, very loud," she signed back.

"I love you, baby bear," I only spoke as Danielle came into the bedroom while I was already in bed.

"I love you more," she spoke. She heard me. She actually heard me. Tears welled up in my eyes and Danielle sat on the bed and looked at me. She smiled hugely as she reached toward me and wiped the tears from my cheeks.

I was really disappointed in the following days. She missed out on so much.

The kids were growing, playing sports, going up to the gym for swim lessons, and often their friends would come over to our house to play. Danielle frequently had to have our girls interpret what the friends were asking her. Most of their friends were patient, some not so much.

Joy was in fifth grade now. In her class was a boy named Charlie Blalack. Charlie was very intelligent, having been home schooled by his Christian mother, Sharon. Sharon had blonde hair, was about the same age as Danielle, and drove the school bus.

One day I came home for lunch and Sharon was there. Scotia is such a small town, I had seen Sharon before, but never really had the chance to meet her. Danielle introduced me to Sharon as I started getting my lunch ready.

I had the opportunity to listen to Sharon and Danielle as they chatted. Sharon had a very calm demeanor and was blessed with a gentle lower-toned voice. It appeared to me that Danielle was understanding a lot of what Sharon was talking to her about. I was so happy to see that Danielle was making a friend with this wonderful, kind lady.

Sharon and Danielle became fast friends. The two of them worked on small craft projects together and who knows what else. I'd often come home from work and find Sharon and Danielle finishing up on some sort of project. Sometimes they would abruptly quit speaking as though they were either talking about Sharon's husband, Dave, or maybe even me.

Dave was a kind Christian man. He and I became good friends. Sharon and Dave's two sons were the same age as Aleace and Joy. Joy was a cheerleader for the Scotia Bears and Charlie was on the basketball team.

Sharon and Dave also lived in Scotia. Dave worked in the bungalow. The bungalow was centrally located in the lumber company's vast shipping area.

If Sharon and Dave came up to the gym to watch the school's basketball games, Danielle, the kids, and I would always look for them so we could sit together.

I was never sure, but I think it was Sharon who helped Danielle organize and obtain a location so Danielle could teach sign language. I never had the opportunity to attend, but from what I knew, Danielle taught sign language at the Fortuna Park Community Center once a week. Danielle was definitely very organized!

"Jack, can you get me some copies for my sign language class?" she asked me one evening.

"Sure," I answered. That meant I had to go to Fortuna to Horizons Office Supplies. I looked at the papers she needed to copy, and she had a page for fingerspelling and another page with basic words. I was surprised to learn that Sharon helped Danielle with a lot of the planning for sign language. Danielle loved Sharon. Sharon was always joyful and a woman with great Christian values.

"Danielle does such an amazing job in our sign language class," Marge told me one day. Marge was from Fortuna and had heard about the sign language class by word of mouth. I could totally catch the enthusiasm from hearing people, just to have the chance to be taught sign language by a real deaf person.

Danielle miscarried again. We were keeping this pregnancy a secret. I knew, of course, and Danielle had told Sharon. Sharon was so kind in helping Danielle through this time of great sorrow.

"Why does this have to happen?" Danielle cried on my shoulder two days after losing the baby. "I really was looking forward to having another baby," she signed and sobbed.

When I came home from work Danielle had made a beautiful burial box for the tiny baby. She had made by hand a blue satin pillow on which she placed the tiny infant. This pillow was carefully laid in a cigar box.

It was obvious to us that this baby was a boy. He was close to the size of a large walnut and he had blue eyes which could be seen through his tiny eyelids.

"Please bury him in the backyard with my other baby," Danielle asked me sadly. I gathered the kids and asked them if they wanted to help me bury a baby that their mom had but it was born too early and he went to heaven.

"Papa," Lamay asked me as Joy held the tiny coffin that Danielle had made, "can we give him a name?"

"Of course," I responded, "I think that's a great idea." I thought a moment and said to all the kids, Aleace, Joy, Lamay, and Christian, as we gathered around the little mound of dirt I had just dug, "Why don't we name him Jason, Mom always loved that name."

"Okay," all the kids responded in unison. We buried that beautiful gift from heaven just as the clouds started to cover the amber setting sun on that sad, eventful day.

I came home from work one day when Danielle handed me a paper from Lamay's preschool teacher.

"Own your own home," the bulletin said. "Government loans available to qualified families."

Danielle asked me to call the number on the bulletin. I had seen similar pipe dreams before. Danielle and I liked the idea of owning our own home, but having four kids and one worker put us in a bind when it came to saving lots of money.

The lady on the telephone asked me a lot of questions about income and the size of our family. We ended up qualifying for a three percent government loan. The loan could not exceed 100,000 dollars. That amount included the lot and the home. Yikes, this prospect of having our own home didn't seem doable with these figures, but Danielle and I were determined.

The kind lady who handled all the incidentals about the government loan was named Rosa. Rosa took a liking to Danielle when we came into her office at Humboldt Hill. "You have to find a contractor and the lot yourself," Rosa told me. "It's hard to find a contractor willing to do it, but I have a few resources that just might work for you. I normally don't recommend anyone but I want Danielle to own her own home," Rosa said softly.

I found a lot in Rio Dell. I inquired with the city as to who the owner was and gave them a call. I talked with Julie Manzi about the empty, blackberry-loaded lot on Riverside Drive. The lot was about a third of an acre and of an odd diameter.

"We weren't really thinking about selling the lot at this time, but I'll speak to my husband and I'll call you back," she stated.

"I talked with my husband," said Julie when she called back the next day, "and because Danielle is Pete's daughter, we have decided to sell the lot to you."

I called the contractor I had located earlier with Rosa's help, and told him about the lot I had found.

It took us about a year and a half to move up the list in order for the government funding to be secured to us, and finally, with all our ducks in a row, we were ready to move ahead. I looked at several house plans books and due to the odd shape of our lot, most of the four-bedroom, two-bath houses were far too large for the lot.

Julie, the lady who owned the lot, stopped by our place in Scotia one day with a book of plans. "I know it's not common for lot owners to help with plans, but I saw this cute little house in this book and thought it might be something that you could fit on the lot," she said.

Danielle loved the home design. I had to do some resizing on some of the rooms but I eventually got the plans in order. The new plans were then inspected and passed by the government housing office.

We needed to save money any way we could. I worked out a deal with the contractor in which he would give me odd jobs to do on the house, after work and on the weekends. By doing this work myself, we could have nicer finishes on the interior of the house.

I hand-dug the perimeter foundation. I also tacked in all the insulation for the internal and external walls. One very big job given to me was to put the roof on the house.

When we were younger, Pete often asked me to help him from time to time with the repair of some of his rentals. I had helped Pete roof the house on Main Street in Rio Dell where Danielle and I lived when we were first married. Even so, roofing our new house was a daunting task.

It seemed to me that I never sat down to eat with my family anymore. I'd get home from work, drive over to the new construction on Riverside Drive, and complete any work that the contractor had asked me to do. I would then come home, take a shower, eat, and go to bed.

I was missing my family greatly, but Danielle understood how important it was for me to help out with the new house. Sometimes she would drop me off, run back home, get me dinner, and bring it with the kids to this unfinished home of ours.

The contractor's wife, Lauri, was a Rio Dell native and knew Pete and Alice's extended family very well. Lauri took Danielle with her one day to buy the fixture over the dining room table and a few other girlie finishes for the home. Lauri was just a little older than me.

Lauri helped me paint the exterior of the house and was very keen on making sure Danielle was pleased with what we were doing.

One day near the end of the construction of our new home, I watched Danielle and Lauri as they carried on a conversation. Danielle used some speech and Lauri used some homemade sign language. I was busy doing some other task when I noticed Danielle getting ready to leave and Lauri gave Danielle a great big hug. *Danielle is an easy person to love,* I thought.

Chapter 25

It was Friday, April 1. I took Lamay and Christian along with Danielle and we went to the new house. The contractor had poured the concrete driveway earlier that day. I had previously asked him if we could put my kids' footprints in the wet concrete. "It's your house," he said, "do whatever you want." I wrote the date in the concrete, April 1st, 1994, and placed Lamay's feet into the semi-hard concrete, then Christian's.

Danielle was so excited about our new house she began to tear up. I embraced her, wiped the tears from her cheeks, and we prayed and asked God to bless our family and thanked Him for all he had done for us.

It was finally moving day. Dave and Sharon had a van and a trailer. Dave, Sharon and their two boys helped my family move from Scotia to Rio Dell.

Danielle and I were trying to think of a way to thank everyone who helped us move. Danielle suggested, "Why don't you make your enchilada casserole?"

"Oh, you mean chilaquiles?" I said.

"Yes," she signed.

Chilaquiles are basically mashed up enchiladas presented as a casserole. Boy, did those chilaquiles hit the spot that beautiful spring day!

"My mom brought this over," Danielle said. "I want to go." Danielle handed me a letter that was addressed to Danielle Silbernagel. I read the letter. It was from the California School for the Deaf class reunion committee. California School for the Deaf was having a class reunion for the years 1970 through 1975. Alice got the letter, as it was sent to Danielle's old address. It was a good thing Alice had not moved or Danielle probably would have never received the letter.

This was Danielle's first school reunion that we were in a position to attend. Danielle was just so excited. We made the plans.

Aleace and Joy were going to be staying with Gramma Alice since they couldn't miss school and weren't really interested in traveling with us anyhow. We would be bringing Lamay and Christian with us.

The event was being held at a hotel with a large banquet room in Emeryville, California, so Danielle asked if we could stay at that hotel. I booked a room for two days and we drove down to the city and checked in.

I lay down to take a short nap with the kids, but Danielle was so excited that she decided to go downstairs to see if she could find any of her old schoolmates.

I heard the door opening and looked up to see Danielle coming in with a lady who looked about the same age as Danielle. "This my roommate, Patty Riley," Danielle excitedly signed and said to me.

I got up and signed, "Nice to meet you. Danielle has told me so much about you."

"Really?" Patty signed, with a huge smile on her face. Patty looked at Danielle and signed "Handsome," as though I was invisible. *Hello, I'm right here,* I thought.

Danielle said she was going back with Patty downstairs and that she would be back in a little while.

"Wait, wait," I signed. "Are there a lot of friends from Berkeley school down there with you guys?"

"Yes," Danielle and Patty signed at the same time. Danielle was on top of the world as she and Patty's hands were a-flyin' as she exited the little room.

Danielle finally came back to the room to find the kids and me watching cartoons. "So many people are here from Berkeley school," Danielle signed.

"How many people from your class?" I asked.

"Too many to count," she signed.

We relaxed a short time and then got ready for the dinner. We were part of a big, sit-down banquet that was organized by the deaf school committee. As part of the banquet they provided each of us with a choice of chicken, beef, or fish. My whole family ordered the beef.

Lamay and Christian looked so cute all dressed up for the semi-formal dinner. I wore a beige long-sleeved shirt, a nice sports coat, and brown corduroy pants. Danielle had on a beautiful black and white dress with a flower pattern. She looked stunning. *Her hair is turning gray now,* I thought.

I had been around deaf people many times in our eighteen-year marriage, but I had never been to a deaf gathering this large. There were about a hundred people sitting around ten or twelve round tables. Danielle, the kids, and I were seated with Patty Riley, her husband John, and Sherry Brown and her spouse.

Danielle was truly, truly content as I watched her sign and laugh and tease along with her old roommates. Danielle had always had a wonderful, comical sense of humor.

I'm a big teaser; Danielle is a bigger teaser.

Danielle was so animated all the way home telling me about this and that and who was married and who was divorced. "Patty has a boy and a girl," Danielle told me as we drove. "Sherry Brown doesn't have any kids, but she wants one." Danielle finally fell asleep as we passed through Laytonville.

I checked the rearview mirror and thanked God for such beautiful blessings. I was looking at the two wonderful kids in the back seat. I thought of our two other girls at home with their grandma, who were growing and becoming beautiful, astute young ladies.

Out of all the people in this beautiful world, I often thanked God for giving me Danielle. Sometimes I found it difficult to think of my life without her. *I love you,* I thought. In my mind, she signed back, *"I love you, more."*

Aleace brought home a flier one evening and asked me to check it out. "College night," the flier said. "Eureka High School." The event was to take place at 4 p.m. the next Saturday.

Aleace was now a sophomore at Fortuna High and I thought it a good idea for us to attend this event because she was our firstborn and I had never been down this college-seeking road before.

On Saturday, the Eureka High School gymnasium was full of tables with each college represented by a name banner taped across the front of the table. It seemed as though there were roughly thirty colleges represented there in the gym.

Aleace and I casually walked by several of the tables. College of the Redwoods, Humboldt State University, and Oregon State were some of the many colleges represented.

As Aleace and I strolled the rows of tables, I read a handout that was given to me as we entered the gym.

"Mija," I said to Aleace. "They're holding a lecture in one of the other rooms about private colleges. Do you think we should go?" In the back of my mind, I knew there was no way in heaven that I could afford a private college for her education, but Aleace was a good student and I thought I should hear about the many different options.

"Sure," Aleace said.

I looked at the giant clock in the gym and said, "We had better go look for the class, it starts in ten minutes."

She and I stopped one of the many attendants working in the gym and asked them where the classroom was.

"PRIVATE COLLEGES," the handwritten sign on the open door read. We went inside and took a seat. I looked around and there were only five other people there as we all looked at the gentleman standing near the front of the room.

"My name is Dr. Plourde." Dr. Plourde was middle-aged, graying at the temples, and he wore black-framed eyeglasses. He started, "I am a local chiropractor but my biggest interest is that I am a private college recruiter. I represent many colleges as you will find out on this handout."

Aleace and I read the handout. Bowdoin, Wheaton, Wellesley, Brown, and Mount Holyoke were some of the private colleges listed. Dr. Plourde then explained to us that these private colleges back east were dying to have students from all over the United States, especially Humboldt County. Colleges did this in order to make their schools more diverse, and especially to enhance the experience of the students.

"How are you going to pay for this fantastic education, you're probably asking yourself. Due to the fact that these colleges are in some cases hundreds of years old they have what is known as 'old money.' This old money is given out as scholarships to students who excel in academics," said the man.

I looked at Aleace and smiled as she smiled back. "This is exactly what we were looking for, don't you think?" I whispered as I leaned over to her. Aleace nodded her head in wonderment and we continued listening to Dr. Plourde.

After the talk, one couple began talking to Dr. Plourde with a few questions about their son who was not present. Aleace and I then introduced ourselves to Dr. Plourde and he and Aleace talked for almost ten minutes.

Dr. Plourde asked Aleace her grade point average and what classes she was taking. "Let's make an appointment and you can come to my office and since you have a few years to get ready, we can talk about what college would best suit your educational goals, and more importantly, which college would give you the biggest scholarship."

I took Aleace to talk to Dr. Plourde at his office in Eureka and he gave her several packets from different colleges. "I know it's early, but I think you would fit in quite well at Wheaton College in Massachusetts. You have a lot of catching up to do in your AP classes, but we still have time," said the quick-talking man.

I overheard him tell her about several other things that he wanted her to start doing and then he said to her, "Call me the beginning of next year and we'll talk again and set up a plan. I promise, if you do what I ask of you, you will go to a private school."

Aleace graduated with honors and true to his promise, Dr. Plourde helped her get accepted to Wheaton College while also receiving a $25,000 annual scholarship.

Grandpa Pete and Grandma Alice were proud and overjoyed at the prospect of their first grandchild attending a private college back east.

Pete traveled with Aleace to Wheaton College. He helped her set up her dorm room by building a few shelves for her desk and he also purchased for her a new Apple computer. Our oldest was well on her way.

Chapter 26

Danielle had always been the one who got the two younger kids to school. We decided that we would keep Lamay and Christian in Scotia School even though we moved to Rio Dell.

Lamay was always a great student. She holds that kind of intellect that is vivid, quick, and detail oriented. Lamay always got excellent grades in all her subjects. I could always count on Lamay to help out Danielle when it came to conversations with other grownups. It's peculiar, but when we see old pictures of Danielle as a baby and Lamay as a baby, they are practically impossible to tell apart.

Christian was diagnosed with ADD in the third grade. Attention deficit disorder was explained to me by his special ed teacher in this way: Imagine yourself sitting in front of thirteen different television sets and trying to make sense out of all this commotion all at once. This was what Christian's brain was trying to do in this world.

I learned that if I wanted him to clean his room, take his dirty clothes to the laundry, and make his bed, I had to give him fewer orders and to give him instead, one task at a time. It was easier for him if I said, "Take your dirty clothes to the laundry. Okay, now make your bed. Good job, now clean your room."

There came a time when the special ed teacher advised me to take Christian to the doctor and perhaps start him on Adderall. I was always more of a natural remedy kind of man so this suggestion just hit me like a brick. Maybe we could change his diet. Maybe we could get him to exercise. I was hoping that we could tackle this ADD without medication.

In the early days computers used dial-up connections. They were very slow but we didn't know any better. I went online and did a pile of research on ADD in order to make an informed decision to help our son go through this life with as little trouble as possible. After days of research I finally went to our local pharmacist, Merilyn. Merilyn had always been a good friend. Merilyn had a quick wit and was a wordsmith. I asked Merilyn about Adderall and ADD. She was very aware that I was against doping Christian.

"Jack," Merilyn said, "everything we've learned as of late shows that Adderall allows the brain functions to work more fully. It allows the brain connections to run correctly as though a light switch has at last been turned on."

Danielle and I had a lot to think about. What Merilyn said about the light switch being turned on made more sense than all the research I had been doing.

"Danielle," I said later in the evening, "Christian's brain works different than most people his age. Merilyn at Palco Pharmacy told me if we get medicine for him that it will help his brain work better. What do you think we should do?" I signed.

Danielle had always been the one who pondered. I, on the other hand, tended to research the problem. I watched her think about it awhile, then she eventually stated, "Let's try the medicine and if it doesn't work, we'll try something else."

We started Christian on low-dose Adderall and adjusted the dosage as the years drifted along. He performed better in school and seemed to be able to follow along better when he was given chores.

Joy started College of the Redwoods as soon as she graduated from Fortuna High School. As a matter of convenience, she was now living with Grandpa Pete and Grandma Alice. Danielle had mentioned to Joy one day that it would be nice if she stayed with Pete and Alice on the weekends so she could help them out a little. Grandpa Pete and Grandma Alice were in their late seventies now. The weekends quickly turned to full time. Joy loved living with her grandparents and they, in turn, loved having Joy around.

Aleace's graduation from Wheaton was coming up soon, so I had to organize the trip for all of my family to travel cross country. The graduation date was in May, and Danielle and I figured that we should make this a family affair. We planned for Joy, Lamay, and Christian to come along. My parents were in a situation where they also would be able to attend. Grandma Alice really wanted to go, but was having medical issues and would not be able to travel. Grandpa Pete stayed home as well.

We stayed at a hotel near the college and the big day arrived. Danielle was so proud of Aleace as she marched in and was seated with the rest of her graduating class. Aleace was graduating with honors.

The day was very warm and humid. While we watched the ceremony, I could smell the magnolia blossoms emanating from the trees surrounding the grounds where the ceremony was to be held. The graduates' chairs were centered while the chairs for the visitors were placed on the peripheral. Shade was provided by tall elm trees with evergreens planted irregularly about.

Danielle wore a beautiful beige wide-brimmed hat which matched her outfit perfectly. We all stood, whooped and hollered when Aleace's name was called as she proudly walked onto the stage wearing her blue cap and gown. She also wore silver and gold ropes signifying her academic honors.

Danielle stood and showed Aleace from afar the deaf applause. The deaf applause is when one holds both hands high into the air and flips the hands back and forth from the elbow joint. Aleace waved back, confirming that she had seen Danielle. I watched Danielle beaming; she was so very proud of Aleace that beautiful spring day.

While Aleace was at college she met Leon. Leon was a kind, gentle man and he and Aleace met online. Aleace used her head when meeting this stranger for the first time. They had arranged to meet each other at the Museum of Fine Arts in Boston. They fell in love and a few years later got engaged and decided to have their wedding in Scotia.

St. Patrick's Parish in Scotia was where Danielle and all our kids were baptized. Aleace and Leon wanted a small, intimate wedding. Aleace made all the arrangements and Leon's close friends and family flew in from Massachusetts.

Leon and his family stayed at the Scotia Inn. Danielle and I waited at the inn for them to arrive so we could meet and have a nice dinner in the inn's cocktail lounge. Their family arrived a little later than planned and were very hungry.

Danielle met Leon's mom, Terry. Terry was very warm and kind to Danielle. Terry did not know sign language, but she was keenly aware of Danielle's deafness and purposefully spoke slowly so Danielle could read her lips. Unfortunately, lip reading was not Danielle's forte, so I found myself doing a lot of interpreting while they spoke.

"Where were you born?" Terry asked Danielle as we stood in front of the well-manicured lawns of the Scotia Inn. Danielle pointed to the hospital that was situated three blocks away. "Really?" said the surprised Terry. "This is really a small town, isn't it?"

It was obvious that Terry was trying to think of something else she might say to Danielle to carry on small talk. We live near the Pacific coast and May evenings can be cool. This time of year, temperatures in the low fifties are not uncommon.

Terry asked Danielle, "Is it always this cold in the evening?"

Danielle smiled her radiant smile and answered with her standard sarcastic humor, "Really? I was just getting ready to take off my jacket. Phew." Danielle gesticulated as she took her right hand and wiped it across her forehead as though she was wiping sweat from her brow. Terry laughed out loud.

Leon's family arrived a few days early to see the sights and relax. The day before the wedding Leon's dad, Mike, asked if we would take them to see the Pacific Ocean. "Of course," I stated. "It would be our joy. You won't be disappointed."

I took our car and Leon's family followed in their rental. I slowly took Blue Slide Road from Rio Dell so I could show their family the lush green pastures and the thousands upon thousands of milk and beef cattle that stand contentedly along the route of our trek.

We would be passing through the quaint town of Ferndale on our adventure toward the great Pacific Ocean. I wondered if we should stop in town, but thought better of it thinking their time was limited as to what they had planned on doing while visiting Humboldt County.

I was very attentive in watching my rearview mirror so that every time a vehicle pulled up quickly behind Mike's rental car, I would slowly pull over to the side of the road so that the vehicle might pass our slow-moving, two-car caravan.

Black and white cows with bashful brown eyes stared at our cars as we wandered slowly toward the forceful foamy wetness of the Pacific Ocean. I had a feeling that the mighty Pacific would be breathtaking to them.

As we drove up to Centerville Beach, I parked adjacent to the road barrier and got out of the car. Danielle got out as well and motioned for Lamay and Christian to come stand by her as Leon's family exited their car.

"Where's the fire?" Leon's dad, Mike, asked me sarcastically when he came to stand by me.

"What fire?" I asked.

"You drove so damn fast I had a hard time keeping up with you," he said rudely.

"Really?" I responded, a little startled. "I thought I was driving much too slowly and that you really wanted to see the ocean."

Without a word he walked back toward his car as he and the rest of his family huffily climbed over the barrier and onto the sand. I looked at Danielle and signed, "Did you think I was driving fast?"

Danielle signed, "I thought you were driving like a little old lady."

"Me too," I signed.

The ceremony was a traditional Catholic wedding and Aleace arranged for an interpreter for Danielle so she could also enjoy the ceremony. Aleace had contracted a wonderful wedding planner because she and Leon lived so very far away and there were many, many moving parts to this wedding.

The celebrant was Father Thomas Going. Father Going and I were great friends. Danielle and I were very involved with church. I was the music guy and Danielle helped out with the small prayer group which met at St. Patrick's church on Wednesday evenings in the small parish meeting room.

Father Going worked a lot with our small Spanish-speaking community. Although Irish with a brogue, he spoke fluent Spanish and had performed many Mexican weddings and baptisms.

It was time. The wedding planner carefully approached me while I was deeply involved with showing Aleace's bridesmaid's boyfriend how to use the CD player.

Aleace was nowhere near me as the planner softly asked, "Jack, I know that Grandpa Pete was very instrumental in the upbringing of Aleace. Do you think it's a good idea to surprise Aleace and have Pete and your dad walk in behind Aleace as you and she come down the aisle?"

"I think that would mean the world to her," I responded.

Aleace and I gathered in the vestibule. Aleace was dressed in a beautiful white wedding gown and a white veil and held on to a bouquet of roses, Gerbera daisies and chrysanthemums. As she reached for my elbow Pete and my dad walked in the double front doors behind us.

Aleace turned to see who was coming to the ceremony so late and tears began to well in her eyes. She then realized that not only me, but both of her grandpas would also be walking her down the aisle.

Father Going announced, "All stand," and all eyes turned toward Aleace. We looked down the aisle of our tiny church and Leon's eyes were locked on Aleace.

Aleace, Pete, my dad, and I marched slowly down the aisle. "Look how beautiful," I heard the people say, "her dad and both her grandpas are escorting her down the aisle."

I looked for Danielle and saw her looking at Aleace. Danielle had tears in her eyes. Her baby was grown up.

The interpreter was dressed in a beautiful spring dress. As the ceremony began, she started signing. I watched as Danielle nodded slightly at her. When one is signing an event such as this, it is common for the deaf person to nod in such a way as to affirm to the interpreter that they understand. This is the deaf way; this is deaf culture. Danielle was so appreciative of her oldest daughter for thinking of her special need that beautiful spring day.

After the elegant wedding ceremony, we all drove down a couple blocks to the Scotia Inn for a quaint reception and sit-down dinner. Many of our most faithful family and friends were there. My brothers, Ray and Ron, showed up along with their wives and kids. Sharon and Dave Blalack were there, as was Aunt Flora, Cousin Kelly Boo Boo, and his wife Sandy. Uncle Albert was there and so were Linda and Ron Doebel.

After everyone had eaten and Aleace and Leon had their first dance, Aleace and Leon went to the podium and called up her Grandma Alice.

Aleace, having received a history degree, explained to everyone the fact that her grandmother was a war bride, and resources being scarce because of the war, had never been given any flowers at her own marriage ceremony.

Aleace then reached down under the podium and handed her grandmother, fifty-nine and a half years late, her very own bridal bouquet. "I know it's a little belated," Aleace smiled at her grandma through tears, "but congratulations on your wedding." Not a dry eye could be found that long-ago evening in the Scotia Inn banquet room.

Chapter 27

Danielle was going to pick me up at work. She was an excellent and careful driver. She took her driving responsibility very seriously. Due to the fact that Danielle couldn't hear, communication while she was driving was nonexistent.

I walked to work each day from Rio Dell to Scotia. The trek was two miles and it usually took me twenty-five minutes to get there. On this day Danielle was going to pick me up and we were going to Eureka to pick up a few groceries.

I saw Danielle driving toward me down Main Street in Scotia. So, to tease her as I usually did, I started walking slowly in front of the car as though I was a decrepit old man who could barely move.

I watched out the corner of my eye as she approached. I could see that she wasn't slowing down.

Danielle never teased or pretended while driving the car so I knew I'd better speed up my walk or she would run me down.

"YOU ALMOST HIT ME!" I signed to her as I finished waving both arms at her as she was about to pass me.

Danielle braked hard and signed, "I didn't see you, sorry." It was obviously time to get her eyes checked for some glasses.

Christian was eight years old and he was to accompany Danielle to the optometrist to get her eyes checked and to help out if the people there didn't understand Danielle's speech.

"What did the doctor say?" I asked Christian as soon as I came home from work.

"I don't know," was his reply.

I went to see Danielle and asked her, "What did the doctor say was wrong with your eyes?"

"He wants me to go to the doctor because he wants me to be checked for diabetes," she said and signed.

"That's weird," I said. "Do you need to get glasses?"

"No," was her only response.

I called Dr. Rigney's office in Scotia and set up an appointment for Danielle.

"Danielle went to the eye doctor," I told him, "and they want Danielle to be checked for diabetes."

Danielle and I went to Redwood Memorial Hospital in Fortuna for Danielle to get some blood tests. Danielle hated needles and she wasn't very fun to be around when she had to fast either.

"Danielle is diabetic," Dr. Rigney told us on her follow-up visit.

I was shocked. Danielle was just forty-five years old.

"I'm going to give you a list of the foods I want Danielle to avoid," said the kind doctor. "We're lucky. We caught her diabetes early so we'll try to manage her diabetes by managing her weight and diet."

Danielle changed the way she ate and lost some weight. After a few weeks I would periodically check her blood sugar. It was apparent that Danielle was able to control her diabetes by diet only, just as Dr. Rigney said.

Danielle had another miscarriage. This miscarriage came as we both were now in our mid-forties. Once again Danielle cried for her unborn child. Again, she hand-sewed a soft satin pillow and placed the tiny, nearly twelve-week-old fetus in the lovingly crafted cigar box.

"Jack," she said and signed through tears, "please bury my baby in the back yard."

When we had moved from Scotia, Danielle had me exhume the two babies she lost earlier and re-bury them in our own back yard at our new home in Rio Dell. Danielle and I buried the little unborn baby next to her brother and sister near the base of our most fragrant white rose bush.

"Do you want to give this baby a name?" I asked Danielle as we cried.

"I want to name the baby Emma, after my grandmother," Danielle signed. Danielle reached for me and wiped the tears from my cheeks. I hugged her tenderly in return.

I noticed Danielle was using stronger reading glasses one day. "How many pairs of glasses do you need?" I asked her jokingly as she was trying to read the paper with two pairs of reading glasses on.

"I don't know," she responded, "these aren't strong enough anymore."

I took time off from work and took Danielle to the same eye doctor that she had previously seen with Christian.

"I told your son the last time Danielle was in, to tell you that Danielle needed to come in to be checked every six months," said the concerned doctor.

"He never told me a thing," I responded.

It had been about two years from the last time Danielle was in to see Dr. Gibb.

"She has diabetic retinopathy," said the doctor.

"What is diabetic retinopathy?" I asked.

"With diabetic retinopathy the tiny blood vessels in the eye burst, and as they heal, begin to grow into the clear gel of the eye. If we don't get her down to Santa Rosa to see Dr. Meffert soon, she can lose her sight," said the troubled doctor.

The doctor's office gave me a phone number and address and told me to call Dr. Mefferts office as soon as possible. Dr. Meffert was located in Santa Rosa on Mendocino Avenue.

"Dr. Meffert's office, how can I assist you?" said the receptionist.

"Hi, my name is Jack Saffell and I am calling for my wife, Danielle. Danielle is deaf and Dr. Gibb in Eureka asked me to call and make an appointment with you," I said.

"Please hold," was the response.

"Yes, we were expecting your call. Dr. Gibb has told us about your wife. I will need to obtain some information from you before you come down," the receptionist said.

It took about twenty minutes on the phone to give them our insurance information. We made an appointment for Danielle to see Dr. Meffert in two weeks.

Dr. Meffert was in his early forties, with dark wavy hair. He tried speaking slowly so Danielle could read his lips. Danielle almost always looked to me to interpret, especially with new people. It seemed to me that Danielle was understanding most of what the doctor was saying to her, just as long as he didn't talk too long.

"Let's get Danielle in this chair so I can dilate her eyes and see what's going on," said the calm physician. Dr. Meffert examined Danielle's eyes and also checked her eye pressure.

"Danielle has diabetic retinopathy," stated the physician. "Her left eye is worse than the right. I want to give her laser treatments. If she tolerates them well, then the eye can heal," he said confidently.

The doctor led us into a small room with a large machine inside. "Sit here, Danielle, and try not to move," said the doctor.

I signed to Danielle what the doctor said and Danielle replied, "I'll try."

Dr. Meffert gave me some special goggles to wear while he did the laser treatment on Danielle's eye. As I looked on, I was stunned as to just how many laser shots Danielle had to have done to her eye. The laser machine counted each blast that was given and I could read the counter from where I sat.

It took about thirty minutes for the doctor to administer the laser treatment. The laser counter read 2,197 blasts. I couldn't believe that Danielle's retina was so very damaged.

We went back to Santa Rosa the following month and Dr. Meffert gave Danielle laser treatments in the good eye, her right eye, on that visit. The counter this time read 2,031 laser blasts.

On our third visit to Santa Rosa, Dr. Meffert announced that Danielle needed a vitrectomy. It appeared that both eyes were affected, but he'd start with the worst eye first.

We were then sent home and given a booklet explaining what exactly a vitrectomy was and what we were expected to do after the surgery.

A vitrectomy is when the doctor removes all the vitreous gel from the eye. He will then laser blast the back of the affected eye. This cauterizes the tiny blood vessels and prevents them from growing back to cause blurring or loss of sight.

Danielle had the surgery performed at Santa Rosa Memorial Hospital. I was asked to gown up and assist the surgery nurses with communication for Danielle. Dr. Meffert asked me to stay with Danielle during the operation since Danielle was going to be lightly sedated.

After the surgery, Danielle needed to keep her head down so the gas bubble they put in her eye would remain until the eye refilled with the vitreous fluid made by her own body. This would allow the retina and the back of the eye to heal.

Simply because Danielle was deaf, and sight oriented, keeping her head down for days on end was nearly an impossible task.

Rio Dell is 150 miles from Santa Rosa. Having a place to stay in Santa Rosa was beginning to be a problem. Each visit to Santa Rosa for Danielle's vitrectomy required us to stay seven to ten days due to a problem with pressure in the eye as we crossed over the Rattlesnake summit in Mendocino County, elevation 2,051feet. The doctor explained that the gas bubble in Danielle's eye would expand as we crossed the summit and could cause irreparable damage to the eye.

The cost for Danielle and I to stay in Santa Rosa was easily 250 to 300 dollars a day. This included our room, food, and gasoline. These expenditures caught me completely off guard. *How am I going to pay for all this?* I thought to myself. *First things first. We'll have to get Danielle fixed up and then I'll worry about everything else later.*

Fortunately, because I had worked for Pacific Lumber for such a long time, I had four weeks' vacation coming. Once management heard that Danielle was having a difficult time and needed to have multiple eye surgeries, they were very supportive and then asked if I needed anything to please let them know.

I received the telephone call from Dr. Meffert's office for the date of Danielle's second vitrectomy, the one for the good eye.

I tried very hard to save money on these, what turned out to be many, excursions to Santa Rosa. I once even called Catholic Charities in Santa Rosa. They set us up in a one-bedroom apartment. I told Danielle that they were going to charge us only $25 a night. I was hopeful; Danielle was not.

I drove up to the apartment complex. It was dark and sordid. It felt as though I was looking back in time to the early 1950's. The two-story apartment complex was painted a gloomy gray color with white trim that was flaking off. The second story had an external walkway which was the only way one could access the top dwellings. These rooms were apparently used as emergency dwellings for homeless or mothers and children in desperate need.

I took the voucher that I was given at Catholic Charities and went to check in with the apartment manager. I looked around and found the apartment door which read "Manager." I knocked and a woman in her late fifties answered the door. She said, "Can I help you?" I told her we were told to come here and that they had a room available for us. I also told her my wife was having eye problems, that she could only see out of one eye, and that she was deaf.

The lady gave me the key. I found our room on the bottom floor. I was hopeful that this apartment complex would be a way to save money while we stayed in Santa Rosa.

I went into the room, leaving Danielle in the car so I could check it out first. I opened the doorway and the room stunk of what reminded me of insecticide. I hoped Danielle would be able to tolerate staying here.

I retrieved Danielle from the car. I opened the car door, helping her out as she grabbed my elbow for guidance. Her sight was very diminished at this time and she needed guiding if we walked anywhere except our home.

"I hate this smell," Danielle voiced as we walked into the seedy room. I took Danielle and put her on the well-worn, dark green couch. "I'm going to check out the bedroom. Stay right here," I told her. The bedroom was gloomy and not exactly spotless. I was afraid to sleep in the blankets. I was very concerned that the bed might have bedbugs.

I told Danielle to stay here and that I'd go get us something to eat. "Don't open the door," I warned her. "I'll open it with the key when I get back."

I went to the Mexican takeout place down the street and ordered some street tacos. Street tacos are low in carbs and they're an okay meal for Danielle and her diabetes.

I got back to the gloomy gray apartments and opened the door to our room. Danielle still hadn't budged. "I need to go to the bathroom," she signed. I looked for the toilet and brought her in. The toilet itself was stained with the rust-brown ring that happens when the water source is not clean. I showed Danielle the layout of the tiny bathroom and cleaned the seat with hot water and a towel before I allowed her to sit.

I was afraid to touch anything, so I cleaned everything that Danielle might touch with the dish soap from the dated kitchenette. I was beginning to get the feeling that this dirty hotel was not going to work for us.

"I hate this place," Danielle said. "It feels dirty; it stinks, and the people upstairs are pounding on the floor," she signed. Danielle may not have been able to hear, but she was very much aware of her surroundings.

"Let's test it for the night, then if we don't like it, I'll find another motel tomorrow," I told her.

Neither Danielle nor I had a good night's rest there in that seedy, rank apartment complex. The next morning I found cockroaches.

I turned the key in to the manager and told her thank you.

"How did you sleep?" asked the tousled manager.

"To tell the truth, the people upstairs kept making a lot of noise. They kept pounding on the floor and my wife couldn't sleep," I said. "Thank you anyway."

Danielle and I checked into the hospital. It was Danielle's second vitrectomy. This surgery would be on her good eye, the right eye.

I gowned up so I could be Danielle's interpreter as we entered the operating room. Once again, Danielle was not going to be put out completely, but only slightly sedated. The surgical nurse said, "Danielle, are you comfortable?" I signed into Danielle's hands. "Yes, thank you," she responded.

Dr. Meffert walked into the operating room. "Hi, Jack," said the doctor. "How's Danielle doing?"

"Okay, I guess," I answered. "She really had a hard time keeping her head down after we got home after the last surgery."

"I thought that might happen," he responded. "Do the best you can."

This being Danielle's second vitrectomy, I was able to pay a little more attention to what exactly the doctor was doing.

Dr. Meffert asked the surgical team if they were ready. "Yes, Doctor," was the reply from the anesthesiologist and the surgical team of three nurses.

Dr. Meffert made three incisions into Danielle's right eye. The instruments that were in her eyes looked like tiny metal straws. One was to extract the fluid called the vitreous gel, one was to pump in a special gas, and the other was to surgically remove the microscopic blood vessels that were destroying Danielle's vision.

After Dr. Meffert removed the tiny intruding blood vessels, he would then laser-treat the super tiny blood vessels in the eye to keep them from bleeding. Just as he laser treated Danielle in his office, he now laser treated her here in the hospital. Again, Dr. Meffert gave Danielle over 2,000 laser shots to the minuscule blood vessels.

After the surgery was done, they bandaged Danielle's eye and the team wheeled her to recovery. Danielle slept a little and when she woke, she had to use the bathroom. I escorted her to the restroom, turned on the light, aimed her bottom so she might sit, and helped her use her right hand so she might know where the toilet was located. Since her right eye was heavily bandaged and the left was still recovering from its recent surgery, communication was tough.

We stayed in recovery for about three hours and they finally released Danielle. The kind nurse wheeled Danielle to the front of the hospital. I retrieved the car, got out, and opened the passenger door. I grabbed Danielle from the wheelchair, under the arms, and helped her to stand. I took hold of her right arm and placed it on the car door. She then reached for the door with her left arm and turned to aim her bottom toward the car seat. As Danielle sat, I placed my hand behind her head so she wouldn't hit her head against the top of the car. Danielle brought in her feet and I made sure her hands were out of the way and closed the car door.

I made sure we both buckled up and then I drove off. "I'm hungry," I heard my beautiful bride say. I drove up to the Mexican takeout restaurant and ordered some street tacos. We ate in the car and after eating I cleaned up the mess that Danielle made. I drove to the motel.

I checked into the Flamingo Hotel in Santa Rosa. The room cost $160 a night. I pulled out my well-worn Mastercard and hoped that the room charge would go through.

The Flamingo had the look of a well-cared for rancho. I asked for a handicapped accessible room with a king-sized bed, and then drove around to where our room was. "Stay here and I'll go check out the room," I told Danielle. "Don't open the car door."

"Okay," she spoke.

I needed to use the card key to open the side gate that would then lead to our room. I walked down the hall, found the room, and using the key card, walked in.

The room was spacious and beautiful. It contained a king-sized bed that had a down-filled duvet. I could see a couch, a table with two chairs, a coffee maker, and the curtain opened to a small courtyard that also had two chairs with a small table.

The bathroom was organized so a handicapped person could be rolled into the shower in a wheelchair if necessary. I thought Danielle might like this hotel room. I went back to the car, retrieved Danielle, and led her to the new room.

I led Danielle to the king-size bed. *This hotel is going to work out just fine,* I thought as I sat Danielle down onto the bed. Danielle felt all around, now using her hands as her eyes. She slid her hands over the duvet and felt the silky soft pillows and then asked me to take her to the bathroom.

I brought Danielle back to the bed and she sat on it. "I love this bed," Danielle signed and spoke to me. Danielle's left eye was so red and bloodshot I'd have been surprised if she could see anything at all.

Danielle took off her clothes and I got her pj's, helped her put them on, and she got into bed. The room had a new flat-screen TV and best of all, there was an outdoor hot tub just outside and down the hall.

I lay down next to Danielle and we both fell asleep. The day's ordeal was difficult. I was very hopeful that these vitrectomies would allow Danielle to keep her sight; Danielle was less so.

I woke up first and took a tour of the hotel. "Top-notch." That's how I would describe this place. It had everything we would need. I went out to look at the hot tub we passed by earlier as we were walking to our room.

"Danielle's going to love this."

I went back to the room and sat down on the bed. It may seem strange, but every time we get into a bed, Danielle slept on the right side and I slept on the left. In this way, because Danielle took off her hearing aid before going to bed, I could fingerspell into her hands because she couldn't see what I was signing to her.

I gently woke Danielle and handed her hearing aid. She put it on and I signed into her hands and spoke. "Get up, I have a nice surprise for you."

"What is it?" she asked.

"I'm not going to tell you, but here, put on your bathing suit," I said and signed.

"I don't feel like swimming," she said.

"We're not going swimming, but I still want to surprise you."

With my help Danielle got on her swimming suit and I grabbed two of the gigantic towels from the well-equipped bathroom. Danielle grabbed my left elbow and we walked down the hall and out the side door.

The huge, twelve-foot round hot tub was outdoors and covered by a large gazebo. I led her to the gazebo and she turned to me and said and signed, "I smell chlorine."

"That's part of the surprise," I said and signed.

I stepped down into the tub first and as I stood on the first step gently pulled her with my elbow down to the first step beside me.

"Hot," she signed.

I had her grab the side of the tub and find a place where she was comfortable. "Hand me your hearing aid," I signed. Danielle took off her hearing aid and as I heard that familiar squeal, I took it from her, placing it on top of the two towels I had thrown down on top of a bench seat that was near the tub.

The hot tub's temperature was too hot for my liking. Danielle, on the other hand, took extremely hot showers at home. Every time I got in the shower at home, I'd have to adjust the hot and the cold dial to a much cooler temperature than what Danielle had used.

I walked over to Danielle and gingerly worked my way down into the boiling water. Well, maybe it wasn't boiling, but it sure was hot. I reached Danielle and touched her arm. She reached for my left elbow and with the jets blowing at our backs, we both relaxed.

I was kinda dozing off when I heard Danielle ask me, "Can we get a hot tub for our home?"

"Why don't we just get a pool put in our backyard instead?" I signed into her hands.

She reached for me, found my arm, and gave it a good smack. I reached for her face between my two hands and kissed her beautiful lips. "I love you," I signed into her hands.

"I love you more," she signed back.

After about a half hour we got out of the boiling hot tub and I toweled off Danielle and then myself. Danielle looked so helpless as she just stood there waiting for me with her eye all bandaged up and having difficulty seeing out of the other.

We walked back to our room. Whenever we checked into a new room, I would physically show Danielle where the toilet, shower, and vanity were within the bathroom, so she could, within her mind, know the layout and, if need be, go to the bathroom without my assistance.

Danielle came out of the bathroom. Danielle knew if she stood at the bathroom door and angled herself just right, she could take slow steps, slowly wave her arms out in front, and she would find her way, blindly, to the bed.

Danielle was tired and said she was going to lie down for a while. I made sure she was safe and secure and signed to her that I was going for a short walk. I always enjoyed walking, plus it gave me a chance to pray my rosary and to think about the many difficult events that we were experiencing.

On my walkabout I happened to walk right by the Catholic Cathedral for the diocese of Santa Rosa. I hadn't realized that we were so close to the cathedral while staying at the Flamingo Hotel.

I walked up to the side door and it was open. I went into St. Eugene's Cathedral, dipped my middle finger into the holy water, blessed myself with the sign of the cross, and then genuflected.

I took a seat and knelt down, made the sign of the cross, and prayed, "Oh my God, I am heartily sorry for having offended Thee, and I detest all my sins, because I dread the loss of heaven and the pains of hell, but most of all because I've offended Thee, my God, Who art all good and deserving of all my love. In choosing to sin and failing to do good, I have sinned against You and your church. I firmly intend, with the help of thy grace, to confess my sins, to do penance, and to amend my life. Amen." This prayer which I prayed when I went to church is called the Act of Contrition.

I prayed for Danielle's recovery. I prayed for my kids at home and at college. I prayed for my mother-in-law, Alice, to have good health so she could care for our other kids. I prayed that Danielle would heal and stay strong and that I accept all that our Lord has in store for us.

"Teach me your ways, oh Lord, teach me your ways." Before I stood, I asked, "Jesus, give Danielle and me your strength in these difficult times. I love you. Amen."

I got back to the hotel and Danielle was sleeping. I lay down next to her and laid my arm across her and spooned her closely. I felt her left hand blindly reach for me. "I love you," I silently signed. "I love you more," she signed back, blindly.

I thought about her surgeries and what her life would be like if she lost her sight. I lay there on that king-sized bed, next to my sweetness and life, as anguished tears left my eyes.

Danielle had four more vitrectomies in hopes to keep her vision. It seemed the doctor was beginning to lose hope. Danielle loved staying at the Flamingo Hotel, so each time we had to go back to Santa Rosa for another prearranged surgery, we would always stay there in that luxurious, handicapped room.

Dr. Meffert, as a last-ditch effort, had us go back to Dr. Gibb's office for a lens replacement surgery of Danielle's left eye.

Danielle had damaged the left eye lens, which caused the lens to become extremely cloudy. Dr. Mastroni, a doctor from Dr. Gibb's office, performed the lens replacement surgery in Eureka.

This surgical procedure was a lot easier on Danielle. Dr. Mastroni carefully, surgically removed Danielle's left eye lens and replaced it with a new, clear lens. The operation was very successful and Dr. Mastroni was well pleased.

"I can see your face," Danielle said as she looked straight ahead and saw through her metal eye patch. The eye patch had holes in it and Danielle was using her peripheral vision.

"You're getting gray hair," she said to me as we drove down Henderson Avenue. I was elated that she could finally see me. We had been through a lot these several last months just trying to keep Danielle's sight. I decided then that I would be content even if Danielle had sight in just one eye.

Danielle was now forty-six years old. We were waiting in the waiting room of Dr. Gibb's office. Once a month Dr. Meffert would drive to Eureka from Santa Rosa to see his many patients who had driven the 150 miles to Santa Rosa so he could perform surgery on them.

Danielle's name was called. I tapped her shoulder and as we stood Danielle would grab my left elbow so I could lead her while we followed the nurse into the room to be examined.

Dr. Meffert explained that day to Danielle and me that she was the kind of person who, after each surgery, developed excessive amounts of scar tissue, which in turn would then render the previous surgery useless.

"Near Santa Rosa there is a camp for patients who have lost their sight so they might learn how to live as a blind person," said Dr. Meffert.

"Are you saying Danielle is now completely blind?" I said in disbelief.

"Jack, we've done all that we can do," said the remorseful doctor. "Danielle has had six vitrectomies and one lens replacement. It's just not fair to keep trying to save her sight, making Danielle endure any more surgeries."

I stared back at the doctor in shock, not knowing what to say. I finally said, holding back the tears, "But I'm not ready to give up, she's too young, she has too much life yet to live."

"Jack," the doctor said, "there is nothing more we can do."

We left the doctor's office. I carefully led Danielle back to our car, opened the passenger door, and helped her into the car, making sure she didn't hit her head on the door jamb as she sat. I walked around the car, got into the driver's seat, and looked at my beautiful wife. She stared straight ahead with unseeing eyes.

I contemplated how I might reveal to Danielle this terrible news. I thought of the things Danielle would no longer see. What about any grandchildren we might have? What about our other children getting married? How could I tell my beautiful, faithful love that she was permanently blind?

"Danielle," I said and signed slowly into her hands, "you're never going to see again." I began to sob and Danielle reached up to feel the tears streaming down my face. She gently pulled my face to her and tenderly kissed the tears from my cheeks.

Chapter 28

    I walked to work every day. I was fortunate enough that my boss allowed me to use the company truck to come home at noon each day to give Danielle her lunch, to check on her, and to make sure everything was fine.

    Sharon and Dave Blalack now lived across the street from us in Rio Dell. Sharon would come over from time to time to visit with Danielle.

    Danielle now relied heavily on her new digital hearing aid. I'm not exactly sure if and what Danielle could hear, but it was apparent that she was trying hard to hear when others talked to her. If she didn't quite understand what Sharon was saying, Sharon would spell the word in Danielle's hand by using the standard ASL alphabet.

    I called Danielle's audiologist and asked her, because Danielle was now blind, if she thought that we should get a hearing aid for Danielle's other ear.

    I also asked Danielle if she thought getting a hearing aid for her right ear would help her. "I don't know," she stated.

"Let's test it out and find out if you like it," I said.

Danielle signed, "I don't care," and we left it at that.

Danielle's audiologist was named Dr. Julie. Dr. Julie knew sign language and Danielle was happy that she could sign to her since signing was easier and more natural to Danielle than talking. If Dr. Julie didn't understand what Danielle was signing, she would look at me and I would tell Dr. Julie what Danielle was saying.

Danielle and I had to learn how to walk together now that she was sightless. If we had to go into a store, she naturally would grab my left elbow. I would then take natural strides while Danielle walked beside me.

On one occasion while Danielle and I were walking back to the car from the pharmacy, she happened to be holding my right elbow because the curb was to our left. Curbs are difficult to navigate when one is blind. On this one occasion I was walking briskly, as I always did, and stopped too abruptly. Danielle, on the other hand, continued her stride straight over the curb.

Down she went as I desperately tried to hold on to her to keep her from falling. I was beyond mortified. Due to my absent-mindedness Danielle was writhing on the ground and I felt terrible.

"I'm sorry, I'm sorry," I said and signed to Danielle as I tried to help her up. She looked so helpless lying there on that dirty parking lot pavement.

"I'll never let that happen again," I said and signed to Danielle with tears in my eyes as we sat in the front seats of my car. "Did you hurt yourself?"

"I think I hurt my knee," she said. I checked out her knee and she had torn her pants and her knee was scraped. I grabbed a napkin from the center console of the car and had her hold it on her bleeding knee. I felt terrible. It was then that I understood precisely how much Danielle would have to depend on me from now on.

Danielle enjoyed going shopping with me for groceries. We'd go to Winco in Eureka and Danielle would hold onto the shopping cart while I pushed us around. "I need shampoo," Danielle said and signed.

We rolled over to the toiletries aisle and I asked, "What kind do you want?"

"Strawberry," was her reply. I then took hold of the strawberry shampoo, opened the cap, and let her smell the shampoo. Danielle nodded, and I knew then that it was the right shampoo.

I quickly learned that stairs would be a difficult obstacle for us when we were out and about. My brother Ray was visiting one summer shortly after Danielle lost her sight, when we came upon a flight of stairs. He watched as Danielle slowly, carefully, took a step, then another, stop, take a step, then another, not really knowing when to stop climbing.

Ray said to me, "Why don't you tell her how many steps there are by tapping her on the shoulder since she can't see or hear you anymore? If you have four steps, then tap her shoulder four times."

"What do I do if we have to go down the steps?" I sarcastically asked.

"Then tap her thigh however many steps you need to go down," Ray replied cheerfully.

Genius, I thought. What a great idea. My brother Ray has always been a keen thinker and Danielle truly loved his sense of humor.

Ray and Danielle were four months apart in age. When she was sighted, Danielle always was amused by Ray's antics. One time we were visiting my mom and dad when Ray and his girlfriend were getting ready to leave on a date one evening. We were all sitting in my parents' living room saying good-bye to them when Ray opened the front door and his girlfriend walked outside. Ray said to his girl, "Good-bye," as he shut the door behind her leaving the poor girlfriend outside all alone.

"Ray, don't be so mean!" I said as we all laughed. I don't believe this girlfriend found it as amusing as we did as she stood outside alone in the dark. "You're so mean," Danielle said and signed to Ray with a big smile on her face. Danielle loved Ray. I'm pretty sure Ray loved Danielle too.

I called the Lighthouse for the Blind one day in hopes of getting some much-needed help. I had asked Danielle if she wanted to learn braille.

"I remember seeing Helen Keller when I was at Berkeley," she told me. I could see her pondering something, and then she said and signed to me, "Jack."

"What?"

"I'm like Helen Keller now," she said, almost startled.

"Yes, you are," I said and signed into her hands, as tears rolled down my cheeks.

The Lighthouse for the Blind is an organization that was developed locally to assist those with low vision or those who are blind. I called and asked them if they could teach Danielle braille so she might read some books or magazines.

Two women arrived at our house one day—a tall, dark-haired lady and a shorter lady with dark blonde hair. I invited them in and they walked to the dining room table and took two seats. Danielle was sitting opposite them and I took the opportunity to introduce myself. I then walked over and stood beside Danielle. The two women watched as I signed into Danielle's hands that two ladies were here from the Lighthouse for the Blind and that they wanted to teach her braille—like Helen Keller used—to read.

I then asked the ladies if they could step over here and meet Danielle. The tall lady came to Danielle and I grabbed Danielle's right hand. "Danielle, this is Ali," I said and signed into Danielle's left hand.

"Hello," Danielle said as she shook Ali's hand.

Then the other lady came over and switched places with Ali. "Danielle, this is Terry," I said and signed into Danielle's hand as she shook hands with Terry.

The two ladies could see that teaching Danielle braille was going to be very difficult due to the fact that Danielle's hearing loss was so great.

Ali and Terry had brought Danielle several items to try to find out if she would be able to learn braille and even some games that other blind people played. While I watched, Ali took out, from a ziplock bag, small black marbles that fit perfectly into a wooden oak block that had six drilled semi-holes into which the small black marbles could be placed. They told me that these blocks were set up so they could show Danielle the placement of the six dots that were used for braille.

In braille one block is called a cell, and each cell has six dots. These dots are arranged with different placements for each letter of the alphabet. Danielle would have to learn the placement for each cell. Fortunately, Ali knew how to fingerspell, which helped Danielle immensely when learning the new braille alphabet.

Ali put me in contact with several different local agencies that could benefit Danielle now that she was blind.

We already had a dog. Squeaker was a black pug cross that we had rescued from the local dog pound about three years earlier. Danielle loved Squeaker.

We always had a dog even when we lived in Scotia. I always felt that because Danielle couldn't hear, having a dog was a good idea so she could watch the dog's antics, and if someone came around the house, watching the dog would alert Danielle that something was amiss.

We received a visit from a local professional dog trainer. The purpose of the trainer was to teach Squeaker to bark when someone knocked at the door.

Danielle, although extremely hard of hearing, could hear, with her hearing aids on, a dog bark. Once the dog barked, Squeaker was supposed to come back to where Danielle was sitting and poke Danielle with her nose, alerting Danielle that someone was here.

I told the dog trainer that Squeaker was not a big barker. After much trial and error, and many treats, the trainer finally got Squeaker to bark and to come back and touch Danielle with her nose when someone knocked on the door.

Squeaker's bark was not very loud. It was kinda like a hoarse squeak; hence her name. Danielle was able to hear Squeaker's squeak so I immediately felt much better about leaving Danielle alone when I had to be at work.

As Squeaker got older it became more difficult for her to do her job as Danielle's hearing dog, so Danielle and I decided to go to the local animal shelter in hopes of finding another small dog which she and I could train and allow Squeaker to retire.

I asked the animal shelter if they had any small female dogs that we might look at that were intelligent enough to learn to be a hearing dog.

Sadly, no dogs fit the bill that day, but I was diligent. I called the animal shelter often, and finally, on one of the days I called, they said that they had a dachshund cross dog and wondered if that might work for Danielle.

I took Danielle to the animal shelter and we went into the kennel to check out this dachshund cross female. The noise was deafening, barking, barking, all the dogs who could bark were barking. I watched as Danielle reached for her left hearing aid and turned it down. The attendant walked us over to a kennel and pointed. There she stood, in the middle of the kennel, shaking.

I opened the kennel door and picked up this poor golden little thing. I handed the seven-pound bundle of shakiness to Danielle. "Poor thing," Danielle said out loud as she kissed and petted the dog. Danielle carefully examined the dog with her touch. I watched as she felt each of the dog's paws. She then stretched out her long tail. She carefully, gently, measured the length of her ears. "I want her," Danielle said.

We paid the seventy dollars that the kennel required for the dog's spay and shots. I put the two passengers in the car, and we found ourselves on our way home with our new bundle of doginess.

Danielle held the dog all the way home. "What does she look like?" Danielle finally voiced as we rode home.

"She's a golden tan color with a dark streak down the middle of her back," I signed with my right hand and said. "Oh," I added, "and she has big, straight up ears."

It appeared that Danielle could hear me speak a little better when we were in a closed room or the car. "She's brown with a stripe?" Danielle asked back.

"Yep, and big ears," I said as I looked at the two passengers, one canine and one who held my heart. Danielle again kissed the brown four-legged pup and said, "Sunny! I want to call her Sunny."

Sunny, it turned out, was made to be a hearing dog. After a couple of days, she finally settled down and I set to work to teach her to bark when someone was at the door and to poke Danielle with her nose.

Repetition, patience, and diligence are required when training a new dog. Sunny had a great bark, one Danielle could easily hear when she had on her hearing aids. Danielle would often lie on the love seat in our living room and Sunny would dutifully lie within Danielle's reach so she could get her ears massaged. Danielle quickly fell in love with Sunny.

A new dog in the house allowed the aging Squeaker to retire. Squeaker, it seemed, had never sought all the attention that Sunny enjoyed.

Sometimes, when it was raining, Squeaker would get lazy and go potty in the house. Danielle, being blind, would sometimes walk where Squeaker had messed and thus make a bigger mess. From another room I'd hear Danielle yell, "Squeaker." I knew what this meant and would run to assist in the cleanup.

Chapter 29

Joy and Lamay both had boyfriends. We were fortunate enough that Danielle had met both boyfriends before she lost her vision.

Joy's boyfriend was named Paul. Paul was a tall, well-built man who had ocean blue eyes and rosy red cheeks. He was very kind and spoke to Danielle as best as he could each time he and Joy came over to visit. Oftentimes, as was the case, Joy had to interpret what Paul said, so Paul would hug Danielle and Danielle would feel his beard and sign "rat." Danielle gave everybody a name sign. Name signs are given to deaf people and the family that they live with.

My name sign is the letter J signed near the right ear. It is made up from the sign "crazy," but signed with a J instead. Danielle's sign is a D signed by tapping the throat area and then tapping again below the rib cage. In the making up of Paul's sign, because Paul liked cats, Danielle decided to use an R instead of an F to sign cat. Danielle jokingly said that using an R this way, changes the word cat to rat. Anyone who signs, knows that this is not the sign for rat. Danielle was, as an inside joke, just teasing Paul with her sign language.

Lamay's boyfriend was named Wayne. Wayne was taller than me, thin, and very caring toward Danielle. One day I came home from work and Lamay was getting some things from her bedroom since she was now living with Grandma Alice, helping her and Pete in their old age. I noticed the kind Wayne sitting next to Danielle, holding her hand.

It seemed this man knew instinctively he was limited when it came to communicating with Danielle and that by holding her hand, he could tell her that he was here and she was not alone. This guy, this boyfriend of Lamay's, was always very kind toward Danielle.

I called Adult Day Care and asked how and if they might assist Danielle. It was my great hope that they could give her something to do during the day. They said that they could give her some crafts to do during the day and they would even have their bus pick her up.

Danielle and I traveled to the facility in Fortuna to see if it was something Danielle might enjoy doing. I was now desperately looking for things that might fill Danielle's life with purpose. Danielle said she wanted to try Adult Day Care.

At the Adult Day Care, Danielle liked working with beads and painting with watercolors. The aides there were always kind and helpful. As with most people, communication there was nearly impossible due to the fact that none of the aides used sign language. Danielle was completely dependent on her hearing aids so she misunderstood a lot and was left out of many of their activities.

The Adult Day Care Center also had a nurse on duty who would check Danielle's blood sugars and advise me via a letter sent home if her blood sugars were high.

Danielle attended Day Care on Mondays, Wednesdays, and Fridays. She stayed home Tuesdays and Thursdays.

I purchased a little wall clock that I put up near the front doorway of our living room in hopes that Danielle would be able to hear the chimes and count out to herself what time it was.

Bong, bong, bong, chimed the clock shortly after I hung it on the wall. It was my hope that Danielle would say, "What's that noise?" and I would say, "That's your new clock so you can tell time now."

After the clock chimed for the first time, I looked at Danielle lying on the love seat and sure enough, after the last bong Danielle said, "What's that?"

"Oh, that," I stated and signed into her hands with a big cheesy grin on my face, "that's your new clock. If you want to know what time it is, just count the bongs."

"Good idea," Danielle said. "Jack," she said after a short time.

"Yes Punky," I replied.

"Thank you for the clock."

I got up and kissed her. "You're welcome."

Lamay moved to Los Angeles with Wayne and before they left, the two of them got married at the courthouse in Eureka. While living in Los Angeles, Lamay went to medical assistant school. She graduated and began work as a medical assistant. Danielle and I were so proud of her.

It took Lamay and Wayne a little while, but they finally were able to move back home. Lamay came over to see Danielle and told her the wonderful news that she was going to have a baby. Danielle just couldn't wait. Lamay continued working as a medical assistant in Eureka for another seven months until it was ultimately just too difficult for her to keep working.

I got a call at work one day from Lamay saying they had a new baby girl at Redwood Memorial Hospital, and asking if I could bring Danielle to the hospital so she could see the new baby. Danielle and I went to the hospital and found Lamay and Wayne in the hospital room holding a beautiful bundle. Danielle sat in one of the hard-wooden hospital chairs.

"Here, Pa, let Mom clean her hands with this hand cleaner," Lamay said. I handed Danielle the hand sanitizer bottle and as soon as Danielle had cleaned her hands Wayne quickly placed the beautiful bundle in her arms.

Danielle took the baby from Wayne and was so gentle. It was obvious that she was a natural when it came to nurturing babies. "Jack," Danielle said to me. "Who does she look like?"

I watched as Danielle carefully felt the contours of the beautiful face of this gift from God. As tears of joy and sadness fell from my eyes, I said, "She looks a little bit like Lamay when she was born and a little bit like Wayne."

"What color are her eyes?" Danielle asked.

"Blue," I said.

"What color is her hair?" Danielle asked.

"Right now, it's brownish but it looks like it might get lighter," I told her and signed into her free hand.

Danielle gently brought the face of our first grandchild near hers and gently, oh so gently, kissed the face of this sweet new baby.

"Lamay?" Danielle addressed her daughter.

"Yes, Mom," she answered.

"What's her name?"

"We named her Nevaeh," was her reply.

I spelled "N-E-V-A-E-H" into Danielle's hands. "I never heard that name before," responded Danielle.

"If you reverse the spelling of her name it spells heaven," said Lamay.

I said and signed Lamay's words to Danielle.

Danielle pondered what I had just signed to her and then said, "Oh, how beautiful."

Chapter 30

The rich, warm, loamy soil glistened as I separated, with my ungloved calloused fingers, those annoying weeds. I tried tirelessly to uproot those prolific invaders from the beautiful multicolored impatiens I had just planted weeks ago, but I found it was not an easy task.

Why is it that those hateful weeds seem to grow ten times faster than the flowers I planted? This must be one of those mysteries whose answers will soon be revealed on ABC's World News Tonight, I thought.

I looked up and saw the police car approaching. I was not at all alarmed when I saw that Chief Graham was rolling down his window. The chief, a well-proportioned, down-to-earth man, was known for his soft-spoken and compassionate nature. I assumed he was just going to say hi as he so often did.

Chief Graham and I had frequently had conversations. Most of them were about gardening. It often seemed to me as though everyone in Scotia and Rio Dell knew me as Jack the gardener from Scotia. Both the chief and I were associated with the town of Rio Dell, he as police chief and I as secretary/treasurer of the Rio Dell volunteer fire department.

But Chief Graham hadn't stopped to partake in small talk, I soon realized. "Kathleen Kemp just called the department to report that your wife is outside walking around the front yard and that she seems confused and is looking for her mom. She needs you to come home now," he said to me.

Because I walked the two miles to work every day, my first thought was to ask the chief for a ride home, but I then thought I should inform my foreman that I needed to go home.

I thanked the chief and then ran over to the Scotia's main office building. I entered the main office, then headed straight to the switchboard operator.

Vickie, a lifelong Rio Dellion, had known my wife and her family all her life. She had always been known as a hard worker and very proficient at everything she did.

I was nervous and tried to calm down before I told her, as calmly as I could, that there was an emergency at home and I had to get hold of Tony, my foreman, as soon as possible. Vickie called Tony's company cell phone and Tony picked me up in front of the main office.

Tony and I had worked together for twenty years. Tony, more than five years younger than me, was, above all other things, calm, patient, and not easily flustered.

I quickly told him what the police chief had told me. Tony stepped out of the company truck, told me to take the truck home, not to worry about anything, and that he'd talk to me later.

The five-minute drive home seemed to crawl as my mind raced. I tried to make sense of the urgent message given to me by the chief of police. Was Danielle sleepwalking? Were they all mistaken and it wasn't my wife at all but somebody else entirely? None of these scenarios seemed to sit well.

As I turned onto Riverside Drive, I could see when I looked straight ahead, that Kathleen Kemp was indeed keeping an eye on Danielle and was following her around the front yard in hopes of keeping Danielle from injuring herself.

I parked the truck along the curb across the street from our house and got out. I said hi to Kathleen. Kathleen and her husband, Arnie, had been our next-door neighbors for the last twelve years that we'd lived in Rio Dell.

Kathleen said, "I just happened to see Danielle outside and I knew she couldn't see. So, I called the police."

"Did she say anything to you?" I asked.

"Yeah, she said she has to go see her mom. I thought that strange because you were not home."

"Kathleen, I have no idea what's going on but I'll get her back into the house. I'll let you know when I know more," I said. "Thanks again."

Kathleen said, "Let me know if you need anything," and she returned to her home.

"Danielle," I signed into her hand. Danielle flinched as I touched her to start signing into her hands. "What's wrong?" I signed and said.

"I have to go see my mom," she said and signed.

"No, you don't," I signed and said.

"Yes, I have to go now," she replied loudly.

"Let's get into the house so you can hear me better," I said and signed.

I walked Danielle through the front door. Danielle immediately went to the bathroom. When she was done, she came and sat at the dinner table.

As Danielle sat, I signed into her hand, "What's going on?"

"I have to go over my mom's house."

"Why do you have to go over your mom's house?" I asked.

"She wants me to go to her house," Danielle said and signed.

"How do you know she wants you to go over her house?" I asked.

"Call her," was Danielle's reply.

I called Alice. "Danielle was outside walking around, and Kathleen Kemp called the cops. Danielle says that you wanted her to come to your house," I told Alice.

"No, I didn't want Danielle to come to my house," she responded immediately. There was a long pause on the other end of the line and then I heard, "Call me and let me know what's going on when you find out," Alice said.

"Okay, I will."

I looked at Danielle and she seemed very agitated. "Do you feel okay?" I asked.

Just then I watched as she began signing with someone. Danielle was furious with this person that she was signing to, who to me, obviously wasn't there. Danielle kept signing to them and telling them to "shut up" and "you're stupid."

I tapped Danielle's shoulder and she winced. It appeared that she had forgotten that I was here standing next to her.

"Who are you talking to?" I asked and signed.

"Irene," Danielle said and signed angrily.

"Who?" I asked again. In all our years of marriage Danielle had never mentioned anyone named Irene.

"Irene, Irene from Iraq," was her response.

"Who's Irene from Iraq?" I asked slowly and calmly.

"She always makes me angry," Danielle responded immediately.

"Are you telling me that Irene from Iraq always makes you angry?" I signed and said.

"Yes," was Danielle's response.

"Danielle, there's nobody here," I said and signed.

"She's right there." Danielle pointed angrily to the empty chair across the dining room table.

I repeated, "Danielle, there's nobody here."

"You're lying to me," she said and signed to me, angrily.

"I don't lie, you know that. I love you; how can you say that I lie to you?"

Danielle slammed the dining room table with her hand. "Irene's right there, you stupid," she said and signed.

I called Alice and told her that Danielle was saying there was a person here, yet there was no one here. "Can I bring her over to your house while I get back to work?" I asked Alice.

Alice was now eighty-six years old and I really didn't have anyone else to turn to at the moment. "Sure," she said, "bring her over."

I took Danielle to Alice's, told Danielle that I would come and pick her up after work, and left.

My mind raced as I tried to put two and two together to figure out what was going on with Danielle. *Maybe her medicine is causing her to suffer a reaction. I'll take her to Dr. Meengs tomorrow,* I thought.

Dr. Meengs was Danielle's doctor. She was so kind and patient with her. Dr. Meengs's mobile clinic came to Rio Dell on Wednesdays. Thank God tomorrow was Wednesday.

I took my car to work that day so I could take Danielle to the clinic first thing in the morning. I got Danielle out of the car and slowly walked her to Dr. Meengs's RV clinic. Climbing the three steps into the RV was always challenging, but because Ray had so cleverly taught me to tap Danielle's arm, it was now second nature to us.

Dr. Meengs greeted Danielle and me and said, "Hi, Danielle, how are you doing?"

Danielle began a litany of the events that she had recently begun to experience. Most of the things Danielle said were just plain weird and didn't make much sense to me.

"Irene wants me to go to my mom's because my eyes are bleeding," Danielle said, eerily.

"Your eyes are bleeding?" the doctor asked.

"Yes, look." Danielle opened her eyes with her fingers so the doctor could examine them.

"They look fine to me," stated the kind doctor.

"My heart is bleeding too."

"Wait, you said your heart is bleeding, Danielle?" asked the doctor.

"Yes, my heart is bleeding inside," Danielle said and signed.

"Let me listen to your heart," said Dr. Meengs. "Everything sounds all right to me," she said a few moments later. "I'm going to talk to Jack for a minute, just wait, okay?"

Dr. Meengs told me that she thought Danielle was having a psychotic episode.

"What does that mean, a psychotic episode?"

"It means that she's having delusional thoughts."

"You mean like hearing voices and experiencing things that aren't actually there?" I said with great distress.

"Precisely," she stated. "I'm going to prescribe her some sedatives," said the doctor, "to see if we can calm down her brain. Right now, it's racing and it seems her thoughts are all over the place."

Dr. Meengs prescribed Ambien CR and told me to give Danielle Benadryl if she needed more of a sedative. I was surprised to learn that Benadryl was used to make people sleep. Dr. Meengs also prescribed a psychotropic drug called Seroquel. She stated that this might aid Danielle by suppressing the weird thoughts she was having. I was cautiously hopeful.

The pharmacy was very kind to us. They had been friends to us for over thirty years now and were aware of Danielle's many medical needs.

Merilyn, our pharmacist, was so kind and said she would stop by the house after work to bring Danielle's new medications, so I wouldn't have to leave her alone in the car while I ran into the pharmacy. I took Danielle home and tried to get her to calm down.

As evening rolled around, I had Danielle sit down at the dinner table while I tried to prepare some dinner. I watched her as I cooked and tried to engage her in conversation. Just then the phone rang. It was Joy and she wanted to stop by and see her mom and tell her some good news.

Danielle, with her hearing aid on, could always hear the phone ring.

"Who's on the phone?" Danielle asked after I hung up.

"Joy," I said. "She wants to stop by with Paul."

"Are you sure you're not lying to me?"

While the chicken thighs cooked in the oven, I walked over to Danielle, touched her arm, and she winced. I sat down next to my love and tried engaging her in a conversation.

"Danielle, why would you think I'm lying to you? I love you. I just want what's best for you," I signed and said.

"Irene said that you are sneaky and that I can't trust you."

Tears welled up in my eyes. I leaned over and kissed her beautiful cheeks.

"Why did you do that?" asked Danielle.

"I kissed you because I want you to know that I will always love you. I don't know Irene but it appears that she is making you confused. Danielle, listen to me closely, you can't believe Irene. Irene is not really here, but I am," I said. "I am here and I'll always be here. You can always trust me; I will never lie to you."

Danielle was silent. There was a knock at the door and Sunny barked and came over to Danielle to poke her. Danielle always acknowledged Sunny when she did the right thing by alerting her. This time, Danielle ignored Sunny.

I opened the door and Joy was there with Paul. "Hi, baby, come in." As always, I kissed Joy's cheek and then hugged Paul.

Joy walked over to Danielle and said, "Hi, Mom, it's Joy and Paul is with me."

"Who?" Danielle asked.

"It's Joy and I brought Paul with me."

Danielle failed to respond.

"What's wrong with Mom, Pa?" Joy asked.

"She's confused and has been signing with people who aren't actually here," I said.

"Liar," Daniele blurted out to me, which caused Joy great alarm.

"Pa, why is Mom acting like that?"

"I took your mom to the doctor today and she thinks Mom is having mental issues," I said.

"Oh, Mom," Joy said as tears rolled down her cheeks. Joy then gave her mom a great big hug and held on ever so tightly. Danielle patted Joy's arm.

"Mom, I have something to tell you. Do you want to hear it?" Joy asked.

"What?" Danielle responded curtly.

"Paul and I are getting married," Joy said, as she signed into Danielle's hands.

"Married?" Danielle asked.

"Yes, Mom, Paul asked me to marry him."

With great excitement and delight, Joy showed Danielle her engagement ring as Danielle felt the contours and bumps of this new ring, carefully.

Danielle seemed to come back to reality for a moment. She said, "You're getting married?"

"Yes, Mom," Joy said and signed, "we're getting married."

"When?" Danielle inquired.

"June," Joy responded. "We want to get married in June."

"Where?" Danielle asked.

"We want to get married in Piercy," Joy answered.

"Good," Danielle said. "I'm happy for you."

I hugged Joy and Paul and said, "I'm so proud of you guys. Let me know what you want me to do as the time gets closer."

Danielle's new medications did not work. She continued to hallucinate and seemed to be perpetually on edge.

I was sleeping late one night when I heard a bunch of noise. I woke up and felt for Danielle. She wasn't in the bed. I jumped up and turned the light on. Danielle was in her closet fumbling for clothes and making all kinds of weird gestures.

I touched Danielle on the shoulder and she was totally startled.

"What are you doing?" I signed into her hand.

Danielle was not wearing her hearing aids. Without her aids Danielle is completely deaf. Danielle signed, "I have to go to South Dakota to see my cousins."

"What are you talking about?" I signed.

She repeated, "I have to go to South Dakota to see my cousins."

Danielle did have first cousins in South Dakota but in our thirty-one years of marriage, I had only met

Danielle's aunt and uncle when they came to visit Pete, Danielle's dad, about twenty years ago.

"It's two thirty in the morning and I have to go to work tomorrow. Can't you do this in the morning?" I asked.

"No, I have to do it right now," she signed.

I went to the medicine cabinet and got Danielle an Ambien and a Benadryl. I gave them to her with a glass of water.

When Danielle became blind, any time I had to give her medication I'd tap her cheek and she'd open up her mouth like a little baby bird. Now I placed the pills in her mouth and handed her the glass of water.

"Danielle, please get in bed; you frighten me when your mind is this way," I signed.

"All right," she snapped with irritation. I helped her into bed and settled down next to her. I held her hand and signed "I love you" into it when I felt that she had finally settled down. She signed back, "I love you more," and finally fell asleep.

"Jack, you need to take her to Sempervirens in Eureka," said Dr. Meengs during our next visit. "She's not responding to my treatment. We have to find out what's going on. The doctors there are trained extensively in these things."

"All right," I replied. "Dr. Meengs," I then said, "seeing Danielle this way is so painful. It's like I can't do anything that's helping her."

"Jack, you're a fine husband and we all know you love her deeply."

"I do, Doctor," I responded as tears rolled down my cheeks.

I drove Danielle to Sempervirens in Eureka.

"I don't want to go to the crazy hospital," Danielle informed me in the car.

"Danielle, you need to see a doctor that knows how to help you with your mind. Your mind is sick right now."

"No way," she said.

"Okay, I promise," I said. I felt terrible having promised her this because I had never lied to Danielle and I didn't want to start lying now. But I had no other recourse. "This isn't the crazy hospital," I said. "It's another doctor's office." I'm pretty sure that because I'm a horrible liar, Danielle knew exactly where we were.

I walked Danielle into Sempervirens that cold winter morning hoping upon hope that Danielle would finally get the medical care she so desperately needed.

We walked up to a window with a sign above it which read "Receptionist."

"Good morning," I said to the plump figure behind the sliding window. "My wife is suffering mental problems and I'm wondering if somebody could see her?"

Without looking me in the eyes, the lady grabbed numerous pages of paper and clipped them to a clipboard. "Fill these out completely, then give them back to me," she stated.

I waited, standing there, until she eventually looked into my eyes. "Thank you!" I said with a big smile. I'm not sure, but she looked like a person who didn't get a lot of smiles on a daily basis.

While I filled out the forms, Danielle was agitated and kept signing to someone. Many times, I asked her to stop signing, but she was so irritated that she just ignored me.

I walked back up to the window. The receptionist looked at me, smiled, and said to have a seat and that someone would be with us in a few minutes.

"Danielle Saffell," said a small, thin woman with short dark hair. "How do you do; my name is Jennifer Weatherbee. I will be helping you today. Please follow me."

Danielle and I followed the lady into a small room that had a table with six chairs placed around it. "Please have a seat," she said and took the chair at the head of the table. "What seems to be the problem?" asked the kind lady.

"Danielle is having problems dealing with reality," I replied.

"No, I'm not," Danielle blurted out. "I'm not crazy."

"I never said you were crazy," I signed into her hand.

"You told the lady that I'm crazy," Danielle said, harshly.

"You can't hear very well and I never would say that, Danielle, I love you."

Jennifer was fascinated as she watched Danielle speak while I returned the answers by signing into her hands.

Jennifer addressed Danielle. "Danielle," she voiced.

"Yeah," Danielle said.

"My name is Jennifer, I'm very happy to meet you. Why are you here today? What looks to be troubling you?" the lady asked as I interpreted.

"Irene told me that Jack lies all the time and my heart and eyes are bleeding and my medicine is poison," Danielle said. I looked at Jennifer and she didn't seem fazed in the least. "Why do you think your medicine is poison?" Jennifer asked, calmly. Danielle did not answer.

"Danielle's starting to compulsively wash her hands. When I feed her dinner, she pushes her food away, then pulls it back and forth repeatedly," I said. "Oh, and she's lost all interest in the activities that she used to love doing."

Jennifer asked many questions and learned a lot. Some were about our family dynamics. She asked how long Danielle had been deaf. She wanted to know how long Danielle had been blind. She asked me if Danielle had ever been diagnosed with schizophrenia in the past.

"I'm going to have one of our doctors see Danielle, so wait here. I'll be right back," said Jennifer.

A few minutes later she returned. "Jack? Could you please bring Danielle this way?"

Danielle and I walked with Jennifer down the hall and got on the elevator. We stopped on the third floor and got out.

The three of us walked down the hall to an office. Jennifer led us in and introduced us. "Jack, this is Dr. Wolk. He'll help you now."

"Hello, Doctor," I said. "This is my wife, Danielle. Danielle is deaf and blind."

"Nice to meet the two of you," he said. "Please take a seat."

We left Sempervirens that morning slightly more confused than when we first got there.

The psychiatrist said that Danielle was psychotic and that he was going to prescribe her some psychotropic medications in order to calm down her erratic thinking. I did learn that there were many such medications on the market and that it may take some time to find the right medication that suited her.

We went back to Sempervirens for three more appointments. Danielle was no better off than when we first set foot in there. Honestly, I thought she was getting worse.

Tony, my co-worker, had told his wife about Danielle and how difficult and sad it was for Danielle and my family to be going through such trying and agonizing times. Tony came to work one day and handed me a phone number with the name "Cathy Silver P.A." on it.

"Call Cathy," Tony stated. "Helene has talked to Cathy about Danielle and she said that Cathy would be willing to help you guys out."

Helene was such an angel for helping Danielle. She had seen Cathy on a few occasions in hopes of relieving some of her own anxiety.

I telephoned and talked with Cathy Silver that very day. Cathy made an appointment for Danielle and me to see her later in the week, and in the meantime to call her anytime, night or day, if I needed to talk to someone.

Chapter 31

We sat in the small, neon-lit waiting room waiting our turn. Danielle was seated next to me on a well-worn cloth seat and wooden-armed chair. Danielle was very agitated and was signing periodically to who seemed to be the dreaded "Irene from Iraq."

"Danielle," I signed calmly into her hand.

"What!" Danielle responded harshly as though I was interrupting a serious conversation.

"Who are you talking to?" I asked guardedly.

Nowadays I never knew if Danielle was going to bite my head off if I asked her a question, so naturally, I was on guard.

"Don't bother me!" Danielle signed back with great agitation.

"Are you talking to Irene from Iraq?" I dared to ask.

"Yeah, what do you want?" she signed.

"Nothing, I just want you to talk to me because I'm really here and Irene is not a real person." I stated the obvious.

Danielle stopped talking to me and again seemed to go back inside her head. I had begun to follow Danielle's thought process a little better now because she had been psychotic for almost four months now. Danielle was obviously quite miserable.

"Danielle Saffell," a beautiful woman called from the hall door.

I quickly stood and patted Danielle on the shoulder in hopes of getting her to leave the confines of her inner thoughts and allow me to lead her. "Danielle, it's time for us to go in and see Cathy," I said and signed into her hand. Danielle seemed slow to respond, but eventually acquiesced.

I smiled at the beautiful lady as Danielle naturally grabbed for my elbow and allowed me to lead. "Hi," I said, as I turned my head aside looking at Danielle, making sure she wouldn't bump the coffee table in the middle of the waiting room with her leg.

"I'm Jack. This is my wife, Danielle," I said as we strode toward her.

"Hello," she replied, "my name is Cathy. I'm so happy to see the two of you. Follow me," she said as she led us down a short hall and into a small room on the left.

Cathy told us to take a seat on the couch and to please make ourselves comfortable.

Cathy was in her late sixties, tall and well proportioned. She dressed beautifully. Her slacks were a light violet color which matched her wine-colored blouse and darker purple scarf. I would later learn that Cathy always wore the color violet or some semblance thereof.

The beige couch was well furnished and had on it several throw pillows. I seated Danielle to my left and took the seat nearest to where Cathy's matching stuffed chair was arranged. Danielle grabbed one of the throw pillows and hugged it meaningfully.

"Hello, Danielle," was the first thing Cathy said as we finally settled in.

I signed into Danielle's waiting hands, "Cathy is saying hello to you."

"Hello," Danielle spoke back to Cathy.

"What seems to be the problem today, Danielle?" Cathy asked.

"Jack says Irene is not a real person, but she is," Danielle stated to Cathy.

"Danielle, who's Irene?" Cathy immediately seemed to know exactly what questions to ask to get Danielle to respond.

"Irene is my friend," Danielle spoke back to Cathy.

"Where does Irene live?" Cathy asked Danielle.

"Irene is from Iraq," Danielle replied.

"Irene is from Iraq?" Cathy repeated.

Danielle said, "Yes, and she's real."

"Okay," Cathy said. "Danielle, I'm going to talk to Jack. If you have any questions, please don't be afraid to ask, okay?"

"Fine," Danielle said.

I watched as Danielle returned back into her own thoughts as Cathy and I began to talk.

"How long has this been going on, Jack?" Cathy asked me directly, as she looked straight into my eyes.

"Three, maybe four months now," I responded.

"Tell me what you have done to help Danielle these last four months," Cathy inquired.

"When Danielle first started talking to Irene from Iraq, I took her to see her doctor in Rio Dell, Dr. Meengs, but the medicines she prescribed didn't work at all."

"That's a lie," Danielle said out loud, startling Cathy and me. We looked at Danielle but I kept on talking to Cathy.

"Dr. Meengs told me to take Danielle to Sempervirens, but each time we go to our appointment at Sempervirens they have a new doctor. Each new doctor seems to have their own agenda and changes Danielle's medicines and says we have to start all over," I told her. "I'm very frustrated and Danielle is miserable."

"Okay," Cathy said. She paused before continuing. "I too am going to change her medicine, but you'll find with me that I'll always be available if you need me."

"Thank you very much," I said as I began to tear up. Cathy reached for a tissue and handed it to me.

"I can see you're at your wits' end," she said softly.

"Yes, this whole process is so frustrating, not only for me, but especially for my beautiful bride," I told her, after blowing my nose.

Cathy talked with me for about half an hour, wanting to know how and when Danielle went deaf, how and when she became blind, and all about our family's state of affairs.

"Jack, have you ever heard of a cochlear implant?" Cathy asked me during our conversation.

"Yes," I responded. "I looked into one about seven years ago. Danielle and I went to UCSF and had several tests to see if Danielle would be a candidate for one. But after the tests, they said that they didn't think Danielle would benefit from one at the time."

"Was she blind when she took in those tests?" Cathy inquired.

"No," I replied, "she was sighted."

Cathy gave me instructions to call UCSF again and to tell them the Danielle was now blind and that I wanted her to be evaluated again to see if the cochlear implant might benefit Danielle now that she was blind.

Cathy told me that she was going to start Danielle on a psychotropic medication called Zyprexa. Zyprexa, she said, concentrates on the part of the brain that causes the schizophrenia, and in time, it hopefully would alleviate Danielle's confusing thoughts.

We left Cathy's office, and I finally had a feeling that we might now make progress. I was also given homework in that I would have to rekindle our association with UCSF with the goal of possibly getting Danielle a cochlear implant.

I picked up the Zyprexa at Palco Pharmacy and began giving it to Danielle along with her other vitamins and medications. Danielle and I visited Cathy every week for a couple of months and Danielle slowly started calming down. The Zyprexa appeared to be working. Danielle slowly came back to reality more and more.

Danielle and I had an appointment to go to UCSF in November.

The otolaryngology office had moved to Sutter Street in downtown San Francisco. Danielle had a disabled placard and it was not very helpful that day. I had to park two blocks from the office. One advantage that we now had was that Danielle was prescribed a wheelchair by Dr. Meengs. Thank God for the wheelchair. She could still make her way, attached to my arm, if we walked, but any hump or irregularity on the sidewalk was an enormous obstacle.

We met with Colleen Polite, the same audiologist we worked with several years before. She remembered Danielle and was saddened to find out that Danielle was now blind. "How did Danielle lose her sight?" questioned the kind lady.

"Diabetes," I responded. "It happened rather suddenly."

Danielle again took the needed tests to determine her chance at getting a cochlear implant. "I'll email you when the tests come back and after I've had a chance to talk to our team," said Colleen.

Just as promised, Colleen Polite emailed me with the news. "Please call me at your earliest convenience," she said in an email. "We have determined that due to her new blindness that Danielle is indeed a candidate for a cochlear implant."

I called and made the appointment for Danielle's operation.

Danielle, however, did not want the cochlear implant. "I don't want some other hearing aid," she stated.

"Danielle, it's not another hearing aid," I responded, "it's different. Colleen Polite will explain it better than I can, next time we visit her."

Then Squeaker had a heart attack.

I called and called for her to dinner late one evening after I got home from work. She would not come. I looked throughout the backyard and finally found her slumped over near our fence.

How am I going to tell Danielle? I thought to myself.

I took Squeaker to Danielle and said, "Danielle, sit up for me, okay?" Danielle was reclined on the loveseat with a great throw pillow behind her head. Danielle sat up and I placed the poor sickly Squeaker on her lap. The Squeak was still breathing, but just barely. Her tongue was hanging out of her mouth, but she didn't appear to be in any pain. Danielle quickly recognized the little bundle of fur.

"What happened to her?" Danielle asked as tears started coming from her sightless eyes.

"It looks like she had a heart attack or a stroke," I said sadly.

"Oh no," she cried out. "I love her, I love her," was all she could say. "Poor Squeaker," Danielle signed to her faithful, cherished companion. Danielle held on to Squeaker and would not let go.

"I'm going to put Squeaker's bed in the washroom so she can have quiet," I told Danielle. Danielle, holding her beloved companion, carefully followed me into the washroom.

Danielle felt about where I had placed Squeaker's bed in the washroom and carefully placed the flaccid little bundle of love in her bed. Danielle knelt down, kissing and petting her beloved friend and companion. She cried and cried and cried before she finally retrieved Squeaker's blanket from our bedroom and placed it over her so she could be comfortable.

Before Danielle and I went to bed, Danielle checked on Squeaker and her breathing was very labored. "I love you so much, Squeaker. Thank you for helping me, I'm going to miss you so much. I love you."

Squeaker passed away sometime during the night.

"Jack," Danielle said to me in the morning. "Could you please bury my Squeaker next to my babies in the backyard?"

"Of course," I said. "It's hard when the things we love die," I told her.

"I know," she said softly. I buried Squeaker next to our beautiful babies in the backyard.

"Danielle," I said, after doing what she had asked. "Squeaker's buried next to your babies."

"Thank you," she said as the tears again rolled down her cheeks.

I caressed her face between my hands and kissed her lovingly. "I love you," I signed to Danielle.

"I love you more," she signed back.

Chapter 32

Danielle and I traveled to San Francisco to the UCSF hospital on Parnassus Avenue in downtown San Francisco. What a madhouse.

Danielle told me on the way down to UCSF about her times in school at the California School for the Deaf. She told me of the many times she and her friends played jokes on each other and of some of her old boyfriends.

She told me in particular of a boy named Denny and how much she really loved him. But he was older and her mom would have gotten mad at her if she ever found out that she had a boyfriend.

Danielle told me of times when she was a little girl and how her grandfather, Giovanni Mela, would use homemade sign language to communicate with her. "He always smoked cigarettes," Danielle said. "He rolled them up in his hands," she gestured.

We had to be at the hospital really early so we had to leave the Flamingo Hotel in Santa Rosa at five in the morning. We signed into the hospital and it wasn't very long until they had Danielle all gowned up and ready to wheel into the operating room.

"Jack? Could you please put on a gown and stay with Danielle while we get her sedated? The other nurses and I don't sign, but there are a few things we'll need Danielle to do once we're in the operating room," a kind nurse asked me.

I gowned up and held Danielle's hands as we were wheeled into the operating room.

The room was cold. The nurse in charge told me that they were going to slide Danielle over onto the operating table. I signed into Danielle's waiting hands and she signed okay and shook her head up and down. "Tell Danielle that she might feel a poke," said another nurse. I complied. "Tell Danielle that we are going to give her some medicine that will put her to sleep," said the anesthesiologist. I again signed into her hands. Before the medicine took effect, I signed "I love you." Danielle slid off to sleep as she began to sign, "I love you mo…"

The surgery took about three hours. I waited in the crowded waiting room and prayed several rosaries. I prayed for Danielle to benefit greatly from the cochlear implant. I prayed for my family at home. I prayed that Danielle would be able to hear with this new device. I thanked God for all his graces, for mine and Danielle's beautiful life together. I prayed and gave thanks for the good times and the bad. Most of all I prayed for our future and what it might hold. "Jesus, I love you, I love you, I love you."

Danielle was groggy and hungry. I stood by her side while she reclined on the hospital bed. "How do you feel?" I signed into her hand.

"Painful," she signed back. I reached into my pocket and handed Danielle her hearing aid. I watched Danielle as she fumbled about trying to place the aid in her left ear. I took the aid from her and slid the earmold into the ear canal. I then placed the flesh-colored hearing aid over her ear and asked her if she wanted me to turn it on. She sleepily signed yes with her right hand, and I turned on her aid.

As I expected, she jerked back as the hearing aid immediately increased the volume of the room. "Too loud," Danielle signed to me as I carefully tried to turn down the tiny computer. "These new digital hearing aids are now simply tiny computers," Danielle's audiologist had told me when she got it.

We stayed in the hospital three hours and were told to go home and that I should call Colleen Polite in about six to eight weeks to set up some other appointments.

We went to the Flamingo Hotel in Santa Rosa to stay the night in one of Danielle's favorite places. I let Danielle sleep late into the morning. I woke her to take her to the restroom and to tell her that I was going to Mass and not to open the door for anyone.

I went to daily Mass at the Cathedral. I went there ahead of time so I could pray the rosary with the other daily communicants. I had often brought Danielle with me to Mass when we were staying in Santa Rosa when she was having her eye surgeries. We were fortunate enough to have made friends with several of the daily communicants there at the Cathedral.

I loved going to Mass every morning. While in the pew, on my knees, I often contemplated on the life of Jesus. I stared upon the crucifix and pondered how dreadfully painful the crucifixion itself was. I often ponder how God is love. I believe, if I understand this correctly, that God does not represent love; rather, God *Is* love.

That God Himself loves me so much that He gave His life that I, little, insignificant me, might have eternal life in heaven. I again prayed that Danielle would heal well and that she might hear Nevaeh's beautiful voice one day and any other grandbabies that we might have in the future.

It was now Valentine's Day. I went to Mass in Scotia. While I was there, Danielle secretly taped several heart-shaped cutouts all around our master bathroom.

As soon as I got home from Mass I went into the bedroom and changed my clothes. I had to relieve myself so I went into the bathroom. There, on every nook and cranny in that beautiful bathroom, were hundreds of heart-shaped craft-paper cutouts. The sheer volume of pink and red hearts was overwhelming. It must have taken Danielle days to cut out each and every heart. They were all over the walls, all over the mirror, all over the shower door. I was completely overwhelmed.

"Danielle," I said loudly as I walked back into the dining room. Danielle was seated with a huge grin upon her face. "I love it, I love it," I signed into her hands. "How long did it take you to make all those hearts?"

"Not very long," she said. "Just a week."

"Danielle," I said and signed into her hands.

"What?" she signed.

"Guess what?" I said and signed.

"What?" she said.

"I love you," I said and signed.

Danielle signed back, "I love you more," as I gently grabbed her face between my hands and kissed her beautiful lips.

Danielle had an appointment with Cathy Silver the next day. Cathy was very pleased with Danielle's reaction to Zyprexa. "I was hoping this medication would help bring her back to reality," she said.

We were driving home from Arcata and I hadn't heard from Alice all day. Alice usually called me at break time at work just to see how Danielle was doing. I had called Alice at lunch time, when I went home to give Danielle lunch, but she still didn't answer the phone. I thought I'd try calling her on our way home from Cathy Silver's, to check on her and to find out if she needed anything.

Flora answered.

"Hi, Flora," I reluctantly said, knowing that Flora had never answered Alice's phone before. "Is Grandma there?"

"Jack," Flora said calmly, "my sister passed away, probably last night."

"We'll be there in about half an hour," I told her.

I started tearing up, knowing I had to tell Danielle that her mom had just died. "Danielle," I signed into her hand and said.

"Yeah," she said back.

"Your mom passed away last night," I signed slowly and calmly.

"What?" Danielle said and signed.

"Your mom passed away last night," I said and signed again.

That moment in time still stands frozen in my mind. I remember I could smell the fragrant odor of the hundreds of eucalyptus trees that line the beautiful Humboldt Bay. I could see the irritated and choppy waves as they tossed about in their cold moist environment. I heard Danielle scream, "MY MOMMY, MY MOMMY!"

I called Joy on her cell phone. "Mija, I have some sad news to tell you," I said. "Your grandma passed away last night."

"Oh, Pa," she said. "Where is she?" she asked through tears.

"She's still at home. Flora's there with her," I said. "I'm bringing your mom there if you want to meet us there."

"Okay," she said.

"Love you," I said.

"Love you too," said the sad granddaughter.

Next, I called Lamay and told her, and then called Aleace in Massachusetts and told her. "I'll be there as soon as I can," Aleace said. I called Christian, but he didn't answer and I didn't want to leave this sad message on his phone. I finally reached him just as we pulled into Grandma's driveway. I told him of his grandmother's passing and hung up.

Just as I got out of the car Joy pulled up. I embraced her and she ran over to Danielle's side of the car. "My mom died," Danielle signed to Joy, as they hugged.

"I know, Ma," Joy sadly signed back.

I walked Danielle into her mom's house and Flora greeted us. She told us that Alice was still in her bed and to go back there. I walked Danielle down Alice's hall and to her room.

There, still in her bed, was Alice. I took Danielle's hand and placed it on Alice's head. Danielle sat on her mom's bed and tenderly, with great love, felt around and caressed her mom ever so gently. Danielle said, "I love you, Mom," as she stroked Alice's beautiful silver-white hair. "Please give my love to my Nonna and Nonno."

I was sitting across from Grandma's bed and Joy stood over her mom as she and Danielle cried together over the great loss they would have to endure.

"Let's do the Chaplet of Divine Mercy," Flora said to me. The Chaplet of Divine Mercy is recited similar to the rosary, so Flora and I prayed together for the poor soul of Alice.

Aleace arrived in a few days and we had a beautiful rosary and funeral at St. Patrick's church in Scotia.

All the girls visited their Grandpa Pete at the rest home. Grandpa was suffering from dementia. The girls told him about their grandma's funeral. They thought he understood that Alice had passed away and he was happy that she wasn't hurting from her arthritis anymore.

We all got together every evening that Aleace was here. Danielle was happy that all her family was together and everyone had a good time, but she was sad that it had to be because her mom had died. Aleace went back to Massachusetts and life got back to normal after a few days.

I was at the pharmacy getting Danielle's medicine nine days after Alice died. Autumn, the pharmacy technician, said, "Sorry to hear about your father-in-law."

I obviously thought she misspoke and said, "Oh, you mean about my mother-in-law."

"No," Autumn said slowly, "didn't your father-in-law pass away last night?"

"I don't believe so," I said.

"You better call to find out," she told me.

I went outside and called Flora on my cell phone. "Flora, did Pete die last night?"

"He did," she said.

I went home and told Danielle. "Danielle, I have something important to tell you."

"What?" she asked quietly.

"Your dad passed away last night."

"You mean my dad passed away last night?" she said and signed.

Danielle then calmly said something quite profound. "My mom wanted him to come and live with her in heaven."

I again called all the kids together and Aleace returned from Massachusetts. Pete had an amazing funeral at St. Patrick's church. Pete was in the Coast Guard as a young man. Danielle's wonderful, patient father was laid to rest with honors and as they lowered his casket into the ground, he was given a twenty-one-gun salute. Danielle jerked back when the rifles were shot.

"What's that?" Danielle asked me after all the shots were taken.

"The soldiers were shooting their rifles to honor your dad for his service to our country."

"That's beautiful," Danielle said and signed.

Peter Joseph and Alice Mary Silbernagel were eighty-seven and eighty-six years old, respectively. They were married for sixty-seven years and died nine days apart. God rest their dear souls.

Chapter 33

Summer was here and Danielle was super excited when Joy told her about all the plans that she had for her wedding.

Danielle and I went shopping for a new dress. Danielle was getting gray by now. I really liked her peach-colored dress that she wore for Aleace's and Lamay's weddings, but Joy's colors were more in the green hues. I finally found a dress that Danielle liked at Ross Dress for Less. It was a pastel green and Joy thought Danielle looked beautiful in it.

Joy and Paul had sent out invitations a couple months prior to their wedding. Most, if not all, of my immediate family were invited, my mom and dad, my two brothers and their many children. Joy was kind enough to even invite my mother's brother and his lovely wife, Uncle Carlos and Aunt Nancy. Paul has a large family and even some of his Carnegie kin from back east were planning on attending.

Joy and I were busy that week, picking up the many family members who were flying into the tiny Eureka-Arcata airport for this upcoming special occasion. My mom and dad were flying in on Wednesday, so Joy made sure to be there to pick them up. While Joy was waiting at the airport, her future mother-in-law, Linda, also showed up.

While Joy and Linda waited for the passengers to deplane, upon seeing her Nana Alice and her Apple Jack, Joy ran to assist them as they both now needed wheelchairs. Nana, being the talkative type, said to Joy, "Mija, we met the nicest couple on the plane, and you know what? They are coming to Humboldt County for a wedding too. Isn't that a coincidence?"

Joy needed to retrieve her car from the parking lot, so, being a beautiful summer day, she left her beloved grandparents parked in their wheelchairs under the overhang of the entrance to the airport.

When Joy pulled up to pick up her grandparents, she noticed they were talking to a beautiful older couple about their age. When Joy came around the car to load her Nana and Apple Jack, her Nana said, "Mija, this is the couple who I was telling you about. This is Ruth and this is Bob."

"Gramma Ruth, Grandpa Bob," shouted Joy. "Nana, these are Paul's grandparents. The nice couple you have been talking to this whole time are Paul's grandmother and grandfather."

The happy occasion arrived. Joy rented a cottage near the Benbow Inn and had her makeup girl and her many bridesmaids present.

"Don't worry, Pa, we can get dressed at the cottage. I just want Mom there so she can enjoy the pre-wedding party," Joy said to me on the phone.

The trip down to Benbow took about an hour from our house. I got all our clothes ready, packed my guitar, and we arrived at the cottage about mid-morning.

The cottage was cheerful and well equipped. It had a small kitchen, bathroom, and bedrooms that Joy and her bridesmaids could use.

As always, steps were one of Danielle's nemeses. I got Danielle out of the car and walked her up to the cottage. There they were, three challenging steps which led into the cottage. I cautiously approached these three culprits with Danielle.

"Danielle, there's three steps here," I signed and said.

"What?" Danielle objected. "Three steps?"

"Yeah, we have to go up into the cottage and it has three steps," I said and signed.

"I don't want to go in," she answered.

"You can't stay out here by yourself," I said, smiling, having known Danielle was going to object to the stairs.

I again encouraged her by saying, "Come on, let's go in, don't be a party pooper."

"I don't have to go poop!" she replied loudly. Joy, the bridesmaids, and everyone gathered all started laughing, knowing because of Danielle's deafness that she so often misunderstood things, and this was one of them.

As the big event neared, Joy had all of us move outside and sit in the chairs placed all around. While we sat around visiting, Joy put on some music. Joy well knew that Danielle could hear music somewhat, with her new digital hearing aid.

As the old song "Cherish" by The Association started to play, I got up and asked Danielle if she wanted to dance with me. To my surprise Danielle stood up and reached for me. I slowly danced her around the little concrete patio. Danielle had an amazing grin on her face and as I looked about, Joy and her bridesmaids were smiling at the two of us dancing. Joy and some of the girls even had tears flowing from their eyes because they realized just how much Danielle was missing at this special event.

After we got ready, I took Danielle to Piercy, where the wedding was to take place. At the wedding venue, Joy and Paul had rented a couple of tents and the wedding party was able to dress in them.

Joy's wedding dress was full-length white satin which laced tightly down the back. Her shoulders were exposed and she wore her hair up with baby's breath and a beautiful, perfectly placed gardenia.

As the start of the wedding drew nearer, I asked my brothers Ray and Ron if they would escort Danielle down the aisle to her seat. My mother, father, and many of my immediate family members were to be seated to the right of the wedding pair. Ray and Ron made sure Danielle was safely seated next to my mom and dad.

Joy and I got into the carriage. Yes, a beautiful, horse-drawn coach. The guests could hear the clopping of the draft horse's hooves but the carriage was purposely driven just out of view.

The venue had, in that location, a dirt path in which the horse and carriage could meander, slowly towards the expecting trove. The short trip on this path would take the bride and me about ten minutes to reach the ceremony.

I began to tell Joy the whole narrative about the day she was born. I told her how her mom would not let me leave her side. I then said how the nurse had me find another nurse because she had given up breathing. I then let her know how I went to the chapel and asked God if he would please spare the life of this beautiful baby girl of ours. Lastly, I told her how the physician stated that the fact that she was alive was truly a miracle and how close she really was to dying. We both had tears flowing from our eyes as I pulled some Kleenex out of my black tuxedo pocket.

Christian, Lamay, Aleace, and baby Nevaeh along with Becca and Stephanie, Joy's best friends and maids of honor, had been previously transported by the coach, to the venue.

Our beautiful daughter Lamay was now five months pregnant with our second grandchild. Baby Nevaeh was the flower girl and as she was only fifteen months old, Lamay found it easier to simply hold our lovely granddaughter as she threw out the hundreds of fresh rose petals along the path toward the stage.

The stout draft horse came to a halt under the huge redwood gazebo. I jumped out and helped Joy exit the carriage. I looked about the venue. It was a large grove of magnificent Redwood trees. Toward the front of this open area was a low stage made from concrete and large river rock. I looked to the stage and saw the beaming Paul and his groomsmen waiting.

I checked out the bride from head to toe and adjusted this and a little bit of that and she reached for my elbow as we stood about fifty feet from where Paul and his five groomsmen were standing.

The ceremony went flawlessly and our beautiful daughter and new son-in-law were now wed.

One beautiful, strange thing happened. Right in the middle of the ring exchange a huge yellow swallowtail butterfly fluttered all around the seated guests and eventually came to land on the shoulder of the bride. Everyone gathered there gasped out loud. Aleace, standing near her sister, the bride, uttered loud enough for most of us to hear, "Looks like our grandma came to enjoy the wedding too." It took me a few seconds, but I signed into Danielle's hands that a beautiful yellow swallowtail butterfly had just landed on Joy's shoulder.

"A butterfly?" Danielle asked quietly.

"Yes," I signed back. "A yellow one."

"That's my mom," Danielle signed.

Chapter 34

A cochlear implant helps deaf people hear. Paul and Joy had kindly driven Danielle and me to San Francisco so Danielle could have her cochlear implant turned on. The cochlear implant consists of many components, but for practical reasons, let's call them the inner workings and the outer workings.

The inner workings, the parts that were implanted earlier in Danielle's skull, behind the ear and under the skin, consist of a receiver which is linked to an electrode array. The electrode array is carefully wound through and along the damaged nerves of the spiral cochlea. When turned on, the electrodes will now stimulate these damaged nerves that were unable or unwilling to do their job naturally when stimulated by sound. Now, with the cochlear array, the nerves will be electronically stimulated.

The outer workings consist of a microphone, speech processor, and transmitter. The transmitter is held in place onto the receiver/stimulator, which is under the skin, by a magnet. The transmitter is connected to the speech processor by a thin wire. When in place the outer workings look like an over-the-ear hearing aid.

Now, with everything in place and turned on, the microphone will pick up the external sound. The sound is then sent to the speech processor. The speech processor sends the sound to the transmitter. The transmitter sends the sound to the receiver/stimulator. Finally, the receiver/stimulator sends the sound to the electrode array, which then tickles the damaged nerve hairs along the cochlea and tells the brain that it is hearing something.

The sound which the deaf person now receives from the turned-on cochlear implant is said to be somewhat mechanical in nature, but it does, with lots of practice, give the deaf person a perception of sound, which they then must learn to identify.

Paul quickly stopped in front of the concrete building to let Danielle and me out. Her handicapped placard was useless because there were no parking places anywhere close to the building.

I got out, retrieved the giant wheelchair from the back of their vehicle, opened the passenger door, and locked the wheels of the chair so I could assist Danielle carefully out of the car. I grabbed Danielle's hand and had her turn around and into the cushy seat and quickly moved her away from the vehicle and closed the door.

Paul and Joy waved good-bye as they began their adventure in looking for the elusive perfect parking place here in the giant, busy streets of the up and down city of downtown San Francisco.

I rolled Danielle and the big wheelchair onto the sidewalk and realized I was really glad I brought the chair because this sidewalk had many of those pushed-up cracks in it which are always hateful obstacles when trying to walk Danielle along.

"UCSF Department of Otolaryngology - Head and Neck Center," the sign read as we approached the newly reconstructed building on Sutter Street.

The building was cold and proud looking, as it stood stoically greeting its many patrons. It seemed to laugh at me as I began to fight the sturdy steel-rimmed glass door leading into its lobby.

"There's got to be an easier way to do this," I said out loud and to myself as I strained to hold the oversized thick glass door open and simultaneously push Danielle in with her gigantic wheelchair.

I backed us out and turned around to face Danielle toward the street thinking I'd attack the door with my butt, holding the glass door open as I charged Danielle and her ample chair and me into the lobby.

A very strong man in a white lab coat who apparently watched my losing battle was kind enough to help me defeat that unwilling door. "Thank you," I feebly mumbled as I was already very frustrated that I couldn't find the stupid blue handicapped door opener thingy that was supposed to be hanging on the outside of the building somewhere near the front.

I rolled Danielle in and parked her and her shopping cart–sized wheelchair facing the lobby. I backed it up against the wall so I could sit down in a chair beside her and sign to her while we waited.

Joy and Paul sauntered into the building about ten minutes after Danielle and I had taken our place. "Were you able to find a good parking place?" I asked the perky couple.

"No, we had to park three blocks away and it looks like we will have to go back and move the car if we are here longer than an hour," Joy said. "We went to Starbucks and got you guys some coffee," she said as she and Paul handed us our drinks.

They sat near us so we could wait and talk to Danielle. Joy was keen on getting her mom to understand her since Joy was an excellent finger speller and would spell into Danielle's practiced hands.

"Where are we?" Danielle asked Joy. I was kinda bent out of shape thinking Danielle had asked Joy and not me.

"PA-SAYS-YOU-HAVE-BEEN-HERE-BEFORE," Joy spelled and spoke into Danielle's waiting hands.

"Oh," Danielle responded. "I forgot," she signed back to Joy. I think Danielle was just trying to think of something to ask Joy so they could have something to talk about while we waited.

We had waited about fifteen minutes when Dr. Colleen, a really beautiful, petite woman in her late thirties, with straight black shoulder-length hair and high heels, opened a door that led from another section of the lobby and gracefully walked over to Danielle.

Dr. Colleen stooped down eye to eye and signed into Danielle's experienced hands, "How are you doing today?" I stepped back, hypnotized, watching those fluidic, poetic hand movements. I was happy, smiling inwardly, grateful that this nice, beautiful person could also speak to my dearly beloved wife.

"No way," signed Danielle at one of our many previous appointments in San Francisco as I told her she'd have to undergo surgery so the doctors could implant the internal workings of the cochlear implant. After much convincing and promises and chocolate, she finally consented.

Today, at last, Joy, Paul, Danielle, and I were back in San Francisco for the final step in getting the cochlear implant. I was so overjoyed I could barely contain myself.

Dr. Colleen led the way as Danielle and her team followed the leader down the hall and to her secret room filled with gadgets, gizmos, and lights. Joy and Paul went into the room first, followed by me and Danielle and her motor-home-sized wheelchair. I carefully rolled Danielle and the colossal chair next to where Dr. Colleen was seated.

Dr. Colleen had always been so very kind to us. Joy introduced herself and Paul to Dr. Colleen. The doctor was genuinely pleased to finally have met one of Danielle's four children.

"Your mother has told me so much about you and your siblings," said the beautiful doctor.

"We're so excited that this day has finally come," Joy said enthusiastically.

"Yes, I'm very excited too," said Dr. Colleen.

Dr. Colleen placed the external unit on Danielle's ear, plugged it into one of the gadgets on her desk, and said, "Here we go," and turned it on. We all held our breath.

Danielle never even winced. We looked at Dr. Colleen, thinking something was terribly wrong, and she said to us, "We have to start out very slowly or Danielle could be overwhelmed by all the noise.

"Jack," the doctor said to me as she handed me a small, thin gizmo. "This is a handheld controller which controls the implant. The more Danielle uses the implant the better she will get at hearing sounds. To her the sound will not be exactly as we hear it, but the sound will soon become recognizable to her."

Dr. Colleen then gave hugs and encouragement and detailed instructions as to how she wanted me to slowly increase the volume, "at a snail's pace," she said, of the implant over the course of the coming months. Danielle and I were then rolled out into the lobby, followed by Paul and Joy, and then sent home.

We left the Cochlear Implant Center on Sutter Street that gorgeous, happy day in San Francisco and were told to practice listening and to attempt to use the new device as much as possible.

Joy, being a coffee connoisseur, asked if we'd like to grab another coffee at the Starbucks before we left the enormous city. Luckily, Paul found a parking place just down the street from the tiny Starbucks. He parked, we all got out, and I pushed Danielle down the street and watched her carefully, hoping she might hear something now that her new cochlear implant was turned on.

I also had to watch out for foot traffic as it seemed that it was lunch time and everybody and their dog was out trying to find some lunch.

I skillfully maneuvered the giant wheelchair as a seriously pudgy lady walked toward us with loud, clacking, noisy high-heeled shoes.

"What's that sound?" Danielle asked of Joy. We all were mesmerized that Danielle had heard something unusual.

"That's a lady walking by in high-heeled shoes," Joy said.

"High-heeled shoes?" Danielle asked loudly.

Joy signed into her hands, "Yes."

Danielle made a face and voiced, "That's weird."

One glorious sultry evening many months after our last trip to the big city with Joy and her handsome groom, Paul, I got home from work and slid open the patio door, leaving the screen door closed in hopes to keep out those hateful, pesky, springtime flies.

While I was preparing dinner, in the corner of my eye, I caught Danielle exhibiting unusual head movements that made me pay closer attention and watch her more intently than usual.

Danielle was moving her head about in odd directions as though trying to figure out something quite puzzling. The more closely I watched, the more obvious it was to me that she was really hearing something.

As hearing people, we hear sounds which we know are unimportant for us at that moment. Perhaps we can hear the neighbor mowing their lawn next door or a garbage truck outside picking up garbage. As hearing people, we filter out these random sounds and know that they are not sounds we need to acknowledge right now to make our life work and stay organized.

But, if you have never heard before, every sound seems important.

I now, consciously, seriously began to focus again on what Danielle might be trying to hear at this very moment, at this time, in this place. When I finally realized what she was hearing, I was greatly overcome. To my wonder and amazement, the loudest, most beautiful white-crowned sparrow song that I had ever heard was coming through the screen door from the patio railing just outside.

I again turned to watch Danielle and just observed how she might react to finally hearing one of God's most beloved, joyful sounds that He has given to us on this beautiful green earth.

"Jack," Danielle voiced as countless tears streamed down my unseen face.

"What?" I answered quietly.

Danielle signed, "What's that noise?"

I was overcome. I was awestruck. I was profoundly moved. I walked over to her, seated at the dining room table, and signed into her waiting hands, "That sound is a bird singing."

"A bird singing?" she signed back with her usual eloquent hand movements, and my heart filled with wonder. "It sure makes a lot of noise," she voiced.

Chapter 35

Lamay called and asked if Danielle and I could watch Nevaeh.

"Pa, I've been in labor for a few hours and I think we'd better go to the hospital," Lamay said on the telephone. I stopped by their house in Scotia and picked up our beautiful granddaughter, Nevaeh.

"Call me when the baby is born," I told them as Danielle and I drove away.

It was early October when our amazingly handsome first grandson arrived. His dad called me as soon as he was born. I asked Wayne, "How much does the baby weigh?"

"I don't know, they haven't weighed him yet."

"You're a fisherman," I said, "how much do you think he weighs?"

Just as fishermen usually overestimate the size of their catch, Daddy Wayne looked him over cautiously and said, "He looks about eight pounds."

Ray weighed in at 7 pounds 9 ounces and was 21 inches long.

The proud couple stopped by our house the next day to pick up Nevaeh, and Danielle was able to go outside with me to feel the new baby boy.

She felt his tiny baby arms. She felt his soft, round baby head. Once again, I became very emotional, tears rolling out of my eyes as I watched Danielle try so very hard to imagine with her hands what our beautiful grandson might look like.

We said good-bye to the new parents. I could see our nineteen-month-old granddaughter, Nevaeh, waving bye-bye to us from the back seat as they drove away. "Danielle," I signed and said as we stood there in the driveway.

"Yeah?" Danielle answered.

"Nevaeh waved bye-bye to you."

Danielle cried tears of happiness as she waved back to our beloved granddaughter.

I led Danielle into the house and Danielle sat in her favorite love seat. "Jack," Danielle asked, "who does baby Ray look like?" The fact that she couldn't see our grandchildren was so painful to me that I even found it hard to answer those questions without feeling great remorse.

"He looks so much like Lamay when she was born," I signed and said into her hands.

"He looks like Lamay?" Danielle echoed.

"Yep, but he looks like he's going to be naturally more muscular," I added.

"What color are his eyes?" she inquired curiously.

"Right now, they look kinda hazel-blue, but all babies' eyes change color," I reminded her.

"What color is his hair?"

"It looks reddish brown," I said.

"Reddish-brown?"

"Yeah," I answered. "Do you remember seeing Wayne's beard before you went blind?" I asked.

"Yeah," Danielle recalled, it was kinda red and brown."

"That color," I stated.

"I wish I could see them," Danielle said to me.

"I know, Punky," I said tearfully. "I know."

"Pa," Alease said to me one day while we were on the phone, "I talked with Joy and we want to send you and Mom to Hawaii for your thirty-third anniversary."

"Hawaii?" I answered surprisingly. "Your mom would love that. You know you don't need to do this, right?" I said.

"We know, Pa, but Mom has always wanted to go to Hawaii. You know that."

Aleace called my brother, Ray, and sister-in-law, Carrie, and asked if they might be in a position to go to Hawaii with Danielle and me.

Danielle loved Ray. Ray is the kind of man who is naturally clever. This cleverness shows itself with a great sense of humor. Danielle loved talking to Ray because he made himself understood even though he knew little to no sign language. Danielle was so comfortable around Ray that if I wasn't around and Danielle had to use the restroom or go from one room to the other, Ray was always one to step up and carefully lead Danielle to where she needed to go.

Ray and Carrie, along with our nephews, Raymond and Louis, made plans to go with us to Hawaii for our anniversary. Danielle was so excited. Ray talked with Aleace several times and Aleace got all the plans and itinerary set up for our adventure.

Sharon and Dave Blalack, our neighbors, said they would watch Sunny for us while we were gone for the week. Sharon visited Danielle at least once a week and Danielle loved her like a sister.

Danielle and I rented a car and drove to San Francisco. We hopped on a Hawaiian Airlines flight to Kauai and arrived near evening.

Alease had made reservations for Danielle and me to stay one night at a beautiful hotel near Kapaa. We rented a van for the week we would be there, and it was plenty big enough for Ray's family, Danielle, and me.

I must have driven in circles because I asked for directions several times, but kept on ending up at the same place. It's very difficult for me to drive to a new place because it's as though I'm driving alone. Danielle, being blind, cannot assist when looking for road signs and any other landmarks.

Finally, at around 9 p.m., I found the hotel. It should have taken us less than an hour to get from the airport to the hotel, but it ended up being closer to three hours. Look at the bright side, I now can find our hotel if we ever go back.

The Hotel Coral Reef was very luxurious. Aleace made sure there was a beautiful tropical bouquet of flowers in the room waiting for us, along with a bottle of Martinelli's sparkling cider. Danielle was on top of the world. The bed even had a down-filled comforter which made Danielle feel pampered.

Ray and his family were supposed to fly in the next day about midday, so Danielle and I had a leisurely morning. We took a stroll around the hotel. The gardens were fantastic and immense.

I described to Danielle the beautiful, tropical plants. I had her feel some of the tropical flowers that grew there. She'd grab hold and smell each one as I took her hand and showed her where the flower was. It was hard to express in words just how amazingly beautiful the grounds were around the hotel. "I wish I could see," she said softly. Try as I might, explaining everything to Danielle is greatly colored by the fact that she can't see.

Ray rented a vacation rental by owner house near the Hanalei Bay near Princeville on the north shore of Kauai. I was given instructions as to how I was supposed to retrieve the key to the rental. I went to the VRBO about 10:30 in the morning. The prior tenants were still there when Danielle and I drove up.

"We're so sorry," the blonde, middle-aged lady told me as she came out to see why I was parked in the driveway. "We're running a little late," she said quietly. "We should be out in a couple of hours."

"What did she say?" Danielle asked me.

"They should be out in a couple of hours," I repeated.

"That's rude," was all Danielle said.

Danielle and I drove back to the airport to pick up Ray, Carrie, and the boys. Danielle wanted to stay in the van. She looked so pleased with herself. She had the window rolled down and was just feeling the warm tropical breeze as I found a shaded parking spot to park in. "Don't speak to anybody," I warned her as I left my beautiful bride seated in the van.

Ray's plane was fifteen minutes late.

"Let's get something to eat," Ray said as he took the helm with Danielle sitting in the front passenger seat.

"Is that you, Ray?" Danielle asked as Ray got in the driver's seat.

"No," he said, "I'm Joe, I'm going to be your chauffeur for the entire time you are in Hawaii."

"Oh, Ray," Danielle said.

Danielle turned toward the back seat and said, "Hi, Carrie."

"Hi, Danielle, how are you?" Carrie said as Ray started driving us to the north shore.

We got to the VRBO house and Ray and I got the key and went in to check out the house while Danielle, Carrie, and the boys stayed in the van.

"Why are there so many stairs?" I asked Ray as I counted them as we ascended.

"I guess it's the new building code that the new houses have to be ramped up on these tall stilts just in case of a storm surge," he said.

"Danielle's not going to be a happy camper," I said to Ray.

"She'll get used to them," he said. I was hopeful.

We checked out the house and went back to the van to get everybody out and take in the luggage. Carrie and the boys grabbed a lot of their stuff and headed up into the house.

I grabbed Danielle and told her that the house was beautiful. "There's a lanai all the way around the house. There's chairs and tables so we can sit outside and enjoy ourselves," I told her. "But," I said and signed with caution. "There's one little problem."

"What?" she asked quietly.

I slowly signed and said, "There's thirty-two stairs that we have to climb up."

Danielle stood there thinking. She was speechless. She finally said, softly, "Did you say thirty-two stairs?"

"Yeah," I answered.

"Shit," was all she signed.

Danielle and I climbed the Mount Everest of Kauai and finally made it into the house. Danielle felt all about the kitchen, which had a granite breakfast bar. There were couches and comfy chairs around the living room and the view of the ocean was spectacular.

"Can you see the ocean from here?" Danielle asked.

"It's beautiful, Danielle," Carrie replied.

Everybody found their rooms and I had Danielle lie down for a little while until I got all the luggage brought up to this beautiful, three-bedroom, two-bath house on stilts. Danielle was exhausted and was sleeping by the time I brought everything that we needed up to the house.

"What are we going to do for dinner?" Carrie asked those of us gathered in the living room.

I looked at Ray. Ray and Carrie love coming to Hawaii. It's easily the happiest place on earth for their family. Ray knows all the yummy restaurants and street vendors here on Kauai.

"Why don't we grab something that we can eat here at the house so Danielle doesn't have to climb all those stairs anymore today. Maybe after her nap, she'll want to walk to the beach or something," Ray said.

Ray looked at me and said, "We should have thought about all those stairs coming up in this house when we were looking for the perfect VRBO."

"I was just so happy to be coming to Kauai it never even occurred to me," I answered.

We had a few adventures planned for this vacation. We were planning on riding inner tubes through an old coffee plantation, riding an all-terrain six-wheeled vehicle through the Kauai back country, and horseback riding on the north shore of the island. We also planned on visiting Poipu Beach, Hanalei Bay, and Kapaa as part of our Kauai trip itinerary.

I went into our bedroom. Danielle was calling me. "Yes, Punkin Pie, did you want something?" I signed into her hands.

I was looking at her hearing aid and cochlear implant on the nightstand so I knew speaking was not going to help much.

"Where are we?" Danielle asked. "I have to go to the bathroom."

I helped Danielle up and took her to our own bathroom, which was connected to our beautiful room. As she was on the throne, I grabbed her hearing aid and helped her put it on.

"Yeah?" she said groggily as the aid squealed once she had it turned on.

"We're in Hawaii, don't you remember?" I said and signed.

"Yeah, I remember," Danielle answered, still groggy.

Danielle was still sedated with all her medications due to her mental illness. Although the medicine, Zyprexa, was working, it didn't take away all of the issues that she was facing. It was up to me, Cathy Silver said, to keep

Danielle sedated just enough where she could enjoy life but still not want to talk to the dreaded "Irene from Iraq."

Danielle took frequent naps. It was good and well that Ray and his family were here. All of us combined could keep Danielle engaged in conversation. "What?" was a word that we often heard Danielle repeat when the bunch of us were conversing.

Our sister-in-law Carrie, was always so patient with Danielle. Carrie learned a few signs, but her voice, if Danielle listened carefully with both the aid and the implant on, was a voice that Danielle could understand most of the time. Oftentimes Carrie would lead Danielle to the restroom while we were out and about on Kauai. I could hear Danielle asking Carrie questions and really trying to carry on a conversation.

It was Sunday and Carrie had picked a special church for us to go to, to celebrate Mass.

"St. William Mission Catholic Church," was what the sign read as we all got out of the van to go in. It took some time for us to get into the church because the walk around the church was mostly grass and Danielle couldn't walk on spongy grass very well.

Ray took Danielle's left arm and I was on the right.

"Where are we going?" Danielle asked.

I looked at Ray and he looked at me. "Why didn't you tell your wife we were going to Mass?" Ray said.

"I thought I did," I answered Ray.

"Well, obviously you didn't," he let me know.

When we are together Ray is always the boss. This dynamic stems from the fact that Ray and I are eleven months apart. I was born with severe nearsightedness. Ray was born with perfect vision. When we were four and five years old, I would ask Ray many, many questions. "What does the moon look like? Can you really see the stars in the sky? What does Mr. Willie Mays look like?" All these questions Ray would answer by showing me pictures in books or newspapers.

Ray was always clever that way. "Ray, what do mountains look like?" I asked one day.

Ray grabbed a book out of our set of encyclopedias and found a picture of Mount Fuji. "Look," he said, "that's a mountain." Even today, every time I think of mountains, I think of the beautiful, snowcapped Mount Fuji.

We had to sit in the back of the church because there was standing room only. I wasn't aware that there were so many people here on the north shore in May.

I noticed some musicians near the front of the church but because we arrived right at 9 a.m., I wasn't able to hear them warm up. Since I play guitar and sing at Mass, I usually am very curious as to the kind of music that would be played during Mass. Perhaps it would be a guitar Mass, maybe they would be playing the piano, maybe they might even have a full choir. I was in for a huge surprise.

The head musician said, "All stand," as the music began. Hawaiian music; the whole assembly was singing in Hawaiian. I was deeply moved. Carrie looked at me as though to say, "Beautiful, huh." I cried throughout all the music choices. Not only was the whole Mass music done in Hawaiian, but many of the responses were also in Hawaiian. With Danielle at my side, holding my left elbow, my brother and his family with us, I would find that this day would never be far from my thoughts. If only coming to Mass today and hearing the beautiful Hawaiian music was what we had come to Kauai for, I would be satisfied.

One day on Poipu Beach, while Carrie went snorkeling and Ray and the boys swam, Danielle sat on the beach. I walked up to her. She looked so cute. She was sitting on a blanket with a beautiful tan colored sun hat on and a short-sleeved blouse. She was content.

Danielle was just enjoying the beautiful Hawaiian day. While I watched, wild baby chicks were pecking around where she sat. I could see her hearing something, but she wasn't sure what it was. We had found a place where she could sit out of the sun so she wouldn't get sunburned.

I sat next to Danielle and she reached over to feel who this might be. "Who are you?" she said and signed.

"I'm your boyfriend," I joked.

I could see the wheels turning in her head as she said, "Brad Pitt?"

"Nope, sorry," I answered, "guess again."

"John Travolta," she said.

"Almost," I said. Danielle knew that when we were young many people would often say I reminded them of John Travolta. "Sorry," I said, "it's only little ol' me, the man who loves you." I then put my hand in her hand with the sign for "I love you." Danielle signed back, "I love you more."

"Danielle, the water looks so beautiful here, let's get up so we can put our feet in the water."

"I don't want to," she said softly.

"Why not? It's such a beautiful day here in Hawaii. Come on," I insisted. "We're not going to be in Hawaii too much longer and don't you want to tell the kids that you went into the water a little bit?" I said and signed.

"All right," she reluctantly said.

I stood her up and we slowly walked to the water. The water was probably seventy degrees, possibly more, as I gently forced Danielle into the delightful moisture-laden foam. I kinda had to pull Danielle around in the water because she kept up quite a bit of resistance against my arm. "Come on, Danielle, stop pulling on my arm, just walk with me," I insisted. She continued to pull against me as I could see she really was trying to enjoy herself.

"Danielle?"

"What!" she said.

"Just let me lead you around," I said. I suddenly looked up and not eight feet away from us was a striking Hawaiian sea turtle just floating close by. By the looks of it, I'd guess that it was about four or five feet long.

"Danielle," I said.

"What?" she cautiously responded.

"There's a giant sea turtle close by us."

"Really?" she said. "I wish I could see."

"I know, Punky, I'm so sorry you can't see anymore," I said, with tears in my eyes.

"What does it look like?" she asked.

"It's so beautiful. It has a hard greenish-brown shell and kinda green and brown dotted flippers and it has sad brown eyes," I answered.

"Poor thing," Danielle said.

"Danielle, stop pulling against me and just walk with me in the water," I said again with irritation. Danielle always allowed me to lead without hesitation. A few minutes passed by as I scanned the beautiful Hawaiian scenery. Looking to the ocean I could see way out in the distance puffy rain clouds. Inland I could see green plants and trees lavishly dancing all the way up the many mountains. Oh, what a magnificent place. I wished Danielle could see it.

"I'm scared," she said softly.

"What did you just say?" I asked, as the gentle waves continued to make their relaxing swooshing sound.

Danielle said again, louder this time, "I'm scared."

"You're scared?" I asked.

"Yes," she said.

"What are you afraid of?" I asked.

"I'm afraid a shark is going to eat me," she responded.

"A SHARK?" I asked in disbelief.

"Yeah, a big shark," she said.

I looked down into the water and started laughing because the water was just barely covering her ankles.

"Sugar bear," I said.

"What?" Danielle responded with a frightened look on her face.

"The water is just up to your ankles."

"What?" she asked.

"The water is only up to your ankles," I again informed her.

"Please, let's get out of the water," she said forcefully.

I was entirely oblivious that I was tormenting my love, so once again, because I was sighted and she was blind, I was hurting my precious.

I quickly walked Danielle out of the ocean. As I put Danielle back down on the blanket on the beach I said, "Danielle, I'm sorry I didn't think about you being scared of sharks while we were in the water."

"That's okay, you didn't know."

The following day we were going to ride an all-terrain vehicle. Four people took up the seats in the back of the vehicle and Danielle sat in the only passenger seat next to the driver.

"Danielle?" I said as the driver watched me sign to Danielle after having helped her into the seat. "You are going to ride around with the driver, and me and Ray and Carrie and the boys are going to be in the back," I stated.

"Fine," she signed.

The whole day was filled with amazement. We stopped to view the rainiest, wettest mountain on all the islands. Mount Waialeale averages 450 inches of rainfall a year. We also stopped by several interesting landmarks, many of which were sacred to the Hawaiians.

We drove by miles and miles of coffee plantations and for lunch we stopped at a stunningly beautiful lanai-covered area with several picnic benches.

Ray took the boys for a walk. Carrie went exploring down by the river, and I took Danielle to the restroom.

When Danielle was first blind, when she had to go to the restroom, I would wait to find some nice lady who was walking into the girls' bathroom and I would ask her if she would be so kind as to take my deaf/blind wife with her to use the facilities. On one occasion when we were at Macy's in Santa Rosa, Danielle said, "I have to go to the bathroom."

We walked over to where the bathrooms were located. The women's bathroom was on the right and the men's door was on the left. As was customary, I stood near the women's door and waited, and we waited, and we waited. We had waited about five minutes when Danielle blurted out, "I really have to go now," she said.

"Now?" I asked incredulously.

"Yes, right now!" she said.

I looked around harder. Inside Macy's it looked like a ghost town.

I made a difficult decision. I grabbed her hand in my left elbow, then paraded her through the men's bathroom door. "Is anyone in here?" I asked meekly.

"Forget about anybody else," Danielle said, "I have to go now!"

From that time on, any time Danielle had to go to the restroom, I'd take her into the men's facilities.

One time we were at Sears in Eureka and Danielle had to go. I took her with me into the men's bathroom and there was some old geezer in there using one of the urinals. He looked over at us and said hatefully, "You can't bring her in here."

"She's blind," I quipped.

"She's blind?" He ruminated on this, as Danielle and I sauntered past him and into one of the stalls.

We finished our all-terrain tour of Kauai and most of us were really hungry. Ray drove us to a restaurant near Hanalei Bay and we had a delicious dinner and a great time.

We finally went to bed. In the middle of the night I heard Ray say, "Jack?"

"Yeah," I responded sleepily.

"Danielle got up to go to the bathroom, but ended up coming into our room," he stated simply.

"Oh, sorry," I said.

"Not a problem," he said as he led her back to our bed.

Danielle, it seemed, was easily confused as to where we were most of the time. I told her on several occasions to wake me up during the night so I could take her to the bathroom, but it seemed she often thought we were at our house instead.

Our Hawaiian trip was now behind us as we rode the Hawaiian Airlines plane home. Danielle said that she had a great time just before falling asleep on the plane.

"Now you can tell Sharon and your other friends that you got to go to Hawaii and how brave you were when you had to climb all those stairs and how a shark almost ate you when we were in the ocean," I joked. My bride did not answer; she was sound asleep.

Chapter 36

Joy and Paul came by the house shortly after we got home to ask Danielle if she had a great time. "Wasn't Hawaii beautiful, Mom?" Joy asked and signed into Danielle's waiting hands. Paul and Joy had already taken a trip to Kauai the year before and they loved it.

"Yeah," Danielle answered, "but there's too many stairs."

"What?" Joy asked with a quizzical look on her face, "Did you say there's too many stairs?"

"Yeah, in Hawaii, there's too many stairs," Danielle said.

Danielle had always been direct and to the point. *No playing around here*, I thought. Joy looked at me, wondering if Danielle misspoke.

"Pa, what does Mom mean, too many stairs?" Joy asked me with a questioning expression on her face.

"Your mom was a little bit bent out of shape the whole time we were there because our VRBO house had thirty-two steps that we had to climb," I said.

"Why were there so many steps?" she asked.

"Ray said he heard that on the north shore of Kauai sometimes in the wintertime the storms are so violent that the building code for any new construction is that the house must be built on stilts," I answered.

Joy bent down to Danielle's eye level and signed lovingly into her hands. "Mom, I have something important to tell you."

"What?" Danielle responded.

Joy signed slowly, "Paul and I are going to have a baby."

"What?" Danielle said.

"Paul and I are going to have a baby," she said again with a huge smile on her face.

"You're going to have a baby?" Danielle echoed.

"Yes." Danielle reached for Joy and gave her a giant hug and said, "Oh, Joy, I'm so excited for you!" Danielle beamed.

It was summertime and I wanted to take Danielle down to Los Angeles to visit my family. I also had another project I was hoping to accomplish while we were down there.

We drove up to my parents' home and I got Danielle out of the car and walked her up to the house. My mom answered the door, kissed Danielle, and Danielle said, "I have to go to the bathroom."

I took Danielle to the back-bedroom's bathroom because my dad was occupying the front one. Danielle knew the layout of my mom and dad's house so once we were in there, Danielle could be left alone and she wouldn't get lost.

I then walked back to the front bathroom and the door was ajar. I slowly pushed open the bathroom door and my dad was sitting on the throne, fully clothed. He looked at me. I hadn't seen him in several years and he was really showing his age now.

My brother Ray lives a few blocks from our parents' home. My mom found herself having to call Ray several times a week to come and pick up my dad because he had fallen or needed some other kind of help. Ray is so kind.

"Do you know who I am?" I asked my dad as he peered at me from the toilet. I thought he was going to say no, but after a minute he said, "Jackson?" My dad might not be as fast as he used to be, but he still remembered me.

Ray and Carrie came to visit and we sat around the living room just visiting and enjoying each other's company.

Ray went into the kitchen. Danielle was sitting on a soft, comfy chair right next to the kitchen's doorway. As Ray walked back out of the kitchen and by Danielle, being the jokester that he is, he stopped right there in the doorway and gently grabbed Danielle's nose. Danielle immediately knew it was Ray.

"Ray, let go of my nose," she said with a big smile on her face. It was so cute because Danielle's voice sounded funny, like she had a cold.

Ray smiled when just then Danielle took her left arm and swung it right in the direction where Ray was standing. Danielle being blind, had no idea where her swing would land. POW, Danielle hit Ray right in his Mr. Happy and the twins. Ray cringed and all of us laughed because Danielle had no idea she was going to hit him there. Ray doubled over and then carefully let go of Danielle's nose and walked into the living room, taking a seat next to me on the couch.

I searched the massive Los Angeles County phone book and wrote down several addresses that I hoped would be productive for my latest ploy.

Danielle, my mom, dad, and I drove around Los Angeles County looking for the perfect one for Danielle. The first place I got to, I told Danielle and my parents to wait in the car while I went in and took a look around.

I came back in a few minutes, and my mom, knowing my reason for today's trip, said, "Any luck?"

"Nothing," I answered.

I then drove to another place. Nothing was there either.

We eventually drove to Whittier, which is about an hour away from my parents' house.

"What are you doing here?" Danielle asked me as I got out of the car for the third time.

"I'm going in here for a minute, if they have what I'm looking for, I'll come back and get you." I told her.

Danielle looked bent out of shape as I smiled at her annoyance and walked into the animal shelter.

I came back and told Danielle, "I found something. I want you to come and look at it and find out if you want it," I said.

"What is it?" she asked.

"Danielle, it's a surprise," I answered.

"I don't like surprises," she said.

"I think you will like this one," I assured her. "Come on, pleeeeease?" I begged.

I led Danielle into the building and she said, "What's all that noise?"

"That noise?" I said as she turned down her hearing aid. "That's a bunch of dogs barking," I said.

"Dogs?" Danielle asked.

"Yes," I answered. "I think I might have found a new dog for you."

"A new dog?" Danielle asked excitedly.

"Yes," I said. "Come on." I led her out into the kennel area where the attendant already had the dog in an enclosed area with a bench seat where Danielle could hold the cute little bundle of fur.

The attendant handed me the dog and I placed her in Danielle's waiting hands. Danielle began fingering every nook and cranny of this bundle of cuteness. "Jack? Is it a girl?" Danielle asked.

"Yes," I answered.

"What color is she?" Danielle asked.

"She's a silky-terrier mix. She has a grayish body with white around her neck."

"She has gray and white hair?" Danielle asked.

"Yep," I responded.

Danielle felt her little paws. She stretched out her tail. She felt her ears and then brought the gentle dog up to her face and kissed it. "How old is she?" she asked.

"One," I said.

"I want her!"

The shelter said that she wasn't spayed yet and that they could do it tomorrow and said if we paid for her now, we could pick her up tomorrow afternoon.

I took Danielle back to the car, but before she gave up holding the dog, she kissed her again.

"Did you find what you were looking for?" asked my mom from the back seat.

"Yep," I answered. "They want us to pay for her now and come back tomorrow to pick her up after they spay her."

"Your father and I want to take care of the costs of the dog, for Danielle," my mom said.

"Say, say?" Danielle signed.

"My mom wants to buy your little dog for you," I answered.

"Mom wants to buy my dog for me?" Danielle questioned.

"Yep," I said.

Danielle turned to the back seat of our car and said out loud, "Thank you, Mom."

"You're welcome. We just love helping you guys whenever we can," said my mom.

It's always nice to get my parents out of the house, since they don't drive anymore. Going on a road trip, for them, was always an adventure.

We went back to the shelter the next day to pick up Danielle's new dog.

"She just got back from the vet," the attendant said. "She's very groggy." She then brought out Danielle's droopy new dog and carefully handed her to me. "Make sure she doesn't eat for a few hours," said the attendant."

"Okay," I promised. I walked back to the car and handed Danielle her pooped out pup.

I got back into the car and started driving back to my parents' house. "Danielle, what shall we name her?" I said and signed into her hands while trying to drive on the freeway with thousands upon thousands of other crazy drivers.

"I don't know." Danielle signed back.

"Hey, Mom?"

"Yeah," she sounded from the back seat.

"Why don't you name her since you bought her?" I said out loud.

I looked in the rearview mirror and watched my mom as the wheels began to turn in her brain. "She so cute, let me think about it," she said as I dodged and weaved through cars on that crazy freeway.

My mom leaned over and touched Danielle on the shoulder. "Danielle?" my mom said. "Do you like the name Cheena?"

Danielle heard her loud and clear. Danielle seemed to always hear better while we were in the car. Danielle repeated, "Cheena?"

"Yes," my mom said.

"What's that mean?" Danielle asked.

"In Spanish it means curly hair," she said. "When I was a little girl, I knew a girl named Cheena and she had a lot of curly hair."

Danielle ruminated on the name for a few minutes and then said, "I love it. Cheena," Danielle said, "let's name her Cheena. Thank you, Mom." Danielle beamed.

Joy visited Danielle often. It seemed that being pregnant had given Joy some introspection and she wanted to be around her mom asking questions and wanting to know how we dealt with the challenges of raising four kids.

"We're headed to the hospital, Pa," Joy said in a phone call I received at work. "I'll call you when we know more."

Paul called later and said that they had just had a baby boy. "Is it okay if I bring Danielle over to see him?" I asked.

"My mom and Scott are coming in about an hour, do you want to come over about the same time?" he asked.

"Sure, we'll see you in an hour," I said.

I gathered Danielle up. She was so excited. We drove to Redwood Memorial Hospital in Fortuna and walked up to the maternity unit.

We rang the doorbell. "Yes, can I help you?" answered a female voice through the speaker.

"I was hoping to see Joy and Paul and their new baby."

"Are you a relation?" the nurse asked.

"A proud grandma and grandpa," I answered.

She pressed the buzzer and we walked through the double doors marked "PUSH." I learned from going to the UCSF Department of Otolaryngology that if I had to push the door open and I was pushing Danielle in her wheelchair, I would always use my derriere to push open the door and then I could pull Danielle through it backwards.

I started pushing Danielle down the hall when I saw a man with a smile from ear to ear holding a precious gift from God. "Hi, Paul," I said as Danielle and I approached.

"Come on in," he said.

"Hi, Mom," Joy called from the bed.

"Hello, Joooyyy!" Danielle always said the kids' names in a singsong voice when she was extremely happy. "How's your baby?"

"Super amazing," Joy said as I pushed Danielle next to Joy's bed.

Danielle and Joy talked while I looked at Paul, who was holding the newborn. I don't know why, but when I see my grandchildren for the first time, tears well up in my eyes and start rolling down my cheeks. "He's really very beautiful," I said to Paul.

"Paul," Joy said, "I want my mom to hold my baby."

"Have Danielle clean her hands, then put her in that chair in the corner," Paul said to me, matter-of-factly.

When Danielle was all sterilized and seated comfortably, Paul placed our second grandson in Danielle's waiting arms.

Danielle tenderly felt the contours of that beautiful baby's face. She felt the softness of his newborn head and asked, "Jack, does he have any hair?"

"Not very much, he looks like Joy did when she was born," I answered.

"Who does he look like?" Danielle asked.

"I think he looks like Paul's brother Jeremy," I answered.

"And he looks like you too, Pa," Joy added.

"What's his name?" Danielle asked as she looked in the direction of Joy.

"Carnegie," Joy responded.

"What?" Danielle asked me. I spelled C-A-R-N-E-G-I-E into Danielle's free hand. "I never heard that name before," Danielle said.

"That's Paul's family name on his dad's side," I told her.

"Oh, Carnegie," she said. Carnegie weighed 7 pounds 14 ounces and was 19 inches long.

I looked at Joy. She was crying. "What's wrong?" I signed to Joy.

"I want my mom to see my baby," she signed back.

"I know, mija, I do too," I signed tearfully.

Cheena was the best hearing dog ever. It took about two weeks for her to learn the ropes of hearing-dogdom. Sunny was a good teacher, so I can't take all the credit.

Sunny liked sleeping at the foot of the loveseat while Cheena was a natural lapdog. Cheena didn't exactly sleep on Danielle's lap. Cheena loved sleeping on Danielle's chest.

Any time Danielle had to go to the restroom, Cheena would jump down and follow Danielle. Any time Danielle got up to go to the dining room table, Cheena would sit near Danielle's feet. Cheena was truly an amazing working dog. If there were awards given out for dogs who really love their masters, Cheena would win the blue ribbon.

Lamay often found time to come to visit Danielle while I was working. This not only pleased Danielle immensely, but it also helped me not to worry about her down time and helped prevent her from going back into her mind and start talking with the dreaded "you know who."

When Lamay visited, she would bring Nevaeh and Ray. Danielle loved her grandchildren more than anything. Nevaeh, now four years old, would run up to Danielle, who was lying on the love seat, and say, "Hi, Grandma, guess who I am?"

"Um, Cinderella?" Danielle would say.

"No, guess again."

"Sweet Pea?" A nickname Danielle had always had for Lamay.

"Nope. Guess again."

"Could it be my beautiful Nevaeh?"

"Yes, Gramma, I'm Nevaeh."

"I love you, Nevaeh," Danielle would say in her singsong voice.

"I love you, Gramma," Nevaeh would say as she sat on Danielle's legs and played and joked around with her.

"Is Ray here too?" Danielle would ask.

"Yeah, he's right here," and Nevaeh would jump off the love seat and pick him up under the arms and bring him to her.

Ray, two years old, would reach for Danielle and kiss her. Danielle would love him back.

Tricia was Danielle's Special Needs Trust trustee. A special needs trust was set up by Danielle's loving parents with the foresight to Danielle's well-being, just in case I died or became incapacitated.

A special needs trust helps the handicapped person by setting up a trust that could be executed by a trustee. This trust lets the trustee help the handicapped person purchase important items. It also keeps the funds unavailable to the handicapped person in case a foreign entity should try to sue or deviously steal the handicapped person's money.

Danielle asked me to call Tricia one day and ask her if there was enough money in the trust to buy a new couch and loveseat.

I called Tricia "How's Danielle doing?" asked the kind trustee. "I think about Danielle and you all the time and always hope you guys are doing okay."

"With a trustee like you," I said, "we can't help but be okay."

Tricia had me order the couch and loveseat, which she paid for.

"Call Tricia and tell her how much we love the sofa and loveseat," Danielle told me a few weeks after Costco delivered our new furniture.

"You're welcome," said Tricia. "Keep taking good care of Danielle. Thanks to you and your family, I never have to worry about Danielle."

"I promise," I jokingly said. Tricia laughed and we hung up.

Chapter 37

Danielle was ecstatic. "Guess what?" she said to me one day after I got home from work.

"What?" I said. I thought she was going to tell me about Judge Judy's episode today.

Danielle enjoyed listening to Judge Judy. She didn't understand anything the judge said, but listening to the television kept her mind occupied. If Danielle told me something about Judge Judy, I would try to agree. But sometimes, if it was way out there, I'd try to correct her. "Are you sure?" she'd ask me. "Well, maybe not, I don't know, I just got home from work." I would say.

"Guess what?" she said again.

"Your new boyfriend came by while I was at work?" I joked.

"Nope, guess again," she said.

"You bought a lotto ticket and won a million dollars," I said.

"No," Danielle finally said. "Joy's going to have another baby."

"A baby," I said excitedly. "Yeah, and she said the baby is due near your birthday."

"Oh, how wonderful," I said. "I better call her and say congratulations."

Danielle was right, Joy's due date was near my birthday. Our second granddaughter was born on October 30, four days after my birthday. What a wonderful gift.

Paul called and said Joy wanted Danielle to come and see the new baby. When we got to the hospital, Carnegie, now seventeen months old, was crawling around the bed with Joy while Paul held on to the beautiful bundle.

"Sit down, Mom, I want you to hold the baby," Joy said. I helped Danielle sit in the corner chair and Paul handed Danielle our second granddaughter.

Danielle carefully fingered the angel soft face of her new granddaughter. "Jack, who does she look like?" Danielle asked as she tenderly felt this precious gift from God.

"I think she looks a lot like Joy did when she was born," I said. Tears again streamed down my face as I watched Danielle concentrate, with monumental effort, to see this baby with her fingers.

"Joy," Danielle said.

"Yes, Mom."

"What's the baby's name?" Danielle asked.

"Dalynn," Joy responded. "We named her Dalynn."

I immediately knew where the new parents had gotten the name. It was a combination of Danielle (Da) and Linda (Lynn).

"Danielle," I said and signed into her free hand. "The baby's name is made up of your name and Paul's mom's name."

"'Da' for Danielle and 'Lynn' for Linda. Oh, how clever," Danielle signed.

Dalynn weighed 6 pounds 11 ounces and was 19 inches long.

We visited with Joy and Paul, Carnegie and the new baby for a while, and then we headed home. I could see that Danielle was thinking about something quite seriously. "Danielle?" I asked on the drive home. "What are you thinking about?" I signed.

"I'm just thinking about our grandchildren," she said. "Jack, do you know what?"

"What?" I answered.

"Do you realize that I have never seen my grandchildren?" she said.

"I know, Punky, it always breaks my heart when I watch you trying to see what our babies look like with your fingers," I said.

"But you know what?" Danielle asked.

"What, punkin?" I said.

"When I feel the new baby's face, I am feeling the face of God," Danielle said and signed.

Tears rolled down my cheeks as we drove home that early winter's eve.

We do not choose the time of our passing, He does.

Danielle died two weeks before Dalynn was to celebrate her first birthday. She had a massive heart attack and fell on my shoulder.

We had Danielle's funeral at our beautiful church in Scotia, the very church where Danielle was baptized as a baby. The whole church was filled with all her relatives and the many friends who deeply loved her.

Danielle and I were married thirty-nine years, five months, and one day.

"You are precious to me."

"God made me for you."

"I adore you."

"You are my splendor."

"I love you, Danielle." … "I love you more," she said and signed.

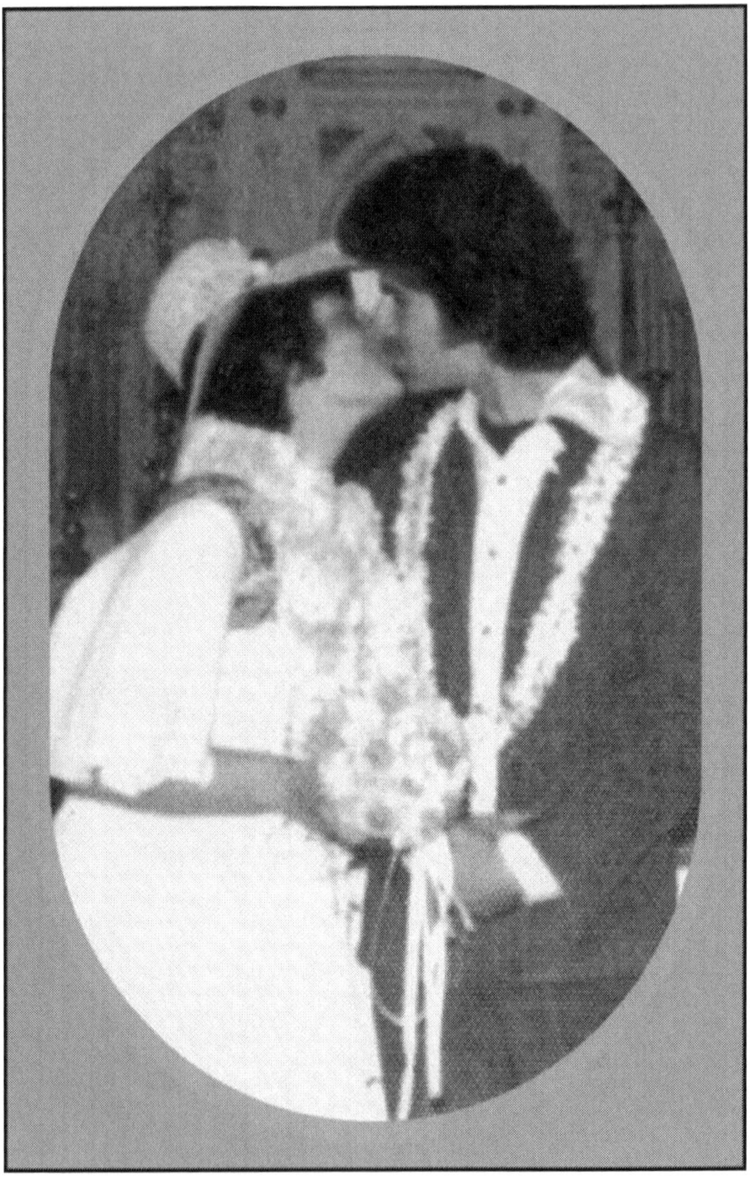

Acknowledgments

I would like to thank Uncle Albert and Aunt Flora (Egidia) for their fond memories and great help in the writing of Danielle's early years. We will always love you.

I'd like to thank my editor, Christine LePorte, for her superb guidance.

To my friends and proof readers, Nitta Schwartz, Susan Pryor, Sheila Hall, Sarah Pascascio, my sister in law Carrie and her neighbor Ciony, for their love and encouragement and keen attention to detail.

I'd like to thank Humboldt State University's Library and Humboldt County's Historical society for their assistance in researching Danielle's early years.

I'd be amiss if I didn't thank Fremont's School for the Deaf in helping me answer some of the questions I had when Danielle lived at the California School for the Deaf at Berkeley.

And to my friends and family who helped with simple wording and phrasing, thank you so much.

Made in the USA
San Bernardino, CA
29 November 2019